The United States

Living in Our World

LIBERTY

The United States

Living in Our World

RESEARCH, EVALUATION, AND WRITING

PAUL F-BRANDWEIN
Director of Research
Harcourt Brace Jovanovich

NANCY W. BAUER
Adjunct Associate Professor
University of Pennsylvania

CONSULTING SOCIAL SCIENTISTS

BURTON R. CLARK
Sociology, Professor
Yale University

THOMAS R. FRAZIER
History, Professor
Baruch College of CUNY

JAMES LOWELL GIBBS, JR.
Anthropology, Professor
Stanford University

NATHAN GLAZER
Professor of Education and Sociology
Harvard University

CHARLES V. HAMILTON
Political Science, Professor
Columbia University

WILLIAM R. HOCHMAN
History, Department Chairman
Colorado College

FRED KNIFFEN
Anthropology and Geography,
Boyd Professor Emeritus
Louisiana State University

BEN W. LEWIS
Economics, Emeritus Professor
Oberlin College

GEORGE O. ROBERTS
Professor of Social Sciences
University of California, Irvine

CENTER FOR THE STUDY OF INSTRUCTION
San Francisco

HARCOURT BRACE JOVANOVICH
New York Chicago San Francisco Atlanta Dallas *and* London

CONSULTING SPECIALISTS

DARRELL F. KIRBY
Professor
College of Education
New Mexico State University
Las Cruces, New Mexico

FRED ROSENAU
Far West Laboratory for
Educational Research
and Development
San Francisco, California

BELL I. WILEY
Professor Emeritus of History
Emory University
Atlanta, Georgia

CONSULTING TEACHERS AND SUPERVISORS

MARION ASHWORTH
Supervisor
Beaumont, Texas

ROSALIND BEIMLER
Assistant Superintendent
for Instruction
American School Foundation
Mexico City, Mexico

PHYLLIS I. BUSH
Dean of Learning Resources
California State University
Chico, California

JAMES CROWSON
President
Jackson Area Council
for the Social Studies
Jackson, Mississippi

WILLIAM GUARDIA
San Antonio Independent
School District
San Antonio, Texas

SISTER LUCIDA MOELLERING, C.PP.S.
Teacher
Archdiocese of St. Louis, Missouri

MARILYNN WENDT
Elementary Principal
Waterford Schools
Pontiac, Michigan

ACKNOWLEDGMENTS

The publisher wishes to acknowledge the assistance of **Larry DiStasi** and **Joseph Alvarez** as special consultants in the preparation of this book.

For permission to reprint copyrighted material, grateful acknowledgment is made to the following sources:

Harcourt Brace Jovanovich, Inc.: Excerpt from *The People, Yes* by Carl Sandburg. Copyright © 1936 by Harcourt Brace Jovanovich, Inc.; renewed 1964 by Carl Sandburg; "Chicago" from *Chicago Poems* by Carl Sandburg. Copyright © 1916 by Holt, Rinehart and Winston, Inc.; copyright © 1944 by Carl Sandburg; "Lands of Hillside Farms" based on a section in *The World Around Us* by Zoe Thralls. Copyright © 1956, 1961 by Harcourt Brace Jovanovich.
Holt, Rinehart and Winston, Publishers: "In a sacred manner I live" from *Bury My Heart at Wounded Knee* by Dee Brown. Copyright © 1970 by Dee Brown.

Photographs: Woodfin Camp, © Eva Momatiuk & John Eastcott 1978: 26BL; Woodfin Camp & Associates, © Daily Telegraph Magazine by C. Bonington: 27BL; Woodfin Camp, © Eva Momatiuk & John Eastcott 1978: 28, 32; Paul Kane, *Indian Camp Colville,* © Royal Ontario Museum, Toronto, Canada: 66; © 1921 J. L. G. Ferris, © 1948 Ernest N. Ryder d.b.n.c.t.a. Renewal. Archives of '76, Bay Village, Ohio: 127; FPG, © Peter Drake: 256T; © Magnum Photos Inc., Alex Webb: 256B; © 1977 Lou Dematteis: 262, 267L, 269R; © Woodfin Camp, Tony Howarth: 267R; © Stock Boston, Carl Wolinsky: 346R.

Portions of this work were previously published with the title *The Social Sciences: Concepts and Values,* Purple.

PRINTED IN THE UNITED STATES OF AMERICA ISBN 0-15-376954-8

PHOTOGRAPH ACKNOWLEDGMENTS

Key: T, Top; B, Bottom; L, Left; C, Center; R, Right.

HBJ PHOTOS: 44B, 91, 98C, 98BL, 98BR, 126, 142C, 142B, 149T, 149BL, 179, 295T, 295C, 295BL, 319B, 334C, 341, 342, 351TR, 351BL, 351BR.

HBJ PHOTOS by Erik Arnesen: 36, 37, 41, 42, 43, 46, 47, 48B, 50, 94, 98BR, 180, 181, 182, 260, 319C, 323, 340B, 349.

HBJ PHOTO by Patrick Bongartz: 292.

HBJ PHOTO by Wayne Bonnett: 189B.

HBJ PHOTO by Robert W. Cottroll: 243T.

HBJ PHOTOS by Rick Der: courtesy of the Brasserie Restaurant, San Francisco: 44C, 335.

HBJ PHOTOS by Terry Eiler: 12BL, 15T, 17.

HBJ PHOTOS by Jacques Jangoux: 263, 266.

HBJ PHOTOS by Regina Kane: 53T, 340T.

HBJ PHOTOS by Susan Lohwasser: 34B, 79BL.

HBJ PHOTOS by David Powers: courtesy of Britex Fabrics, San Francisco, California: 311T, 311C, 311B.

HBJ PHOTO by Richard Reeves: 57.

HBJ PHOTOS by Elliott Varner Smith: 9B, 34T, 34C, 44T, 53B, 79T, 142T, 284, 289; courtesy of McDermotts, Sausalito: 291B; 305; courtesy of Bill's Hamburgers, San Francisco, California: 306L; 306R, 307, 308; courtesy of Ortmans Ice Cream Parlor, Oakland, California: 309, 310, 312L; courtesy of Dreyer's Ice Cream, Oakland, California: 312R; 313, 317, 318, 320, 321, 322, 324, 325; courtesy of Electrical City Appliances, Berkeley, California: 329, 331L; 331R, 333, 334T, 336, 337, 348, 351TL.

HBJ PHOTO by Burton Stratton: 90.

HBJ PHOTO by Phil Toy: 9C.

HBJ PHOTOS by Tom Tracy: 149BR, 314.

HBJ PHOTOS by Arthur Tress: 9T, 21B, 26BR, 29.

RESEARCH CREDITS: Steve McCutcheon: 2; John Running: 7; Jerry D. Jacka: 10, 11, 12BR, 16; John Running: 15BL, 15BR, 18; Woodfin Camp, C. C. Bonington: 21T; Rapho-Guillumette, Sam Bettle: 23; Steve McCutcheon: 24, 26T, 27TL, 27R, 30, 31, 33; Carol Simowitz: 48T; Tom Tracy: 52; Steve McCutcheon: 54; The Bettman Archive, Inc.: 61; George Catlin, *Bird's Eye View of Mandan Village,* National Collection of Fine Arts, Smithsonian Institution: 62; Sebastiano del Piombo, *Christopher Columbus,* The Metropolitan Museum of Art, gift of J. Pierpont Morgan, 1900: 63; The Bettman Archive, Inc.: 64, 65; Historical Pictures Service, Inc.: 69, 75; George Henry Boughton, *Pilgrims Going to Church,* The Robert L. Stuart Collection, New York Historical Society: 76; The Bettman Archive, Inc.: 78; Lou Dematteis: 79BR; The Bettman Archive, Inc.: 83, 88, 93, 97; Grant Heilman: 98T; Historical Society of Pennsylvania: 100; Historical Pictures Service, Inc.: 103; The Mariners Museum: 104; The State Capitol Building, Austin, Texas: 116; The Bettman Archive, Inc.: 118; Denver Public Library: 119C, 119BL, 123; Henry E. Huntington Library: 119BR; Historical Pictures Service, Inc.: 124; The New York Historical Society: 128; Virginia Museum Photo: 130; The New York Historical Association, Cooperstown, New York: 131; The New York Public Library: 133; Photo by George F. Mobley, courtesy of The United States Capitol Historical Society: 135T; Library of Congress: 135C, 135B; Louisiana State Museum: 138; The Bettman Archive, Inc.: 139; Massachusetts Historical Society: 140; New York State Historical Association, Cooperstown, New York: 141; The Museum of the City of New York: 145; Library of Congress: 147; UPI: 149C; Culver Pictures, Inc.: 150L; The New York Public Library: 150R; Painting by C. T. Webber, courtesy of the Cincinnati Art Museum: 152; Brown Brothers: 155, 156T; Culver Pictures, Inc.: 156B; American National Insurance Company: 159; Museum of the City of New York: 161T; New York Historical Society: 161B; Signal Corps Photo, National Archives: 162; courtesy of The New York Historical Society, New York City, New York: 163; The United States Naval Academy Museum: 167; West Point Academy Collection, USMA: 170; Historical Pictures Service, Inc.: 171; Library of Congress: 175, 176; Culver Pictures, Inc.: 183; Henry Farny from the Taft Museum: 184; The Bettman Archive, Inc.: 186; California Historical Society, San Francisco: 189C, 191T; Culver Pictures, Inc.: 191B, 193; The Bettman Archive, Inc.: 194; Culver Pictures, Inc.: 195L; Drake Well Memorial Park: 195R; Culver Pictures, Inc.: 198; Collection of Mr. August A. Busch, Jr.: 199; The Byron Collection, Museum of the City of New York: 200; Archives of Labor History and Urban Affairs: 201; Henry E. Huntington Library: 202; The Bettman Archive, Inc.: 204, 205, 209T; Steve McCutcheon: 209B; Tom Tracy: 211; Culver Pictures, Inc.: 212; The Bettman Archive, Inc.: 214; UPI: 217; The National Archives: 218; Imperial War Museum, London: 219; Library of Congress: 223T; The Bettman Archive, Inc.: 223B, 224L; FPG: 224R; The Bettman Archive, Inc.: 225; Historical Pictures Service, Inc.: 226L; Library of Congress: 226R; Franklin D. Roosevelt Library: 227; Historical Pictures Service, Inc.: 228; Photoworld, a division of FPG: 229; Culver Pictures, Inc.: 231, 232; NASA: 237, 238; Tuskegee Institute: 239T; UPI: 239C; Free Library of Philadelphia: 239B; UPI: 241, 242, 243B; Lou Dematteis: 244T, 244C; Denver Public Library: 244BL; University of Oklahoma Library: 244R; UPI: 246, 247, 248; FPG: 249; Library of Congress: 250; Betty Lane: 251; California Historical Society: 254T; Library of Congress: 254B; Brown Brothers: 255; Shostal: 259; Tom Tracy: 269L; Grant Heilman: 272; Historical Pictures Service, Inc.: 273L; Denver Public Library: 273R; Minnesota Historical Society: 274; Tom Tracy: 276, 277, 280; The Bettman Archive, Inc.: 278; Grant Heilman: 283; Black Star, John Launois: 285, 286B; Tom Tracy: 286T; Shostal: 291T; Steve McCutcheon: 293; Shostal: 294; Tom Tracy: 295R; D. P. Wilson: 296T; Shostal: 296B; NASA: 297; Library of Congress: 301; Tom Tracy: 302T; FPG, H. Hall: 302B; UPI: 304; Media Generalists: 319T; EPA-Documerica: 334B; Shostal: 338; Connecticut College Photo by Phillip C. Biscuti: 344; FPG: 345; Editorial Photo Archives, Inc.: 346R; Black Star, John Launois: 347T; FPG: 347B; BBM Associates: 352; Minnesota Historical Society: 354; Denver Public Library: 355.

COVER CREDITS: Art by Walter Gaspar; HBJ PHOTO by Rick Der.

ART ACKNOWLEDGMENTS

Jan Benes: 136, 166; Wayne Bonnett: 111; Graphic Arts International: 268; Dick Harvey: 160; Richard Leon: 73, 109, 197, 235, 253, 310; Francis Livingston: 105; Tony Naganuma: 3, 20, 36, 63, 74, 86, 96, 110, 129, 144, 158, 185, 198, 208, 222, 236, 261, 271, 282, 290, 307, 316, 328; Norm Nicholson: 114; Tom Quinn: 4, 6, 13; Jim Sanford: 1, 22, 67, 82, 132, 148; Kazuhiko Sano: 68, 80, 102.

MAP CREDITS: Donnelley Cartographic Services: 8, 25, 38, 40, 66, 70, 77, 81, 85, 89, 91, 95, 101BR, 106, 107, 112, 115, 117, 151, 154, 165, 168, 188, 210, 211, 213, 215, 230, 233, 242, 275, 287, 353, 356–357, 358–359; HBJ Map: 264.

Contents

UNIT ONE

Three Groups of Americans

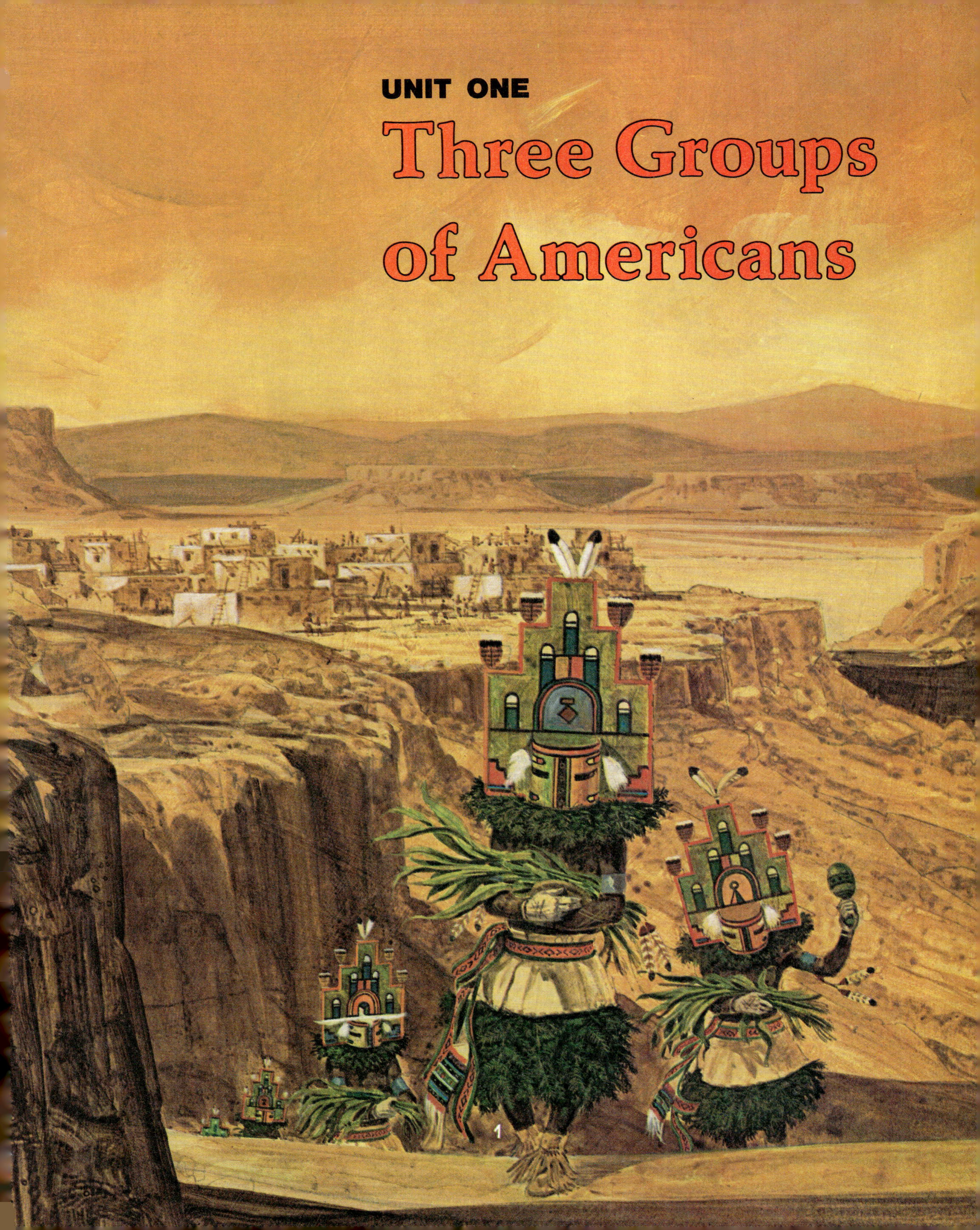

In the Western Hemisphere of the planet Earth are two large continents. One is South America. The other is North America.

In North America there are many different places where people can live. There are the cold, frozen stretches of the north. There are the hot, dry deserts of the southwest. There is the grassy, fertile carpet of the Great Plains.

People have settled in almost all of these places. They have farmed the land. They have fished the oceans, rivers, and lakes. They have built homes and raised families.

Many people live on the North American continent. You will read about three groups of people in this unit. They are the Hopi of the southwest, the Eskimos of the north, and the Mexicans of Tepetongo.

The Hopi of North America

The picture on page 4 shows part of the desert called Black Mesa (MAY•suh) in the southwestern United States. Imagine this place on a morning in August. Children rush through narrow streets to a village square. Other children are already there. Some men and women are there, too. Some people climb ladders to stand on the flat housetops. They all expect something very special to happen today. They look out at the empty countryside and see sand, rock, and bare, reddish earth stretching for kilometers.

These people are the Hopi (HOH•pee). They are Native Americans. The Hopi have lived in these villages for hundreds of years. The people on the housetops can see the desert that stretches far, far away. The villages are on a flat-topped hill called a **mesa.** *Mesa* is the Spanish word for "table." The people on the housetops hope to see something come up the mesa from the desert.

About noon, tall figures appear. In a long line, they come up the road from the desert below and walk through the village streets. The sun's rays sparkle on their bright costumes and painted bodies. The tall, masked figures shake turtle-shell rattles as they move into the open square. All the children stare with wide eyes.

Important Guests in the Village

The Hopi call these tall figures *kachinas* (kuh • CHEE • nuhz). They believe the *kachinas* to be spirits of their ancestors, of animals, of nature. The *kachinas* are important guests on Black Mesa today. They are believed to come from mountains far away. They carry fresh corn plants and green branches to the middle of the square. A chief welcomes them. He then blesses each of the *kachinas* in turn with a pinch of cornmeal.

This begins a ceremony, something people always celebrate in the same way. The Home Ceremony is the *kachinas'* good-by to the village until next summer. They come often each summer.

Suddenly a *kachina* shakes his rattle loudly. The *kachinas* start to dance and sing. Thirty pairs of feet stamp the ground. Thirty voices begin a story, a song, a prayer. With each step, they shake rattles tied to their hands and legs. *Kachinas* dressed as women make music on special wooden instruments.

The song goes on and on. The *kachinas* pray to the gods for happiness to come to the Hopi and all people. They pray for water to make plants grow. They pray for gifts of food and life.

The children listen to every word. From the prayers and songs they learn how troubles come when leaders struggle for power. They learn what is important to their people and to the gods. They must think the right thoughts and wish for the right things. They must value peace. If they can live the right way, the gods will send rain for the cornfields and bring peace and good times to all the people.

The singing and dancing end. The *kachinas* pick up the corn plants and green branches. They take them to the children. The youngest children try to hide from the *kachinas.* Tied to the plants are gifts of *kachina* dolls, toy bows and arrows, or flat sheets of colored corn bread. Each child gets a branch and a gift.

The *kachinas* dance several more times. They must leave when the sun sets. A chief bids them good-by. He says, "Carry our prayers to the gods. Ask for water that gives life to us and to all living things everywhere."

What the Hopi Believe

For hundreds of years the Hopi have performed their ceremonies. Some day you may see the Home Ceremony in a village in the homeland of the Hopi. You will hear the *kachinas* chant the same words. You will see them dance the same steps. Over hundreds of years, the ceremonies have remained nearly unchanged.

Today many Hopi have cars and television sets. They wear clothes made in factories. But they still gather to watch the old dances. Many Hopi still live as Hopi did almost five hundred years ago, before the Spanish, British, or French came to America.

You may have guessed something the youngest Hopi children didn't know. The dancing figures are really men of the village. They are not truly spirits from the mountains far away. Costumes and great wooden masks make them look like *kachinas.* These men belong to a secret club for grown men only. Night after night they meet in a *kiva* (KEE•vuh), an underground meeting room. They practice their dances and chants in the *kiva.* Other secret clubs present other ceremonies at different times of the year. In each club the men make and care for the great masks they will use in their ceremonies.

Young and old Hopi love the *kachina* spirits. They say the spirits watch over the people and take part in the workings of nature and the life of the village. The Hopi have over two hundred different *kachinas.* Each has its own name and its own powers. But *kachinas* are invisible spirits, so men act for the *kachinas* in the human world. When men dance in the *kiva,* each dance sends a prayer or message to the real *kachinas* and to the gods of the earth, the sun, and the skies.

You can see that *kachinas* are important to the Hopi. Their children need to learn about them. Boys and girls are given *kachina* dolls carved from the dry roots of the cottonwood tree. By playing with them, children learn the *kachinas'* names. They learn what each one does for the Hopi. Most *kachinas* are powerful and helpful spirits. There are animal *kachinas* and plant *kachinas,* too. A few *kachinas* cause trouble or are clowns.

When they are about eight years old, Hopi boys and girls are ready to learn to become adults. They go to a secret ceremony where *kachinas* give them new names. At this time children learn that the masked figures are really men taking the part of *kachina* spirits. From this time on, the children themselves may take part in *kachina* ceremonies.

You have been reading about some special ways that the Hopi act and live. You will read about other ways in the pages ahead. All these special ways are called **culture.** Culture is the way a group of people have learned to act, speak, live, and believe. For example, the *kachina* ceremony is one part of the Hopi culture. This ceremony is one of their special ways.

Other features make people special, too. To find out more, try the investigation on the facing page.

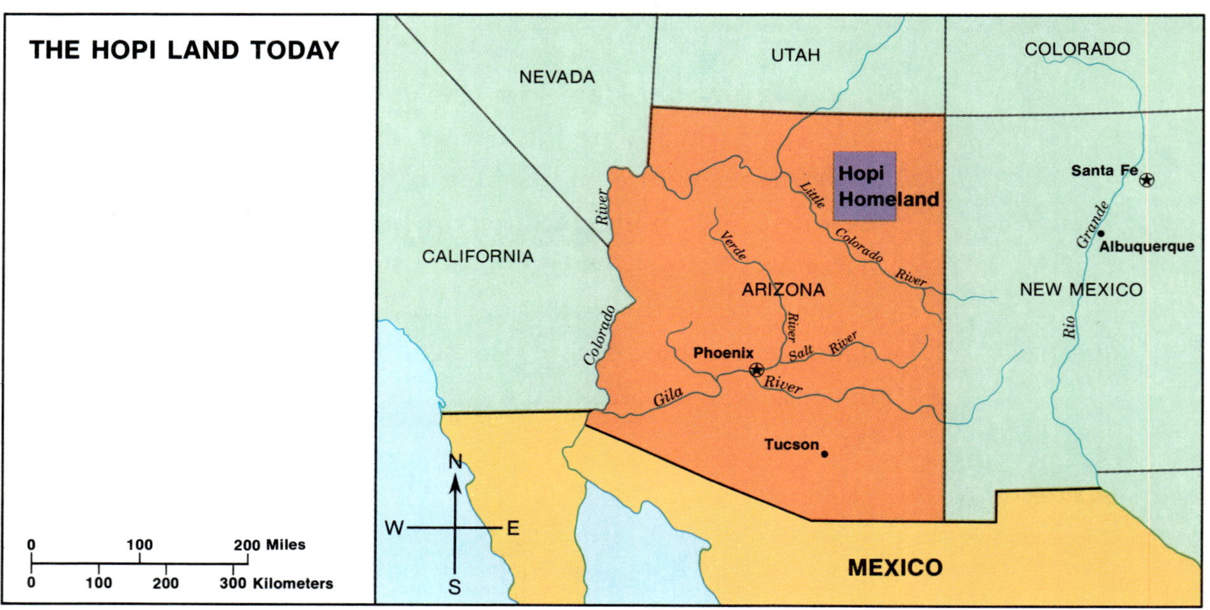

Food for the Hopi

The land of the Hopi gets very little rain. Plants can live only in the few damp places of this dry land. There are few big animals. A hunter must work hard and travel far to find enough food here. Life is hard in this land, but for thousands of years people have been able to **adapt** to this dry climate. Adapt means to change when you have to.

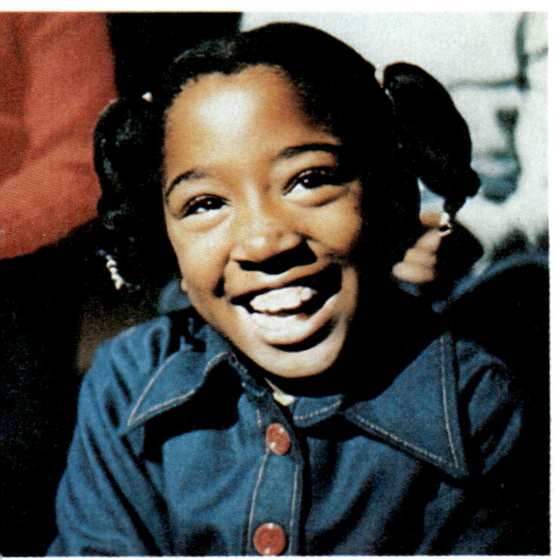

AN INVESTIGATION
into your traits

A special feature of a person is a **trait.** You can tell one person from another by looking at their traits. You were born with some traits called **physical traits.** Others, called **cultural traits,** you learn.

Do you know the color of your skin and eyes? the shape of your eyebrows and lips? These are all physical traits.

Do you wear glasses? Were you born with glasses? Glasses are part of your culture. Wearing glasses is a cultural trait.

1. Which traits are easiest to change, physical traits or cultural traits? Why?
2. Which of your traits are like those of most of your classmates? Why are your cultures alike in these ways?
3. How is your culture different from that of some of your classmates? Why do you suppose your cultures are not exactly alike?

A Problem on Your Own

1. What eye colors do you see in your class? Which color is found most often? Which colors are found least often? Can anyone change eye color? Why?
2. Decide for yourself how you will learn, record, and report your findings to your classmates.

The Hopi have learned to stay alive in this very dry land. They plant crops that grow well in a dry environment. Hopi corn plants are tough and hardy. They grow with little water. Each corn seed sends out very long roots that reach water deep in the earth. Hopi corn grows close to the ground. The wind does not blow it or dry it. Farmers from other places may think the small plants and colored kernels look strange. But this corn is adapted to life in the desert. It is the Hopi's main food. It gives them life. The Hopi call it "Mother Corn."

Hopi corn needs water to stay alive, as do all plants. Hopi farmers know where to plant the corn so it will have the best chance to get water. Sand dunes hold water. So does land at the foot of a hill or the mouth of a canyon. Rain water runs off the hill on to the land below it. Rain water runs down a canyon on to the land at its mouth. So land below a hill or a canyon is a good place for corn.

To guard against a bad year when no rain comes, a Hopi farmer always tries to plant some corn near a spring of water. These springs are found at the bases of the mesas where the Hopi live.

Besides corn, the Hopi grow fine peaches, beans, pumpkins, and squash. They hunt rabbits for meat and skins. Since Spanish settlers first brought sheep to the Southwest, the Hopi have also raised sheep. These animals need little care. They eat plants that grow in dry places.

Many Hopi men spend most of their time in the fields from spring to fall. They plant, weed, hoe, and water their crops. Their sons work with them. By the time a boy is about six years old, he will already be learning to farm. Boys often stay in the field from sunrise to sunset. They look after the sheep and keep birds from stealing corn. They help their fathers in as many ways as they can.

House and Home

Other people who lived in the desert got their food by hunting small animals. They kept moving much of the time, looking for animals. But the Hopi grew their own food and settled in villages. Some Hopi villages are hundreds of years old. Many were built on high land for safety. From high up, the Hopi could watch out for enemies. Early villages in this desert land were often built into the sides of cliffs in the canyons. Later the Hopi built their villages near springs on the mesas. Women had to get water from a spring every day and carry it home.

By Hopi custom, a house belongs to the woman, who gets it from her mother. A husband comes to live at his wife's house. Women build houses and fix them when they need repair. Walls are usually big, flat stones held together by dried mud. High on the walls are one or two small holes for light and air. Sweet-smelling cedar logs hold up the roof. The men bring these logs from mountains far away. Few trees grow on the dry mesas.

Until about one hundred years ago, the Hopi built their houses without doors. They entered their houses through a hole in the roof. To get down to other floors, they used ladders.

Many Hopi houses were apartment houses. A big one had more than nine hundred rooms. Many of the houses still standing are hundreds of years old. The desert has little rain to damage them. The houses are well built and well cared for.

Each home was built with a room for storing corn. The women and girls ground the corn between stones. They did this slow work in the main room of the house. There, too, they baked many kinds of bread from the corn they had ground.

How Hopi Decide

The many members of a Hopi family—grandparents, aunts, uncles, and cousins—form a **clan.** A clan is a large group of people of the same family. Clan members like to live close together. They depend on each other's help. Each clan has its own designs. They are found on old rock carvings. The designs are also woven into sashes men wear when they dance.

A girl lives with her clan all her life. A boy lives with his mother's clan until he marries. Then he lives with his wife and her clan. But he is still a member of the clan he is born into, his mother's clan. He will always go to meetings of this clan.

A clan's chief is an older, wiser man. In a village, clan chiefs and other leaders make up the village **council.** The council makes plans and rules for the village. The chiefs and council do not often tell people what to do. Everyone knows what he or she is expected to do. Hopi are expected to cooperate and to settle their quarrels quietly. Cooperation and peacefulness are cultural traits the Hopi value highly. The village council has very few quarrels to settle.

A man is chosen to serve on the council because he is wise, not because he wants to lead. A Hopi must be asked four times before he is willing to be a leader. The Hopi do not try to stand out in a group. They believe that standing out puts other people in the shadow. A Hopi does not talk about his skill or about races he has won. A Hopi farmer does not try to harvest more corn than he needs. It is enough to be a Hopi, to believe as a Hopi. Nothing more is needed.

Handwork

Taking care of crops is a man's job. But a Hopi farmer has little work in the fields from November to February. During that time he weaves cloth. His family needs the cloth for clothing. He uses cotton from the fields and wool from the sheep. In the Hopi culture, weaving cloth is a man's work. Hopi men take great pride in making the fine wooden looms they use for their weaving.

A Hopi man wears a long shirt with a colorful sash around the waist. He ties a headband across his forehead. A Hopi woman wears a simple dress of rough cloth, usually black or blue in color. The dress is held in at the waist

by a narrow band of many colors. For special days the Hopi often wear fine jewelry with beautiful designs in stones and shells.

Women and girls make the tools they use in their daily work. They make clay pots and bowls for storing food. They make big pottery jars in which to carry water from springs at the foot of the mesa. They also make baskets to carry food.

Like the loom, Hopi pottery and baskets are made to be used. But often they are also made and decorated to be beautiful. The same is true of Hopi masks and dolls. Each clan decorates masks and dolls in its own way. Only members of the same clan may use these masks and dolls, and only clan members may use the clan's design.

The Hopi do only a little hunting. Today they use guns. Long ago they used bows and arrows and curved throwing sticks to hunt rabbits and other small animals. When they had to, they used the bows and arrows against their enemies. But the Hopi have always wanted peace. In Hopi language they called themselves the "Peaceful Ones."

The Hopi had to find ways to stay alive in their dry, rocky environment. Their culture was their way of adapting. But a culture is more than adapting. Their culture also gave the Hopi ideas and customs, a sense of beauty, and hope for the future.

The Hopi Today

About five thousand Hopi people now live in thirteen villages on their homeland in Arizona. They meet more and more people who are not Hopi and not Native American. For three hundred years Spanish settlers and Mexicans were the Hopi's only neighbors. Today, thousands of people from all over the United States travel the new roads to visit the Hopi villages. Hopi people now **interact** with many different kinds of people. To interact means to act together so that each person affects the lives of all the other people.

All about them the Hopi see many things used by other cultures to make life easier. A metal pail, unlike a clay pot, will not break when it is dropped. A Hopi woman does not have to spend hours making it. Driving a truck is easier than walking to a cornfield.

The Hopi now have hospitals in their homeland. There, doctors and nurses help the Hopi care for their health. Some of the Hopi people now live in new houses in villages off the mesas. The Hopi have also built a motel for visitors.

Hopi children go to schools much like yours. They speak English in school and watch television at home. Some go away to colleges where they interact with people who are not Hopi.

Many Hopi have jobs away from the village. They want to earn money. Money will buy them things they hope will make life easier. Some drive to work in town. In their jobs they interact with people whose culture is not Hopi.

Those who work in places far away from the Hopi homeland interact with many people from other cultures. They come back to the village for special ceremonies. They come back to visit with friends and members of their clans. Today the Hopi divide their lives between Hopi and other cultures.

A few years ago, older Hopi in the villages worried about interaction between cultures. They feared that young Hopi might forget the dances and the *kachinas.* But many young Hopi still dance. They are proud of the *kachinas.* They have found that other Americans enjoy the dances and the *kachinas.* They admire the Hopi's peaceful ways. Interaction works both ways.

1. What were the main foods of the Hopi?
2. What was the Hopi's shelter like?
3. From what did the Hopi make their clothing?
4. What tools did they use?
5. What did the Hopi believe ruled events like rainfall?
6. In what kinds of groups did the Hopi live?
7. How did they choose their leaders?
8. How were Hopi people expected to act?

1. How are leaders chosen in your community? How is this different from the ways of choosing Hopi leaders long ago?
2. How have the Hopi learned to survive in their harsh climate?

1. In "Working with Key Facts" you answered eight questions about Hopi culture. Now answer the same questions about your culture.
2. Then make a chart of your answers. Write *Hopi* and *My Culture* at the top of a sheet of paper. Down the left side of the paper, write *food, shelter, clothing, tools, beliefs, groups, leaders, ways to act.* Next to each trait, list the answers you gave for Hopi. Then list the answers for your culture.

Suppose a Hopi boy of eight went to live for ten years with another group of Native Americans. He learned their skills of weaving and making pottery and their ways of hunting and herding sheep. He also learned what they cared about and believed in.

1. Which of the other group's beliefs and ways of doing things might the Hopi boy want to copy?
2. Which of his Hopi ways would be hardest to change? Why do you say so?

The Eskimos of the Far North

The far northern part of North America, near the North Pole, is a land of cold, ice, and snow. Over a hundred years ago, only a few people lived in this arctic land. They are called Eskimos.

Imagine being in the far north during a winter many years ago. Icy winds blow around a village of Eskimo people. No one is outside. Their houses, built half underground, are covered with snow. It is early afternoon, but the sky is already getting dark. The Arctic winter has only a few hours of light each day, and in mid-winter, one or two hours.

One house is the *karigi* (kuh•REE•jee), or men's clubhouse. Inside it is warm and comfortable. Imulak (EE•moo•lak) and his sons sit on low benches, wrapped in robes of caribou skin. They are eating raw seal meat dipped in seal oil. As they finish, they hear noises at the low tunnel entrance.

A man and a little boy from another clubhouse come to visit. In the winter months Eskimos cannot do much hunting. Such visits are a favorite way to pass the time. The visitors sit by a seal-oil lamp to get warm. Imulak gives them some food. He is not just being friendly. Eskimos are expected to share with each other.

After the guests eat, Imulak takes a little carved seal from a soft skin bag. He carved it himself from the white tusk of a walrus.

"Why did you make that seal?" asks the little boy.

Imulak has many reasons for carving animals. He wants the carved seal to bring him good luck on his next seal hunt. He believes that each animal has a spirit, or *inua* (IN•oo•uh), which must be treated with respect. He also believes that some animal's spirit was in the walrus tusk before he carved it. When he gets a tusk, he turns it in his hands and studies it until he knows what lives inside. Then, by carving, he sets free the animal, its shape, and its spirit.

"You ask why I carved this seal," Imulak finally says to the boy. "One reason was to please Nerqivik (NEER•kee•veek)." Then he tells the boy the old story of the magic woman who is believed to live at the bottom of the sea.

An Old Story in Eskimo Culture

Nerqivik is a giant goddess with long, flowing hair. Long ago, the story goes, she was a human girl. Her parents died and nobody else would take care of her. When summer came, the people of her village prepared to move away. They put their belongings into their big, open boats, called *umiaks* (oo•mee•aks), and set out.

Nerqivik saw that the others would leave her behind. They must have known she would starve, but they already had too many mouths to feed. She jumped into the ocean and swam after them. When she reached them, she grabbed the side of a boat and tried to pull herself in. The people in the boat chopped off her fingers.

She sank to the bottom of the sea. Down at the bottom of the sea she turned into a powerful spirit. Her chopped-off fingers became the seal, the polar bear, the walrus, and all the other animals the Eskimos hunt for food.

From her home under the sea, Nerqivik is now believed to rule the animals. She decides when to send them out so Eskimos may hunt them. But the hunters must follow

Nerqivik's rules. For example, after a man kills a walrus, he must offer it fresh water because sea water makes it thirsty. Then he must cut off its head to free its spirit. These actions please Nerqivik, and she will send more animals to hunt. She is also pleased by carved animals. That is one reason why Imulak makes them.

When Imulak finishes his story, the clubhouse is quiet. The visiting man rises slowly to his feet. He half closes his eyes and softly taps his drum. He begins to make up a song and a dance about hunting the seal. The young boys watch and listen. Some day they too will be hunters. Then it will be their time to make up dances and songs.

Imulak picks up a drum. He beats it and hums. He follows the dancer's rhythm. The dancer has no room to leap and jump. He stands in one spot, bending his knees and his back. He sways from side to side in time with his song.

After many stories and dances, the man and his son wrap themselves in their parkas, or coats. Laughing and joking, they leave the warm clubhouse. Imulak and his sons call out, "Good-by! Come again! We want to see your faces around our fire often!"

Living in a Cruel Environment

The Arctic is cold because the sun is always low in the sky. In the middle of winter, for days at a time, the sun never shines at all. It is light for only a few hours. Snow and ice cover the ground most of the year. Except in July and August, it is cold enough to freeze water every night. Few trees grow here because the ground is frozen as far as 300 meters down.

Only in the four warmest months—June through September—does the ice melt on the surface of the frozen ground. Then short grass and a few flowers begin to grow. Such a grassy, treeless area is called **tundra.**

If you had to live in the Arctic, you might have a very difficult time. But Eskimos have lived here for thousands of years. They know how to survive. They know where to find food and how to make clothing and shelter. Eskimo people live and work together in a culture that has adapted to the harsh Arctic environment.

The Eskimos have learned to get their food from the tundra and the Arctic Ocean. Inland are large herds of reindeer that live on the tundra. Birds live on land and near the sea. Walruses, polar bears, and seals are found along the coasts. Whales and fish live in the sea. During the short summers, there are leaves, berries, and seeds to be gathered.

The life of the Eskimos used to depend mostly on successful hunting. Crews of Eskimos hunted whales from boats. Eskimos had to make holes in the ice and wait patiently for fish or seals to appear. Too often nothing appeared. In skin-covered canoes, called *kayaks* (KY•aks), they hunted seals on the sea. They tracked animals across the frozen ground. They learned how to follow signs that you would probably never notice. With dog teams and sleds, they followed herds of reindeer far across the snow and across the vast tundra.

With patience and skill, a hunter was able to bring meat home to his family. The animals of the frozen north also supplied Eskimos with many other things necessary for life.

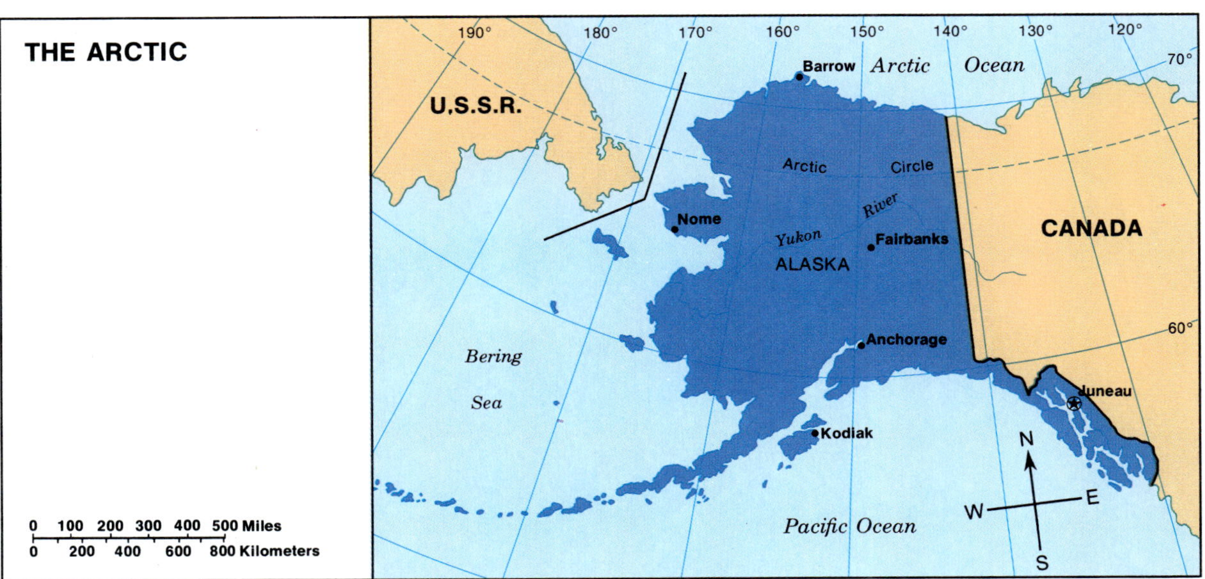

Clothing and Tools

From animals they kill for food, the Eskimos also get materials for making clothes and tools. In the Arctic, a hunter's life depends on strong, warm clothing. He wears waterproof boots, called *mukluks.* If his clothes rip, he may die of cold. Water in a *mukluk* can freeze a foot.

An Eskimo woman knows how to prepare skins and sew them into warm, strong clothing. She must often check them, mend them, and make them stronger. This work takes much time. She can make needles from animal bones or walrus tusks. Sinews (SIN•yooz) in the animal's body can be used for thread or even rope.

Bone, tusk, and horn can be made into spears, knives, fishhooks, and harpoon heads. Both wood from the Arctic spruce trees and ivory can be used to make snow goggles. Sunshine on white snow can be blinding. The wood is also good for making boxes, bows, arrows, and poles for spears and harpoons. Special knives make the Eskimos's many cutting jobs easier. A long knife cuts snow blocks. A curved knife is for scraping and cutting animal skins.

Shelter and Warmth

In the Arctic there are never enough animals in one place to feed people all year long. When the Eskimos lived only by hunting, families had to keep traveling to find food. They traveled alone. For weeks and months they might see no other people.

Sometimes they used skins to make a tent. Other times they used the material nearest to them—snow—to build a quick shelter. Sometimes houses made of snow-blocks are called "igloos," but the Eskimo word *iglu* means any kind of a shelter.

To help keep warmth inside and protect them from wind and storms, Eskimos often build their *iglus* partly underground. These houses are made of materials from the environment, such as earth, driftwood, and sometimes stones. Some walls are made of boards. An extra room or two opens off the long tunnel entrance. A bench along the wall is used for eating and sleeping.

Education and the Family

The family is very important to the Eskimo people. They love children and do not spank them often. In the old days, almost all of a child's education came from members of the family.

A young girl learned to cut and prepare meat, to clean and scrape skins, to chew the skins until they were soft enough to sew. She learned to take care of all the little children in her family.

A boy learned by watching his father. He also learned from other men in the clubhouse. He learned to make fish spears and the other tools he needed. By the time he was twelve, he went with his father on long hunting trips.

A boy learned to depend on himself and take care of himself. He also learned to share. As you have seen, Eskimos shared their food with neighbors. Some day their neighbors might save their lives by sharing their food with

them. Eskimos knew that life was dangerous. They needed to know just what an animal was going to do so they could catch it. They had to struggle to stay alive. You might think that an Eskimo would worry and feel gloomy about this dangerous life. But Eskimos were always expected to be cheerful, even if they did not feel cheerful.

In the old days, Eskimos had no books. On quiet evenings older people told long stories. From them children learned of the past. They heard of great hunts, brave people, and terrible winters when people starved. They learned how heroes made long journeys and escaped from storms by magic.

The Eskimos believed in spirits who had power over people and nature. Nerqivik was a spirit who ruled animals. Children learned the spirits' names, how to please them, and how to be safe from the wicked spirits.

Eskimos Live Together

Eskimo villages were small. They were not built to last long. A family spent all summer hunting animals. They spent the winter in a village with other families. Sometimes a family stayed in a different village each winter.

A village did not have a chief, but some leaders were important. One of the leaders was the *shaman* (SHAH • mun). A *shaman* was a man or woman believed to have power over spirits. Eskimos believed the *shaman* could make people ill or cure them. They expected the *shaman* to have power over weather and tell what was going to happen. A *shaman* in a ceremonial mask might look frightening. People were often afraid of the *shaman,* but they asked the *shaman* to help and to give them advice.

Men's work was dangerous. They went out in their boats with harpoons as weapons to hunt whales and walruses.

The women and children gathered on the shore to watch them go. The men had to work together to stay alive. Still, some men never came home. The captain of the crew owned the boat. He planned the whaling season and led the men on the hunt. Sometimes the captain of a whaling crew was also a *shaman*. Such a man was considered to be a great leader.

The men of a whaling crew had their own clubhouse. They and their sons could relax there. They ate, sang, danced, played games, and told stories there. They also trained their boys and held village ceremonies at the club. Hunters from far away were always welcome to visit the whaling crew's clubhouse.

Culture Meets Culture

In the old days, most Eskimos knew almost nothing of the world outside the Arctic. They believed the Arctic was the whole world and they were the only people in it. Today Eskimos know they are part of a big world.

Many people from outside have brought their foods to the Arctic. They have brought tools to make work easier. They have brought guns to hunt reindeer and seals. They have brought machines and medicines.

Not everything the outsiders brought has been good for the Eskimos, however. The once plentiful seals and reindeer are now scarce. Even with guns, an Eskimo would now have trouble getting enough to eat by hunting. Outsiders also brought diseases like smallpox with them. Many Eskimos died before medicines were able to help them.

The outsiders saw things they liked in Eskimo life as well. They thought parkas and *mukluks* were good for the cold climate and began to make them. They admired the Eskimo carvings and bought many of them.

Eskimo children now go to schools much like yours. They do not spend much time learning to hunt, fish, and sew skins together. They sometimes find it hard to understand the beliefs of the older people. Some parents are sad if their children do not share their beliefs.

Many Eskimos now live in small wooden houses. Snowmobiles pull their sleds. Their boats have motors. Airplanes carry people and mail everywhere. Some Eskimo men do not hunt any more at all. They may get jobs at an airfield or move to a town.

The old ways do not mean as much to these Eskimos. But they are not always at home with the new ways either. They are trying to find a good blend of the old and new.

To find out more about cultural change, try the investigation on page 34.

AN INVESTIGATION
into cultural change

In every culture people use skills to do work. A skill is something you learn to do, like swimming or skiing.

In old-time Eskimo culture, special skills were needed. Boys had to harpoon seals. Girls had to make food and clothing from parts of the seal. As Eskimo culture changed, however, new skills were needed.

Investigate changes in the skills you learn in your own culture. Here are six things that have changed your culture. Down the middle of your paper, list:

an automobile	concrete
a computer	a refrigerator
packaged foods	a light bulb

To the left of the list write *skills before*. To the right of the list write *skills after*.

Before these things were invented, people had to use other skills and tools. You may have to read a book or ask an older person about what these skills and tools were. List them in the *before* column. After these six things came into use, people had to learn new skills to care for them and use them.

List the new skills in the *after* column.

1. What do the *before* and *after* lists show?
2. What differences do new tools make in what people must learn?

1. Describe the land where the Eskimos live.
2. Name five resources on which Eskimos have depended for food.
3. From what did Eskimos make their homes?
4. From what did Eskimos make their clothing and tools?
5. How were Eskimo children taught?
6. In what ways has Eskimo culture changed today?

1. In the Eskimo language, the same word means *if* and *when*. An Eskimo boy would say, "I'll hunt seals if I grow up." What does this tell about how Eskimos have felt about life? What does it tell about the value of being cheerful?
2. In what ways are the changes in modern Eskimo life like the changes in modern Hopi life?

Find Alaska on a globe. The center of Alaska is about 65 degrees north latitude and about 150 degrees west longitude. Use the latitude and longitude lines on the globe to find this point. Then move your finger east along the line for 65 degrees north latitude. Keep going until you come to Finland.

1. What nations does your finger cross as you trace the line?
2. What large ocean does it cross on the way?
3. What can you guess about the climate in Finland?

1. Make a chart of Eskimo culture like the one you made of the Hopi culture. Look back at page 19.
2. How is each Eskimo cultural trait like or different from Hopi cultural traits?
3. What differences does the environment of the Eskimo make in the ways they meet their needs?

The Mexicans of Tepetongo

Tepetongo (Teh • peh • TONG • go) is a village in Mexico. Imagine a home in Tepetongo early in the morning. A rooster crows. A dog barks. Eleven-year-old Ramona gets up when her mother calls. She goes to the kitchen. Her father and older brothers are already dressed and eating breakfast. This will be their main meal of the day. They have eggs, refried beans, rice, fresh *tortillas* (tor • TEE • yahs, flat corn cakes), and coffee.

As the men eat, Ramona helps pack their lunch. She wraps beans and rice in corn *tortillas*. Her sister adds *chile* (CHEE • lay) peppers and fruit. Ramona's brother harnesses the burro. Now the men start their hour-long walk to the field. They will work there all day.

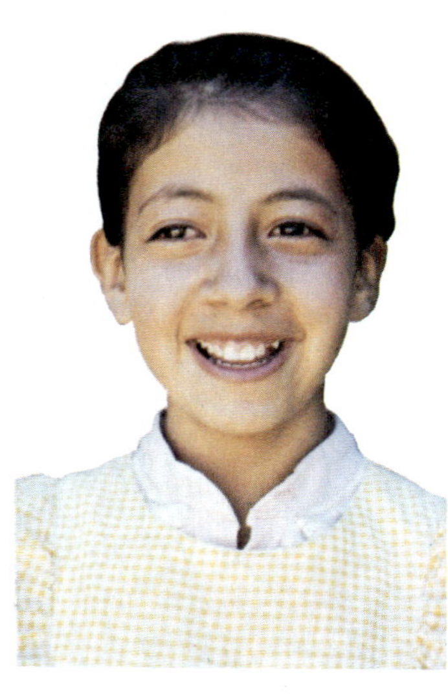

Ramona puts on her good dress for church and school. Her mother takes the girls to church for the six o'clock service. After church, Ramona helps her mother fix breakfast. Then it is time for Ramona to leave for school.

Ramona skips happily through Tepetongo's streets. She likes to go to school, but next year will probably be her last year in school. Most children in Tepetongo go to school only six years. Few have time to go to high school. Older boys must help in the fields. Older girls must help at home.

A Hard Life in a Hard Land

At school Ramona studies geography. She learns that about two thousand people live in Tepetongo. She learns, too, that it is in the state of Zacatecas (sah•kah•TEK•ahs), an area of high mountains in central Mexico. The capital city, also named Zacatecas, is about 120 kilometers from Tepetongo. Very few people from the village have been that far.

The climate at Tepetongo is warm and dry. Rain in the summer is very important. Harvests are small if there is too little rain. Too much rain at the wrong time may wash out crops. Either way, many families may go hungry.

The state of Zacatecas, Ramona learns, has no big rivers and very few small ones. One of its small rivers flows around Tepetongo. In most places people have to dig wells for water. In this dry climate no forests grow, and there is little grass for animals to graze on.

Ramona learns in school about Mexico's many cultures and regions. She knows that Mexicans in other places behave in ways different from the ways of Tepetongo. Life is not easy in Tepetongo. People must work hard just to meet their needs. Almost nothing extra is produced. People grow what they must eat. They are poor, but they are proud that they can take care of themselves. Ramona and her family feel that they lead good lives.

Two Peoples, One Culture

Ramona also studies Mexican history at school. She learns how Hernán Cortés (er•NAHN kor•TES) and his men came from Spain to America. Here they found the rich cultures of the Aztecs (AZ•teks), the Mayas (MAH•yahs), and others. The Spaniards conquered the Aztecs and settled in what is now Mexico. The environment reminded them of Spain in some ways, so they called it New Spain.

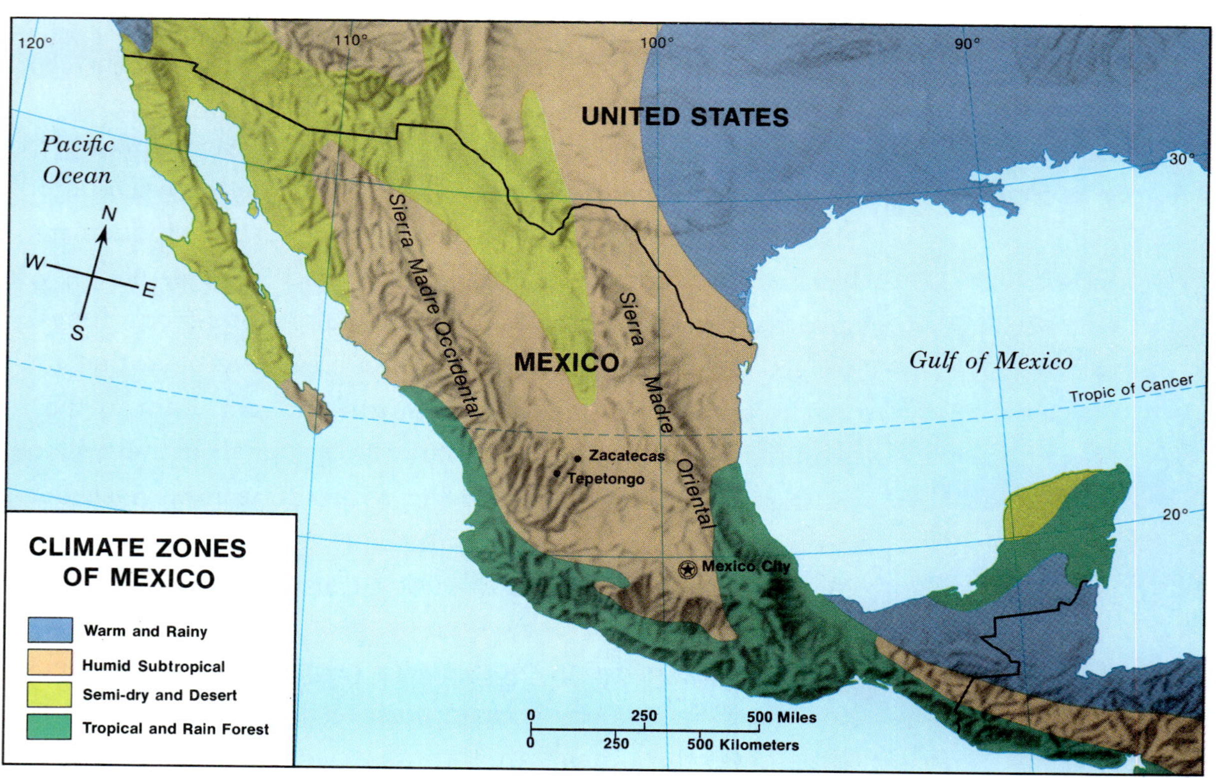

MISSION SAN CARLOS DEL RIO CARMELLO, by Oriana Day. Permission of The Fine Arts Museums of San Francisco

The Spaniards taught the Native Americans their Spanish culture. They taught them to use the Spanish language, tools, and ways of behaving. They taught them about the Christian religion. The Spanish settlers also learned from the Native American cultures. They learned to grow corn, beans, squash, and tomatoes. They learned about chocolate and chewing gum and about Native American languages, music, tools, art, and clothing. They also learned what Native Americans cared about. Two cultures, half a world apart, began changing each other. The peoples of these cultures began to interact with each other.

Slowly a new people, part Native American and part Spanish, came into being. They made a new culture of their own. This culture is both Spanish *and* Native American. The people and culture are called *mestizo* (me • STEE • zoh). While most Mexicans are now *mestizo,* many other people who live in Mexico still belong to Native American, Spanish, African, or other cultures that were brought there.

Ramona's teacher has explained how Mexican people rebelled against Spain in the early 1800s. By then the people felt that they were Mexican rather than Spanish. They did not want to be ruled by a faraway king. They fought for freedom and won it. The colony that had been New Spain became the Mexican Republic in 1823.

During its first thirty years, Mexico lost much of its lands to the United States. These lands are now the states of Texas, New Mexico, Utah, Arizona, Nevada, California, and parts of Colorado, Oklahoma, Kansas, and Wyoming.

Under Spanish rule, even before the Pilgrims came to New England, *mestizo* and Black pioneers settled and brought their culture to all parts of New Spain. The children and the children's children of these settlers remained in lands that are now part of the United States. Their *mestizo* culture became part of United States culture, too.

Women's Roles At home Ramona helps her mother look after the little children, grind corn, sort and cook beans, or prepare *chile.* She also helps sew clothes, linens, or tablecloths. Almost every family in Tepetongo has a sewing machine.

Girls begin the work of women as soon as they can. Until they marry, they spend most of their time at home with their mother and sisters. When they marry, they will know what they need to know as wives and mothers. A wife and mother is highly respected in Mexican culture.

In a village like Tepetongo, a person cares about the family above all else. A husband and wife may own very little, but having children gives them pride and joy. At the center of the family is the woman. She sees that everyone is well cared for. She attends to their needs for food, clothing, shelter, and love. Because family ties are so important, her husband's parents or her own may live in the house with the family. She will take care of them as well.

At home the mother teaches her daughters and young sons the **values** of their culture. Cultural values are the ideas, beliefs, and ways of acting that people care about.

Children in Tepetongo are expected to live in the same way as their parents and grandparents. Children are taught at home to live this way. Teaching and raising the children at home are important parts of the Mexican mother's **role.** A role is a job we do or a part we play in life. Most Mexican girls learn the mother's role from their own mothers.

Boys, Men, and the Land

The father loves his children. But he was taught that the mother is the one to teach young children. He helps her only when she cannot handle a problem alone. As soon as their sons are old enough, he teaches them the jobs they must do in the man's role.

In Tepetongo the men and boys work on the land. A man greatly values his land. It provides almost everything his family needs. It grows crops that feed his family and animals. It provides clay for dishes, jars, *adobe* (ah•DOH•bay) bricks, and tiles for building and roofing his home.

People in Tepetongo live close to their natural environment. They depend heavily on their land and what they can grow on it. To live this way, much work is needed. Working hard and taking care of your needs with your own hands are highly valued. These skills are expected of a man in Mexico.

A young boy is eager to begin working with his father. By the time he is five or six, he will begin caring for chickens or pigs. As soon as he is tall enough, he will want to harness the burro. Besides plowing, planting, hoeing, and harvesting, a growing boy learns other skills. He must be able to make whatever he needs. He must be able to make a house, furniture, a simple tool, or a well.

A young man of Tepetongo tries to be strong, work hard, keep his word, and deserve his neighbors' respect. Someday he will be ready to own part of his father's land. Then he will live the man's role as husband and father.

To find out more about learning cultural traits, do the investigation on page 44.

AN INVESTIGATION
into learning cultural traits

The language you speak is a very important cultural trait in your life. When you were very young, you probably made the same sounds as Mexican, Eskimo, and Hopi babies. You probably made all these sounds before you learned the language of your culture.

Make a list of some of your cultural traits. Begin with language.

1. What language do you speak? How did you learn to speak it? Do you speak more than one language? How did you learn the second one?
2. List five more of your cultural traits. A cultural trait is something you learn.
3. Some traits you learned by using language. People told you things. You asked them questions. Write *L* after any trait you learned by using language. Other traits, like walking and eating, you did not need language to learn.
4. Write *H* after each trait that would be useful if you lived among the Hopi; *E*, among the Eskimo; *T*, in Tepetongo. Write *U* after traits that would not be useful in any culture but your own.
5. Would learning the language and customs of another culture be easiest at the age of five, ten, or forty years? Why do you think so?

Evening in Tepetongo

Ramona begins to prepare *tortillas, chiles,* and *refritos* (ray • FREE • tos, refried beans) for supper. Her father and older brothers come home from the fields, dusty, tired, and hungry. They wash and eat.

After supper they walk to the *plaza* (PLAH • sah), a big square in the middle of the village. The men of Tepetongo gather there to talk business, laugh, rest, and enjoy themselves. The women, girls, and small children go to church.

When church is over, most of the people are together for awhile in the *plaza.* Boys show off how well they ride horses. Young men watch the girls they like. At last the sky darkens. Everybody goes home. Tepetongo's day is done.

Adapting Through Culture

In the rocky soil of Zacatecas, few plants grow well without care. One that does is the *maguey* (mah • GAY) or century plant. It has long, wide leaves with sharp points. On some kinds of *maguey,* the leaves are as big as 30 centimeters wide and 275 centimeters long. *Maguey* leaves have strong, thread-like fibers. Tepetongo people beat the leaves. Then they take out the fibers and dry them.

They use the fibers in many ways. They weave them into mats, rugs, hats, and horse blankets, and twist them into ropes. They also use them to cover roofs and to make dishes for food. From *maguey* Mexicans get *aquamiel* (ah•gwah•mee•YELL), or honey water, to drink. They use the pulp to make candy.

Although few of Zacatecas's resources are easy to use, the *mestizo* culture has adapted to Tepetongo's environment. Men and women have learned skills that are right for Tepetongo. Some of these skills came from the Native American culture. Some came from Spanish culture. Some are a mixture of both. By using whatever they can, the people of Tepetongo have gained knowledge that helps them meet their needs.

The Village Culture

Mexicans have met their needs in another way. They have built villages like Tepetongo around large *plazas* in the pattern of villages in Spain. Around the *plaza,* they built their homes. In the evenings they could be near family and friends. The church stands at one end of the *plaza.* It was one of the first buildings built in Tepetongo. Some villages have changed little since they were built over four hundred years ago.

At times a family will be lucky enough to raise more corn, beans, or other vegetables than it needs. Such goods are sold or traded in the *plaza.*

Ramona's father may offer some extra corn to the leather worker in trade for a harness. He may also sell the corn for money to spend for goods from the general store, the woodcutter, the potter, or the drugstore.

The people of Tepetongo are served by others, too. The president of the village is the head of the village government. The people elect a person they respect to be their president. They want the president to be fair in settling

quarrels. The president names people to a town council that helps govern the village.

The *plaza,* the church, village government, and a strong family life are all important parts of Tepetongo's culture. They are part of the special ways of the people.

A Happy Custom

On June 24, Ramona dresses faster than usual. Today her father and older brothers do not leave for the fields after breakfast. They wait for Ramona and the others to finish their breakfast. Then they all hurry to the *plaza.* It is filled with brightly colored booths, a big Ferris wheel, and carnival rides. Some of the booths have games to play. Others have good food to eat—special fruits, the candied fruit of the prickly pear cactus, and candied *tamales* (tah·MAH·lays).

Everybody is excited, for this is Tepetongo's happiest day of the year. It is the birthday of its special saint, San Juan Bautista (sahn HWAHN bow·TEES·tah, Saint John the Baptist). Every village, town, and city in Mexico has its own special saint. The people of Tepetongo look to San Juan Bautista for protection and care. They honor his birthday every year with this *fiesta*.

Later in the day, dancers will come from another village. They will wear masks and costumes decorated with feathers and mirrors. They will dance using rattles like those the Native Americans of Mexico have used for many thousands of years. Dancing will go on in the *plaza* all day long.

Many people will have firecrackers. There will be the music of *mariachi* (mah•ree•AH•chee) bands into the night.

Tepetongo has other *fiestas.* The *fiesta* of San Isidro (sahn ee•SEED•roh), or Saint Isidore the Farmer, is also very important to the people. It comes each year after the spring rains have helped seeds start to grow in the fields. The new plants will need more rain in July. Then the crops will be good, and people will have plenty of food for the winter. There must not be hailstorms to beat down the young crops. The people pray that this will not happen.

Every day for ten or twelve days, the people of Tepetongo go into the hills near their fields. They hold services in honor of San Isidro. They pray for a good harvest and enough rain to make the crops grow.

Other people you have studied asked for help in getting food, too. The Eskimos carved animals to please Nerqivik. The Hopi used *kachinas* to help with the corn. Because food is so important, many cultures do such things. In its own special way, each culture tries to make sure of a good food supply.

Growing Up

Ramona will have her own *fiesta* on her fifteenth birthday. Then her family and friends will celebrate her Fiesta de Quinceanos (keen•say•AHN•yohs), or fifteen years. They will have a special service in the church for her. Afterward there will be a party. Everyone will then know she is old enough to marry.

A boy and girl must not speak to each other about getting married without their parents' permission. In Tepetongo all these things must happen first:

The boy makes sure the girl is interested.

He tells his own parents he wants to marry the girl.

They give him their permission.

His father arranges to meet her parents.

Her parents must welcome his father's visit.

His father talks over marriage with the girl's parents, at their home.

Her parents agree to give her hand in marriage.

Now the boy and girl are engaged, and he can visit her frequently.

Then the families must plan for the wedding. They have much to do. They set the date far ahead so they can complete their plans.

The boy's father must make decisions. His son will need land. In Tepetongo the father will give his son a piece of family land to farm. The land should have water. It should have good soil. It should be near a road. The boy needs tools for farming, building, and repairing, too.

The girl's family must provide for her. She needs pottery for cooking and storing foods. She needs dresses, linens, and kitchen utensils. She needs a beautiful wedding dress. She and her mother spend weeks making it. Her father will also give land to his daughter and her husband. The bride is expected to bring all these things with her when she marries and moves to a new home.

The new couple will need a house. The boy's family may own one that their son can have. If not, they must build a new one from what they can find in the environment. They can use stone or *adobe* bricks of sun-dried mud for the walls. They can use straw or *maguey* fiber for the roof and poles to hold it up. Poles are expensive because they are brought from the hills, where they are made from tall trees.

At last the wedding day will come. The whole town will come to the wedding. The priest will marry the couple in the church. A celebration will follow in the *plaza.* There will be music and dancing. The parents of the boy will lose his valuable labor. The girl's parents will lose her help at home. The parents will miss the children they know and love so well. But someday they will have grandchildren.

FOR YOU TO DO

Many people leave Tepetongo to find jobs elsewhere. Some go to big Mexican cities. Some come to the United States, where they interact with people of a different culture.

Suppose some people from Tepetongo came to live near you. How would they know what is important to people in your culture? How would they know the ways you and your friends do things? List some ways. What could you learn from them? Name some things.

1. On what do the people of Tepetongo depend for tools? for shelter?
2. How do they teach their children?
3. What is a woman's role in Tepetongo?
4. What is a man's role?

1. Compare the women's role in Tepetongo with the women's role in the other cultures you have studied in this unit.
2. The people of Tepetongo, the Eskimos, and the Hopi ask San Isidro, Nerqivik, and the *kachinas* for help in getting food. Explain why people who live in harsh climates might follow these ways.

Practicing Key Skills

1. Many words in American English are borrowed from Spanish. To find out about some of these words, use a dictionary that tells the languages that words came from. Look up the word *mosquito*. After it shows how to say the word and what it means, it may say this: (Sp., dim of *mosca* fly L *musca*). This means *mosquito* comes from the Spanish word *mosca*, meaning *fly*, and that the Spanish word comes from *musca* in Latin.
2. Now look up these words on your own: *chocolate, banana, coyote, lasso, guitar,* and *tomato.*

1. Now you can make a chart of the cultural traits of the people of Tepetongo. Follow the form of the charts you made for the Hopi and Eskimo cultures.
2. How many of the ways of living you listed for your own culture do you find on the Hopi chart? the Eskimo chart? the Tepetongo chart?
3. Which of the ways of living on your charts would be the easiest for people to change? Why?

Reviewing Key Ideas

Imagine that you suddenly find yourself on a deserted island, that is, an island with no people living on it. With you are boys and girls from each of the cultures we have studied. None of you has brought anything with you. You have been dropped into a strange new environment together, empty-handed. Your problem is to find ways to survive.

Besides water, your first need will probably be food. Will you fish? hunt animals? gather fruit from trees? grow vegetables? How will you decide what to do?

Will you look for shelters—or build them? What kind of shelter might you make? What will you need to make it?

All you have with you are the ideas and skills that each of you has learned in the culture in which you were raised. Your Eskimo friends may want to build igloos and hunt for animals. Your Hopi companions may want to build homes from stones and mud. Your Mexican friends may want to plant crops. Each group will try to use its own culture. But you will all be limited by what you find on the island. As a group, you will have to adapt to your new natural environment.

In your studies, then, you have come to understand this about culture: The natural environment affects the culture that people build.

Other Needs

You and your friends will miss the tools you have used in your own cultures. You will have to find a way to make the tools you need to get food and build shelter. Some of your friends may be able to use old skills to make tools. Or you may find that you will have to invent tools that are new to all of you.

Suppose, then, that you and your friends are able to satisfy your material needs—your needs for food, shelter, clothing, and tools. Recall that these are some of the basic parts of cultures everywhere. Will you then have everything you need? Or will you want to make your life richer?

Perhaps in the evening, when your work is done, you will all gather around a fire. You may sing songs for one another or show each other the dances of your people. You may tell stories or share the art of your different cultures.

To each of you, the music, the dance, the stories, and the art of the others may seem very strange. But the *idea* of such things won't be new to anyone. All of you have known art, music, stories, and dance in your own cultures.

By now you have learned a little more about cultures: All cultures include the same basic parts. They all have ways to get food, shelter, and clothing. They all have some kind of art, music, stories, and dances. But these cultural parts take different forms in different cultures.

Changes in Culture

Suppose that more children in your group come from one culture than from any of the others. Then whose music and dance will you hear the most? Which language are you most likely to speak together? Who is most likely to take the lead in planning the work you all do? You will probably find that the largest group will usually take the lead. Other groups may start to lose their culture.

If the island has very little rainfall, the skills of the Hopi children may be most valuable in helping you survive. The Hopi children might become leaders. The rest of you will learn skills from them. The change in your environment would cause you to change your cultures.

If the island has many animals to hunt, the skills of the Eskimo children will seem valuable to all of you. If the Eskimo children lead in hunting, they may begin to lead in other ways, too. Their culture may be copied by the rest of you. Some of you may start to forget your old ways or your old language. When cultures interact, the group with the culture that best fits the environment may lead over other groups. Other groups may start to lose their own cultures.

By now you know that the forms of culture do not stay the same. They may change slowly or quickly. They may change because the natural environment has changed. Or they may change because people of different cultures interact. Thus, you have learned even more about cultures: Cultural forms are changed by people as they interact with people of other cultures or with a changed environment.

Using Key Words

Use these key words to complete the sentences that follow.

adapt	mesa
clan	physical traits
cultural traits	role
culture	tundra
interact	values

1. The special ways a group of people has of acting, speaking, and believing are all parts of their ____.
2. You are born with certain features, such as the color of your skin and eyes. These are your ____.
3. You learned other ways you have of acting and doing things such as the language you speak. These are your ____.
4. A job we do or a part we play in life, such as being a parent, is a ____.
5. The beliefs, customs, and ways of behaving that a people care about are their ____.
6. The people of Tepetongo developed a culture different from the culture of other people in Mexico because their environment was different. To change to fit your environment is to ____.
7. The Hopi built their villages on a flat-topped hill called a ____.
8. Much of the land in the arctic regions is grassy, treeless plains called ____.
9. When people act together, and the actions of each person affect the others, they ____.
10. People in a family, such as aunts, uncles, and cousins, form a group called a ____.

Focus on the Social Scientist

In this unit you have been learning about the customs and traits of different cultures. Such studies of different cultures are possible because of the work of scientists called **cultural anthropologists.** Dr. James Lowell Gibbs, Jr., a Black American, is a cultural anthropologist at Stanford University. He has investigated the culture of the Kpelle (PELL•eh) people in Africa. He and his wife lived among them for a few years, learning the ways in which the people of this African culture meet their needs.

Their first visit was to a village deep in a tropical forest area. They called on the most important chief who lived in the village. They told him what they hoped to do. They exchanged gifts with him. By building goodwill and understanding, Dr. and Mrs. Gibbs earned the permission of the chief to live and study in his village for seventeen months. Day after day they observed the village people and talked with them. In the evenings they wrote a record of what they learned.

From Kpelle women Mrs. Gibbs learned of their homes, families, cooking, and handcrafts. She heard their stories. She learned what they believed and how they spent their time.

From Kpelle men Dr. Gibbs learned of farming, the ways people settled their disagreements, and the things Kpelle valued. He learned, too, of secret clubs that held secret meetings. He asked no questions about the secrets because he had respect for the beliefs of the Kpelle people. Most cultural anthropologists respect the beliefs of the people they study.

A New View of Cultures

You have read of the cultures of the Hopi, the Eskimo, and the people of Tepetongo. Now read of a boy from Los Angeles named Mike. Notice how his culture is like your own. Notice also how his culture differs from yours.

Mike lives with his parents and his sister, Susan. He begins his school day with the pledge to the flag. For lunch he eats a peanut butter sandwich. He likes to play baseball. When he grows up, he may want to be a musician like his mother. But sometimes he would rather be an astronaut or a baseball pitcher.

Three times a week Mike goes to a special school. There he learns the Hebrew language. He learns of the land where it is spoken—Israel. He learns of Moses and the Ten Commandments. He learns of famous and important American Jews. He reads books and plays written by Jewish writers.

Friday nights, Mike's family has its Sabbath (SAB·buth) meal. His mother prays and lights two candles. His father prays, cuts *hallah* (HAH·lah), which is a special bread, and pours wine. After having the bread and wine, the family eat the rest of the meal. Then they all go to the temple. Like all the men there, Mike and his father cover their heads with a *yarmulke* (YAH·mul·kuh) to show respect for God.

In December Mike and his family will celebrate *Hanukkah* (HAH·noo·kuh), the festival of lights. This holiday is celebrated by Jews all over the world. Each evening for eight days, the family lights another candle on the *Hanukkah Menorah* (men·OR·uh). Each night Mike and Susan get a different present.

Living in Two Cultures

Mike is one boy who lives in two cultures. He is an American and a Jew. He shares many culture traits with most people who live in the United States, where he was born. He also shares the Jewish culture with millions of Jews in many lands. His grandparents and other Jews brought Jewish culture with them when they came to the United States from other parts of the world.

Before Columbus came to America, many different people with many separate cultures already lived here. These were the Native American cultures—Mohawk, Navaho, Sioux, and many more. Beginning with Columbus, explorers and then settlers came to America, bringing their own cultures with them. Parts of their cultures had to change to suit the new environment. Other parts of their culture changed when Native American ways seemed better. Some parts of their culture remained the same.

Over the years people of all these groups have come to share many ways of acting and believing. They have built a new culture that most Americans now share, as does Mike.

Many Americans also keep alive parts of cultures their grandparents and great grandparents brought to America. Like Mike's family, they value the old ways and like to share them with others who feel the same.

In most cities there are people of many different cultures. You will find evidence of these cultures in people's foods, houses, languages, music, dances, festivals, arts and crafts, and churches and temples.

UNIT TWO

The Birth of the United States

It is the winter of 1620. A battered ship called the *Mayflower* rocks gently in the waters of Plymouth Bay. On board are about one hundred English settlers who call themselves "Pilgrims." They prepare to begin a new life in an unknown land that promises both opportunity and danger.

Behind them lies the stormy Atlantic Ocean. And beyond that is Europe and the life they have left. It is a life with crowded cities and fenced-in land. Many people have grown tired of the wars and religious fighting. They are seeking a new life.

To the Pilgrims, the thickly wooded coastline before them looks like an endless wilderness But it is not. Hundreds of groups of people live there. Each group has its own culture and ways of life. A few of these Native Americans know of the new visitors. From the forests they watch the settlers silently and wait.

Europeans Explore North America

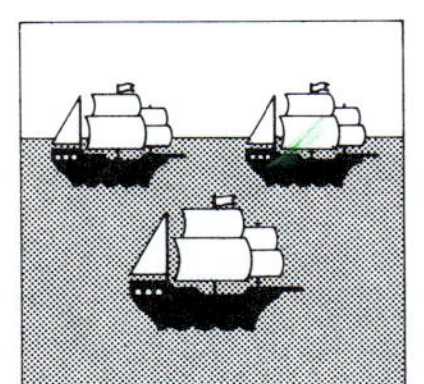

For hundreds of years, European explorers had sailed the seas, seeking new lands. With each discovery, the world they knew grew larger. The Vikings in their long boats had been the most successful. Between A.D. 800 and A.D. 1100, they reached Iceland and Greenland. Some even landed on the northeast coast of North America. They called this place "Vinland."

Such voyages increased in the 1400s. In their fast ships, Portuguese captains sailed south down the African coast. One after another, explorers looked for a sea route to the spices of India and China. Vasco da Gama (VAS·koh duh·GAH·muh), a Portuguese explorer, sailed to India in 1498.

A few years earlier Christopher Columbus, a mapmaker from Genoa, Italy, had made a new plan. He hoped to reach India by sailing west across the Atlantic. Portugal turned down his plan. But in 1492 King Ferdinand and Queen Isabella of Spain agreed to give Columbus his ships. On August 3, Columbus set sail westward.

Ten weeks later, on October 12, Christopher Columbus landed on Guanahani (gwa·nuh·HAN·ee), one of the Bahama Islands. The people he met there he called "Indians," for he believed he had reached an island off the coast of India. He never did realize his error.

What Columbus did was greater than he thought. He had opened the way to a world unknown to Europe. It was to be a world of riches and promise beyond anything he imagined. His discovery gave people in Europe new hope.

Other Voyages to America

After Columbus's success, other explorers sailed westward. In 1497 John Cabot, an English explorer, sailed down the North American coast from Newfoundland to Maine. The same year another Italian, Amerigo Vespucci (uh•MER•uh•goh VES•POOT•chee), made a voyage for Spain. He sailed along the coast of the Gulf of Mexico and around Florida. Vespucci was sure that Columbus had found a "new world," not the Indies. In 1507 the name "America," a form of Vespucci's first name, was chosen to describe this land on a printed map.

Soon other nations sent ships across the Atlantic Ocean. Each nation wanted to make its own claims to land, treasure, and trading rights. Vespucci, now sailing for Portugal, explored the coast of South America in 1503. Giovanni da Verrazano (jaw•VAH•nee dah ver•ə•ZAH•noh) sailed the North American coast for France in 1524. Henry Hudson sailed into New York Harbor for the Dutch in 1609.

Almost everywhere they landed, the explorers were met by the people who already lived there. In these meetings neither side understood the culture of the other. The Native Americans looked upon the Europeans as unusual visitors. The Europeans saw the Native Americans as a simple people who lived in a wilderness. Both sides were mistaken. But it would be a long time before they realized their mistakes.

The Native American Home

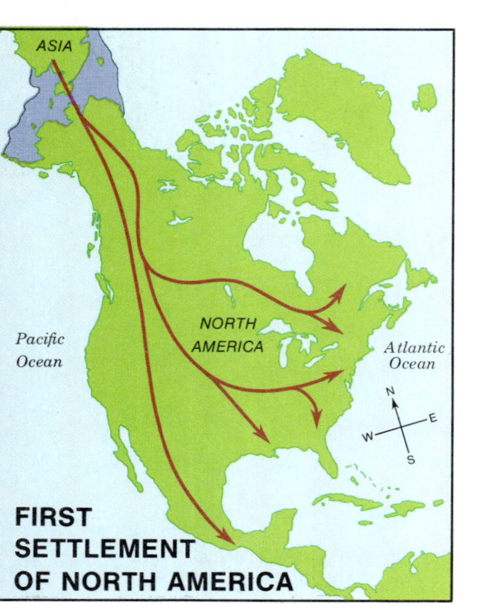

Native Americans had been living in the Americas for at least fifty thousand years before the Europeans came. Their ancestors may have come from Asia over the Bering Strait and down through Alaska. Scientists believe they may have crossed a wide land bridge that once connected the two continents.

From Alaska these early people moved south and east throughout North and South America. As they spread out, different groups developed different ways of life. Some hunted, some fished, some grew crops. They lived in forests and plains, in rain forests and deserts, on seashores and mountains. By 1492 Native Americans spoke at least 160 languages. Together, the different groups of Native Americans may have numbered nearly a hundred million people. That was about twenty-five million more people than lived in Europe at that time.

Different Ways of Life

The cultures of the Native Americans differed. For example, the Shoshone, the Pueblos, and the Aztecs were distant relatives. But in 1492 they lived and acted very differently.

The Shoshone lived in the dry, rocky land between the Rocky Mountains and the Sierra Nevada. The small bands of Shoshone lived a wandering life. They gathered roots and berries and hunted small game. Families usually roamed alone. Often they cooperated with other Shoshone families. There were no chiefs, and war was unknown.

A few hundred miles south, the Pueblo lived in what is now Arizona. They built large cliff cities and grew corn, beans, and squash. The Pueblo lived in several tribes. Each tribe was guided by a council of elders. These elders were usually priests.

Further south and east lived the Aztecs. They had fought and conquered other Native American groups. In time the Aztecs had a rich empire, ruled by a king. They built huge pyramids as temples. They grew many crops unknown to Europeans. The Aztec calendar was more accurate than the one used in Europe. More people lived in their largest city, *Tenochtitlan* (tay•nawch•tee•TLAHN), in A.D. 1500 than in London, England.

The Meeting of Cultures

The Europeans who sailed to America did not understand the differences among the Native Americans. Most Europeans thought the native cultures were simple and the people were much like children. Yet, in the interaction between the two cultures, the Native Americans gave as much to the Europeans as they received.

The Europeans brought to America many skills and tools. They brought guns, ships, horses, metals, cloth, and the wheel. To survive in their new environment, however,

they needed many skills developed by Native Americans. Soon, many settlers began wearing buckskin clothing. They learned native ways of fishing and trapping, planting crops, and traveling by canoe.

Most important were the crops. Corn is one of the most important crops in the world today. It was first grown by Native Americans. By 1492 they had more than seven hundred kinds of corn. Potatoes, tomatoes, squash, beans, and tobacco were also first grown by Native Americans.

Spain and Conquest

It was not corn that Columbus and those who followed him had come for, however. It was gold. In 1519 Hernán Cortés (er•NAHN kor•TES) and four hundred soldiers conquered the Aztecs in Mexico. Francisco Pizarro (fran•SIS•kaw pee•SAHR•raw), another Spanish adventurer, defeated the Incas in Peru in 1532. These and other Spanish conquerors forced the Native Americans to work in mines. They shipped the gold and silver they mined back to

EARLY EXPLORERS
TO THE AMERICAS
England
France
Spain
Portugal
Netherlands
Land Controlled by Spain in 1600
0
1000
2000 Miles
0
1000
2000 Kilometers
NORTH AMERICA
SOUTH AMERICA
Pacific Ocean
Atlantic Ocean
Gulf of Mexico
Caribbean Sea
Columbia River
Colorado River
Rio Grande
Mississippi River
St. Lawrence River
Amazon River
Paraná River
NEWFOUNDLAND
FLORIDA
WEST INDIES
MEXICO
Aztec
Tenochtitlan
Inca
Cuzco
ENGLAND
FRANCE
SPAIN
PORTUGAL
Hudson—1609
Cabot—1497
Verrazano—1524
Columbus—1492
Cortes—1519
Coronado—1540–42
Vespucci—1497
Vespucci—1503
Pizarro—1532
N
S
E
W
140°
120°
100°
80°
60°
40°
20°
80°
60°
40°
20°
0°
20°
40°

FRANCISCO VASQUEZ DE CORONADO, by N. C. Wyeth, Brandywine River Museum, Chadds Ford, Pennsylvania

Spain. One Spanish explorer after another claimed lands for Spain. Some, like Francisco de Coronado (kaw•raw•NAH•daw), spent years searching for seven cities of gold.

Spain sent more than soldiers and explorers to the new world. Missionaries, or priests, also came to teach the Native Americans the Christian religion. Santa Fe, Los Angeles, and San Francisco began as missions built by Spanish priests. Here Native Americans were given food and shelter and taught Christianity.

By 1550 Spain controlled more land in America than any other nation. The Spanish cities grew. Spanish culture spread throughout America. To pass on this culture, the Spanish built schools and colleges. The first colleges in America were begun in Mexico City and Lima, Peru.

1. Where had the Vikings sailed by A.D. 1100?
2. Why did Columbus call the people on Guanahani "Indians"?
3. Where did the name "America" come from?
4. What did the Europeans think of the Native Americans?
5. How did the Native Americans greet the Europeans when they first came?
6. How did the Native Americans get to North America? Where do scientists think they may have come from?
7. What were some differences between the Shoshone and the Pueblo cultures?
8. What did the Europeans bring to America?
9. What did they learn from the Native Americans?
10. What did Cortes and Pizarro seek in America?
11. How did the cities of Santa Fe, Los Angeles, and San Francisco begin?
12. Which nation controlled the most land in America by the middle of the 1500s?
13. Where were the first schools built in America?

The European settlers who came to America were used to their old cultural ways. Many wore fancy clothes and stiff shoes. But soon they began to follow some of the Native American ways.

1. Why might settlers wear buckskin clothing in their new environment?
2. Why might they decide to plant Native American crops?
3. There are many Native American place names still in use in the United States. Can you find one or two in your community? What are they?

A time line is a good way to show the order in which events happened. The time line below shows some key events that took place between 1400 and 1650. Make your own time line on a sheet of paper. Include the events shown on this time line. Then add the following events to your time line.

1. Mayflower lands at Plymouth Bay, **1620.**
2. Vasco da Gama sails around Africa to India, **1498.**
3. Amerigo Vespucci explores South American coast, **1503.**
4. Giovanni da Verrazano explores North American coast, **1524.**
5. Francisco Pizarro defeats the Incas, **1532.**

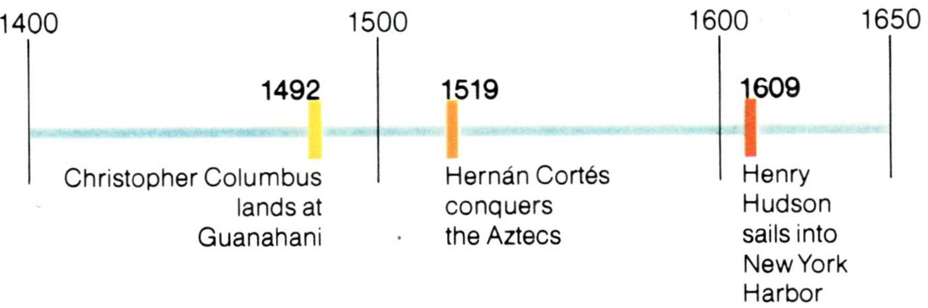

In the 1400s European explorers claimed land in America for their nations. Since the 1960s nations have been exploring outer space. People have landed on the moon, and space ships have traveled to other planets.

Should the nations that land on other planets claim those planets for their nation? What are your reasons for your answer?

2 Settling the Colonies

For many years after Columbus's voyage, Spanish cities and Spanish missions were built throughout America. Spain grew rich on gold and silver from its new lands. Other nations sent explorers to North America, but none could challenge the Spanish claim to America.

Then, in 1588, the English navy defeated the Spanish navy. Many of the Spanish ships were destroyed. Until this time, other European nations had thought it was impossible to defeat the Spanish navy. Now they began to think about empires of their own in America. French trappers set up trading posts along the St. Lawrence River in the early 1600s. French missionaries explored the lands around the Mississippi River. At the same time, people in England were looking to America as a new home.

Although many Spanish people had settled in Mexico, not many lived on the northern frontier in what is now the United States. The French wanted to control the rich fur trade in the forests of the northeast. Not many French settlers came, however. But most of the English came as colonists to settle the land. The English coastal settlements soon had thousands of colonists. They would be very important in deciding the future of North America.

The English Companies

England in the early 1600s was a nation of sharp differences. Its navy was the most powerful in the world. Its nobles were wealthy. But in the cities the poor were begging in the streets. The King and **Parliament** fought for power. Church groups argued about who had the true religion. Many farmers were driven off the land. In the cities there were not enough jobs. People who could not pay their bills went to prison. Many English people looked across the Atlantic for a place where they could be free.

One way to reach America was to join a company. This was a group of people who put their money together to make the voyage. The King **chartered,** or gave land to, these companies to start colonies. Paying members of the company got land when they arrived in the colony.

More than half the colonists could not pay their own way, however. They came to America as **indentured servants.** This meant that someone else had paid their way. In return, they had to work for their masters until they had paid off the cost of their trip. Usually it took seven years.

The First Colony

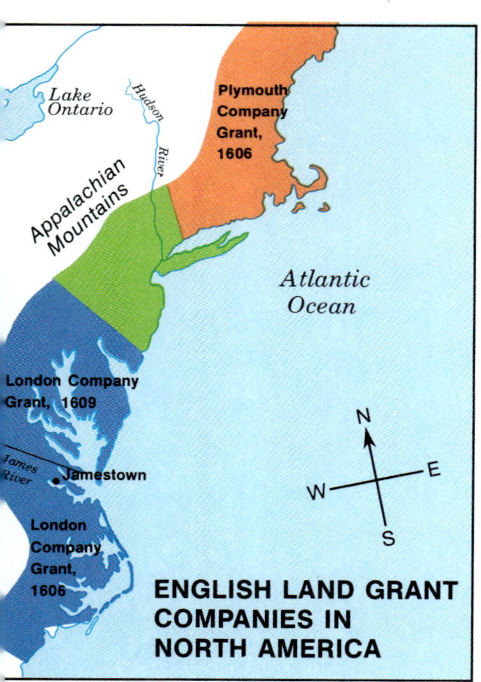

ENGLISH LAND GRANT COMPANIES IN NORTH AMERICA

The first successful English settlement in North America was started at Jamestown, Virginia, in 1607. The settlers did not have an easy time. Many died in the first seven months. The rest survived by planting corn given to them by Native Americans. But the colonists worked hard. Before long they were sending lumber and tar to shipbuilders in England.

In 1612 Native Americans showed the Jamestown settlers how to plant tobacco. Within two years tobacco had become the first cash crop of the colonies. Soon settlers were planting tobacco everywhere along the coast from Maryland to North Carolina. Their large farms were called **plantations.** Ships could sail right up the river to the plantation docks and load the tobacco bound for England.

In the rich soil and mild climate of the southern coast, farming became the main way of life. The plantation was its center. Before long these plantations needed more and more workers. In 1619 Black Africans came to Virginia to

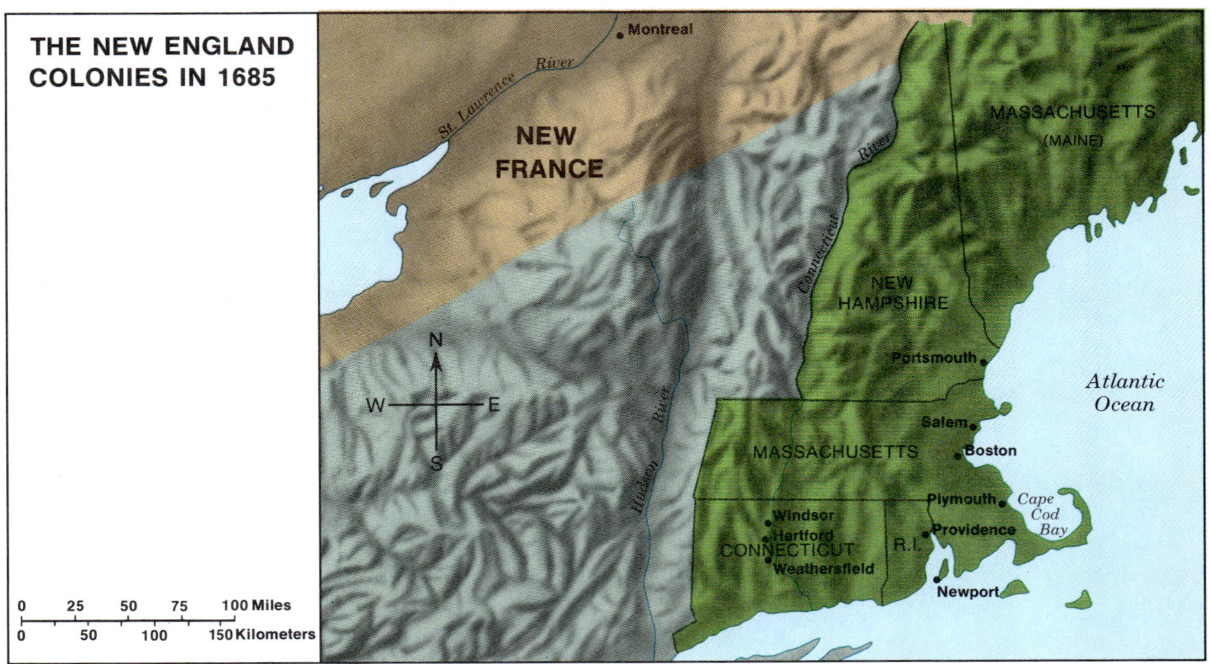

work on the plantations. In that same year Virginia also set up its first representative government. It was called the House of Burgesses.

The New England Colonies

The first English colony on the northern coast was founded at Plymouth, Massachusetts, in 1620. The Pilgrims had been headed for Virginia. When they discovered that they had sailed too far north, they agreed to stay where they were. Their leaders signed the *Mayflower Compact.* This agreement called for a governing body that would make "just and equal laws" for the colony.

The Pilgrims soon found that the northern environment was very different from Virginia. Cold winters and rocky soil made farming very hard. Tobacco would never grow in New England. But the deep harbors made fine ports for ships. The thick forests of hardwood trees could be made into lumber for shipbuilding. The large schools of codfish in the sea made fishing a good industry.

Ten years after the Pilgrims had landed at Plymouth, another colony was started by the Puritans at Massachusetts Bay. Unlike the Pilgrims, the Puritans came with food, clothing, and tools to build their new community.

The church was the center of Puritan life. Men, women, and children prayed and went to church often. They lived by the strict rules set by their ministers.

The Puritans thought that all people were naturally sinful, but that they could save themselves by overcoming their sinful nature. One way of doing that was to work hard. Puritans worked hard and long in the Bay colony.

Puritan rules were very strict. Games and music were thought to be a waste of time, so they were forbidden. People who disobeyed the rules were punished. Often their hands and feet were locked in public stocks for several hours or days. This was to disgrace them before other people. To find out more about obeying laws and rules, try the investigation on the facing page.

AN INVESTIGATION into obeying rules and laws

Rules and laws tell some ways that people should or should not act. But someone must see that people obey these rules or laws.

On a piece of paper, make two lists like the ones below. One list can be the roles of people who try to get everyone to act correctly. The other list can be the ways of acting that show the need for someone to watch.

PEOPLE	WAYS OF ACTING
life guard	children jumping in pool

A Problem on Your Own

Do the people you listed in your chart have to obey rules and laws, too? Does someone make sure that they do? Explain your answers.

A Puritan was expected to work hard, be thrifty, live by the laws, and be respectful to elders. The Puritans believed that if they lived in this way they would be rewarded with a good, prosperous life. Those who did not work hard or were poor were thought to be sinful. At one time poor people were made to wear the letter *P* on the shoulder of their right sleeve. The *P* stood for pauper or poor person.

The Puritans did not allow people to follow any other religion in the Bay Colony. When Roger Williams, a Puritan minister, argued against this policy, he was sent away from the community. Williams founded his own colony at Providence in 1636. It was the first settlement in New England to allow freedom of religion.

Anne Hutchinson, another Puritan, was also forced to leave Massachusetts Bay. She began a settlement nearby on Narragansett Bay. In 1644 the two settlements were chartered as the colony of Rhode Island.

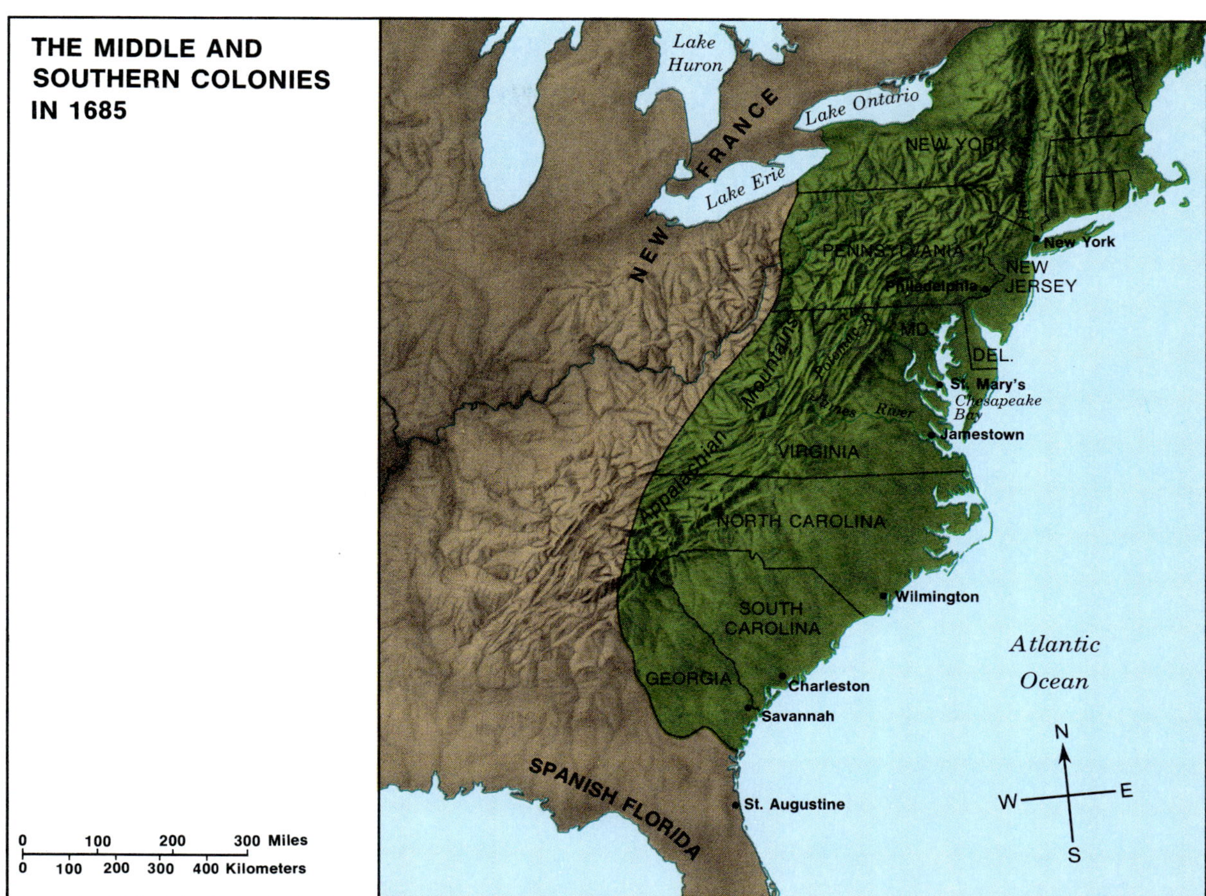

The Middle and Southern Colonies

Between New England and the southern colonies lay New Netherland, New Jersey, Delaware, and Pennsylvania. New Netherland, later renamed New York by the English, was settled by the Dutch in 1624. The other colonies were chartered by the English King.

Some colonies were settled largely by Quakers. The Quakers had been **persecuted,** or punished, in both England and New England for their religious beliefs. Quakers did not have priests or religious rites. They believed all men and women were equal. They opposed war. The Quakers settled mainly in the Pennsylvania colony, which was named after its founder, William Penn.

Farther south, Lord Baltimore started Maryland as a colony for Catholics who were being persecuted in England. Fifteen years after the first settlers arrived at Chesapeake Bay, the colonial assembly passed the Toleration Acts. These laws promised religious freedom to all Christians who came to Maryland.

The Carolinas were settled largely by young English nobles. They started large tobacco and rice plantations and brought Black African slaves to work for them. The Africans adapted better than the English to the Carolina climate and lowlands. The success of the plantations was due largely to their knowledge of herding cattle and growing rice. Their skill with the canoe, the main way of transportation in the colonies, was unmatched.

South of the Carolinas, James Oglethorpe started the colony of Georgia. It was settled largely by poor people who had been freed from prison. Slavery was forbidden.

Spanish and French Influence

South of Georgia was the old Spanish settlement of St. Augustine in Florida. In the West, the Spanish had also settled Santa Fe in New Mexico. But Spain's power in North America had declined after the defeat of its navy in 1588.

French power was growing, however. The French had founded New Orleans and had claimed the Louisiana Territory along the banks of the Mississippi River. In the St. Lawrence Valley, the French settlements of Montreal and Quebec City were growing rapidly. North and south, east and west, the French and English began building forts to protect their claims. They prepared for the long struggle that would finally decide who would control the land in North America.

1. Why did English settlers leave England for America?
2. What was an indentured servant? What did an indentured servant have to do to be free again?
3. What changed life in Jamestown in 1612?
4. How did the Puritans of Massachusetts Bay think people should live?
5. Why were Roger Williams and Anne Hutchinson sent away from Massachusetts? Where did they go?
6. Who were the Quakers? What did they believe?
7. What skills did Black Africans bring with them to the Carolinas?
8. Which two nations wanted control of North America?

The Puritans who settled Massachusetts Bay believed that their way of life was the only true way. When Roger Williams and Anne Hutchinson disagreed, they were sent away from the community.

1. Can people disagree with rules and beliefs in your school?
2. What might happen to someone who disagrees? Would a person be sent away?
3. What happens to someone who disobeys a rule?

The map on the facing page shows the growth of the English settlements in America to 1750. Use the map to help you answer these questions.

1. What geographic features of the land blocked the settlers from moving westward?
2. How did rivers seem to affect settlement?
3. Which colonies had the most settlers in 1700?
4. Which colonies grew the most between 1700 and 1750? Why do you think this happened?

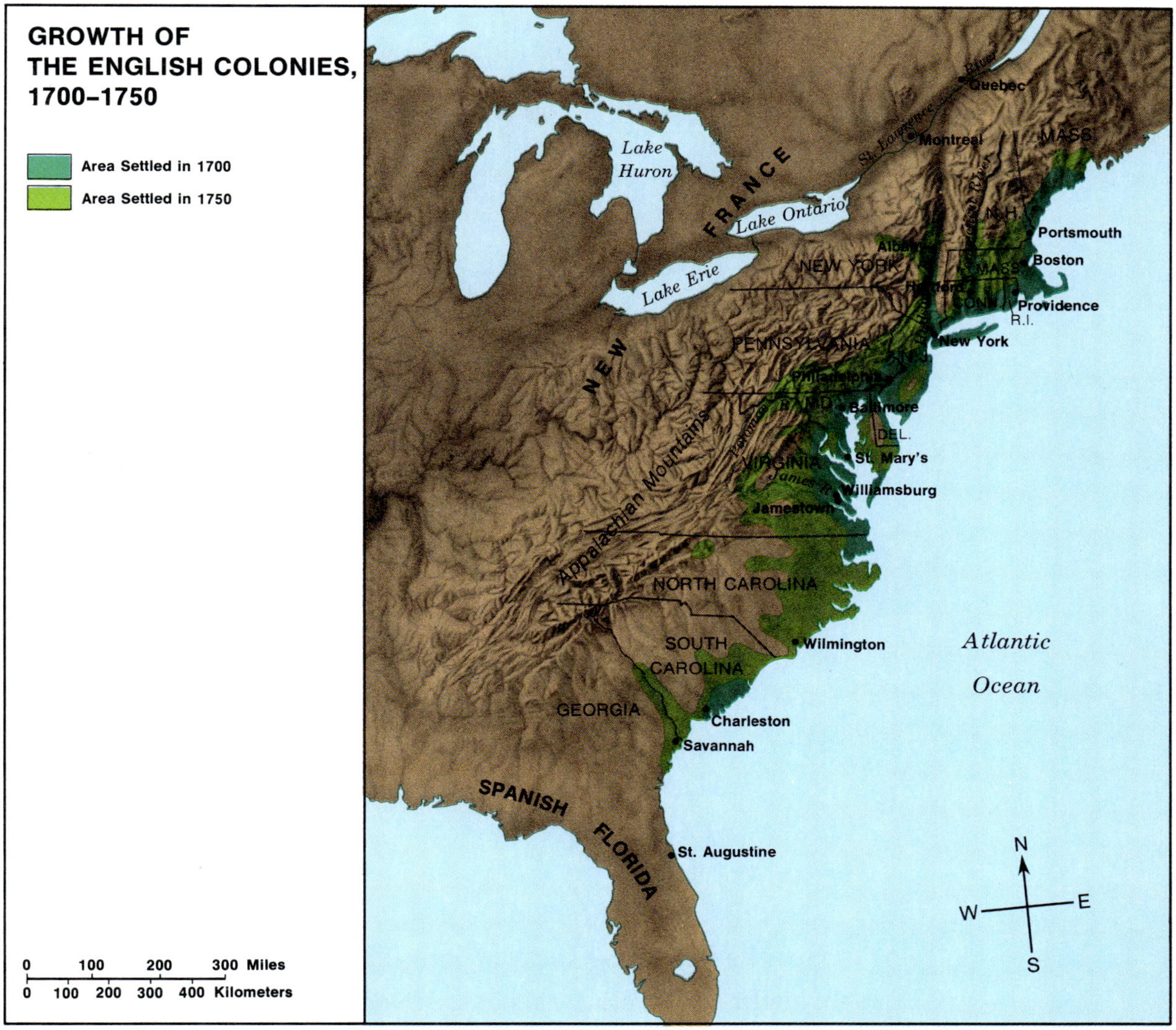

GROWTH OF THE ENGLISH COLONIES, 1700–1750

Area Settled in 1700

Area Settled in 1750

0 100 200 300 Miles

0 100 200 300 400 Kilometers

The Pilgrim village at Plymouth, Massachusetts, has been rebuilt. Each year thousands of Americans visit Plymouth.

1. Why might people want to rebuild an old village?
2. Why would people want to visit it?
3. Is there an old village or part of town near where you live that has been rebuilt? Find out about it. What is it? Why and when was it built?

3 Trouble in the Colonies

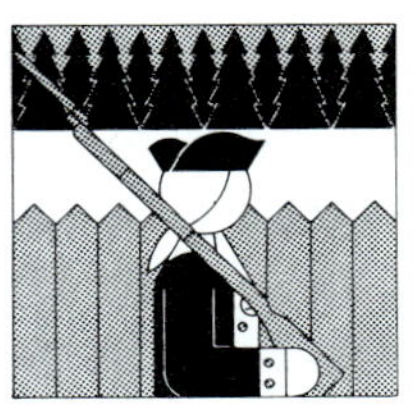

Life changed as the colonies grew. The first colonists had worried about food and shelter. The later colonists were concerned with getting bigger and better. They planted and traded for more of everything—more goods, more comfort, more land, and more profit.

In the north, cities grew. Streets were paved. Homes, schools, and churches were built. Shops of all kinds were opened. Harvard College was founded in 1636 in Cambridge, Massachusetts. By 1750 Philadelphia and New York were almost as large as many cities in Europe.

In the South, the plantations grew. More and more they depended on slave labor. More Black Africans were brought to America as slaves. Everyone lived close to the soil. There were few cities, schools, or churches, and the roads were poor. Each plantation was its own center of life.

This Land Is My Land

As towns grew into cities, many colonists became restless. They wanted to move on, to push over the hills to the next frontier. But the land was not empty. It belonged to the Native Americans, and they did not want to be pushed off it. In Virginia in 1622 Native Americans killed 350 settlers who had built houses beyond Jamestown. The English struck back by killing twice as many Native Americans.

Native Americans and colonists had different ideas about the land. Most Native Americans believed the land was to be shared. The animals and the land were to be used by those who needed them.

To most colonists, however, land was something to be owned. In Europe most land was owned by rich people with large farms. Small farmers had little chance to get land. But in the colonies there was plenty of land. Every colonist wanted some. Land gave a person freedom and a place in the community.

There were other differences, too. Native Americans lived close to the land. They were thankful for the food and shelter nature gave them. They moved with the animals and the seasons. But to the colonists, land was to be cleared and fenced in. They cut the forests down and used the wood for firewood or for building ships and homes. In the clearings, they built homes and planted crops.

Some crops were hard on the land. Tobacco wore out the soil in a few years. When the land was used up, or when a settlement became too crowded, the colonists simply moved on to new land. There was always more land to the west. They knew Native Americans already lived there. That did not stop them. The colonists thought their culture was better than the Native Americans'. They believed they had the right to take what they wanted.

To find out more about uses of land, try the investigation on page 91.

The French and Indian War

During the 1700s English colonists moved further and further inland. Often they ran into other people, especially French trappers. England and France were now the major powers in the northeastern part of America. Spain ruled the land in the south and west. France claimed all the land between the Appalachian Mountains and the Mississippi River. This region was a rich source of furs for trappers.

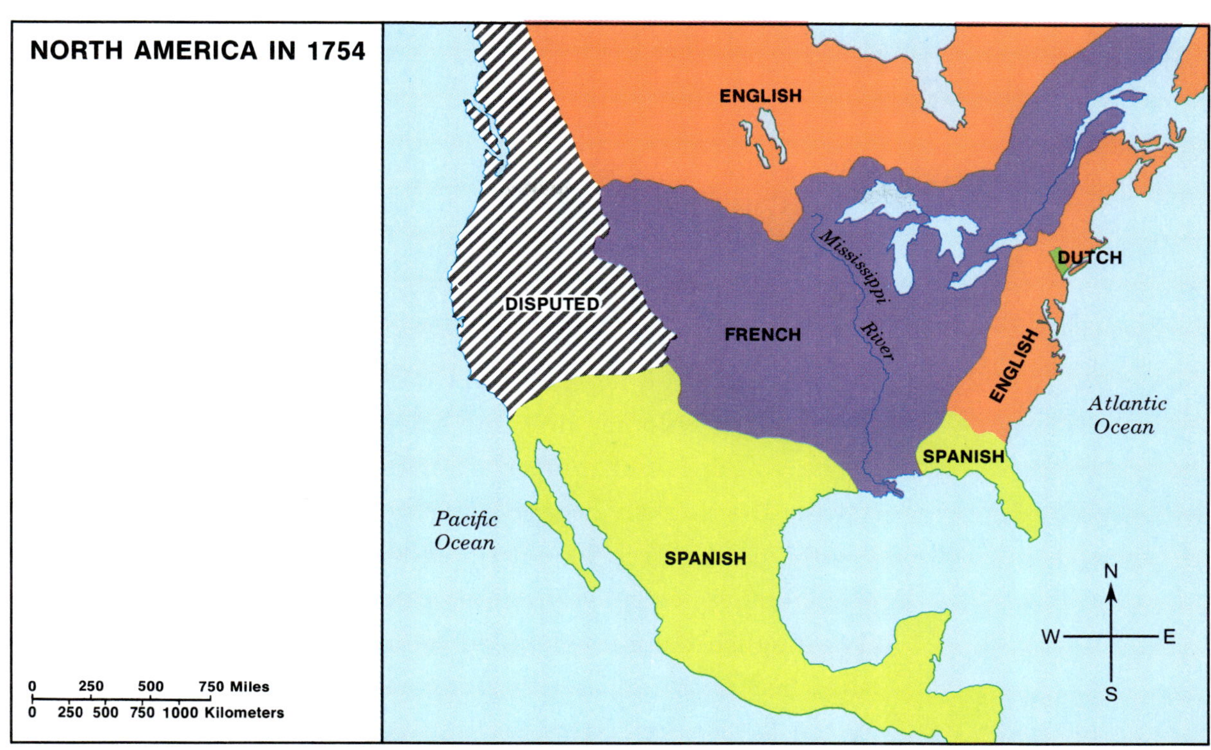
NORTH AMERICA IN 1754
ENGLISH
DUTCH
DISPUTED
FRENCH
Mississippi River
ENGLISH
Atlantic Ocean
SPANISH
Pacific Ocean
SPANISH
N
W
E
S
0 250 500 750 Miles
0 250 500 750 1000 Kilometers

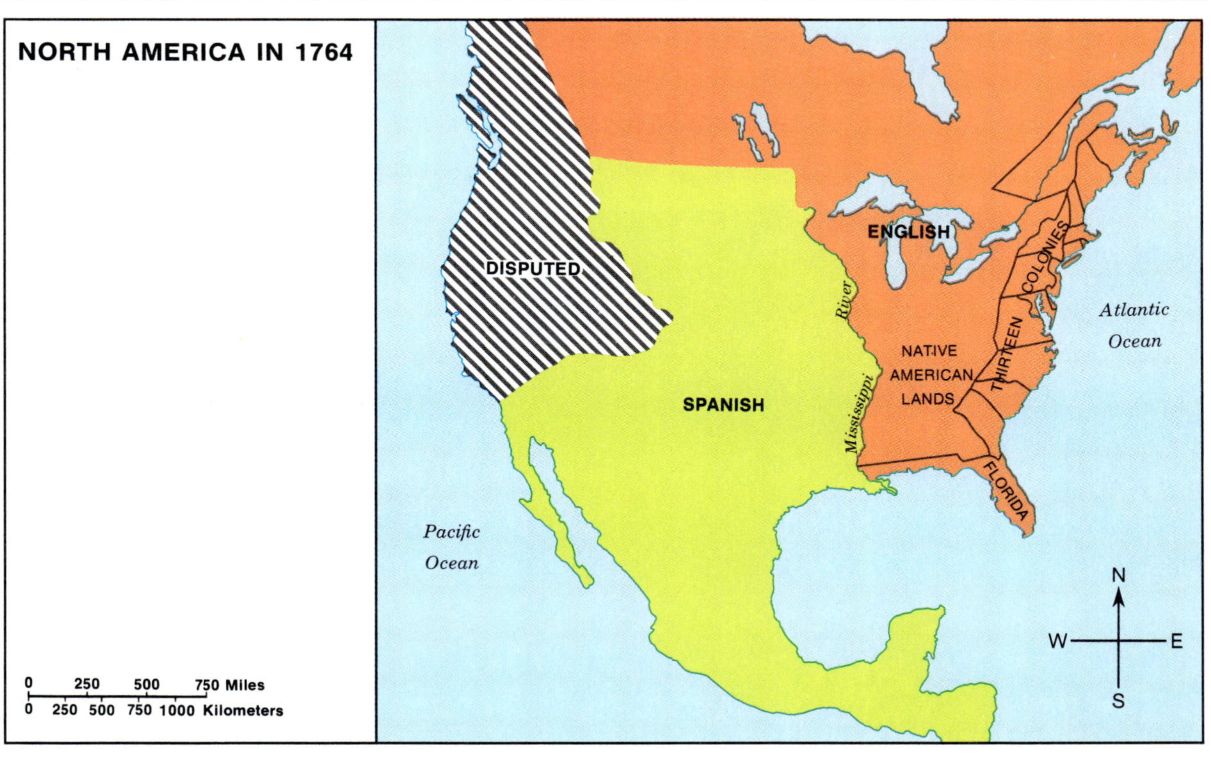
NORTH AMERICA IN 1764
ENGLISH
DISPUTED
River
THIRTEEN COLONIES
Atlantic Ocean
NATIVE AMERICAN LANDS
SPANISH
Mississippi
FLORIDA
Pacific Ocean
N
W
E
S
0 250 500 750 Miles
0 250 500 750 1000 Kilometers

As more English settlers moved across the Appalachians, the French became worried. They built forts in the Ohio Valley. Together with Native Americans, they began to raid and burn the homes of English colonists along the frontier.

By 1754 England sent soldiers to protect the colonies. Fighting began in the Ohio Valley. Two years later war broke out in Europe between France and England. In Europe the war was called the Seven Year's War. In North America the fighting was known as the French and Indian War. In the colonies first one side, then the other, seemed to be winning. But there were more English colonists. After awhile the English began to win.

In 1763 the Treaty of Paris ended the French and Indian War. France lost nearly all her colonies in North America. The English colonies doubled in size. English territory now stretched north and south along the Atlantic coast and west to the Mississippi River.

AN INVESTIGATION
into community planning

A city may decide to divide its land into **zones,** or areas. The land in each zone can be used only in certain ways. Factories, for example, may not be built in a zone planned for homes. What zones do you see on the map below?

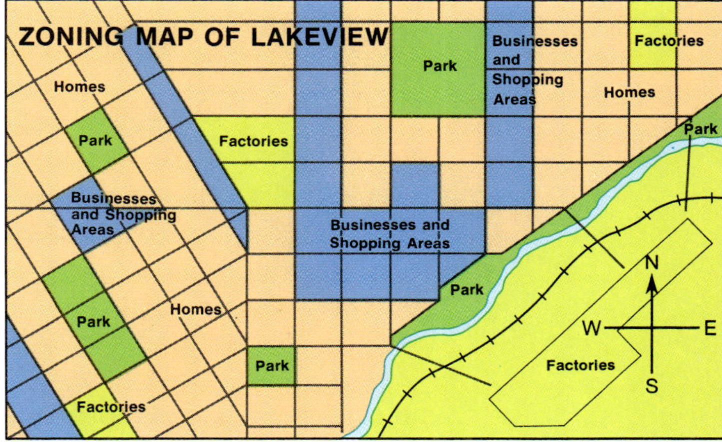

Find out how your community is divided into zones. You can get a zoning map by writing to the chamber of commerce. Try to answer these questions:

1. What different zones do you have? How can the land in each zone be used? Why are there different zones?
2. Who decided on the zones? How can they be changed?
3. Has the zoning of your community ever been changed? How?
4. In which zone is your school?

The Fight over Taxes

The French and Indian War had cost England a lot of money. Peace was also costly. England now had thirteen separate colonies, plus Canada, Florida, and a Native American territory. Each area had to be ruled. The frontier had to be protected. Governors had to be paid, and soldiers had to be fed and housed. All of this cost money. The English government decided to raise some of this money by taxing the colonies.

In 1764 the English Parliament passed the Sugar Act. It added a tax to the price of sugar and other products the colonists had to import. A year later Parliament passed the Stamp Act. It placed a tax on newspapers, licenses, and documents of all kinds. More important, it was the first tax the colonists had to pay on things they bought. The colonists saw the price of each newspaper they bought go up because of the tax. Lawyers, merchants, printers, shippers, and other groups united to protest the Stamp Act. Some questioned England's right to tax the colonies at all.

James Otis, a Boston lawyer, argued that there could be no taxation without representation. He said that Parliament should not pass tax laws for the colonies since the colonists could not elect representatives to Parliament. Others took up the cry. The Sons of Liberty, a citizen's group, burned the records of the Boston tax court. Merchants in Boston and Philadelphia called on people to **boycott,** or stop buying, European goods. Representatives from nine of the colonies met at a Stamp Act Congress. They declared that only the colonists had the right to tax themselves.

Parliament repealed the Stamp Act in 1766. But on the same day it claimed full power over the colonies. The next year Parliament passed more tax laws. These laws said tax collectors could search private homes for goods on which taxes had not been paid. When the people of Boston protested, English soldiers were sent to Boston to keep order.

The Boston Massacre

Parliament had said English soldiers could demand that the colonists give them food and shelter. The colonists said that their homes and businesses were being invaded. On March 5, 1770, an angry crowd in Boston faced a group of English soldiers. The crowd shouted at the soldiers and pushed in on them. Suddenly the soldiers fired into the crowd. They killed four people and wounded three others.

The Boston Massacre, as this shooting was called, shocked everyone. The English pulled their soldiers out of the city. Feelings eased for awhile. But the struggle went on. Parliament and King George III wanted to control the colonies. The colonists wanted to defend their rights.

1. How did the colonists' view of land differ from the Native Americans'?
2. What were some of the causes of the French and Indian War?
3. How did the Treaty of Paris in 1763 change the size of the English colonies?
4. Why did the Stamp Act anger so many colonists?
5. What did the colonists do to protest taxation by Parliament?

Settlers and Native Americans disagreed about land in North America. Even today people disagree about what rights they have on land they own. Zoning laws in most communities try to limit what people may do with their property.

1. Does a person who owns land in your community have the right to do anything he or she pleases with the land? Why?
2. What are some limits in your neighborhood on how people can use land?

The map on this page shows the English and French forts where fighting took place during the French and Indian War. Use the map to help you answer these questions.

1. What forts did France build on Lake Ontario?
2. What English fort was built on Lake Ontario?
3. What English fort was nearest to Fort Ticonderoga?
4. Which English forts were west of the Appalachian Mountains?
5. Who had more forts?

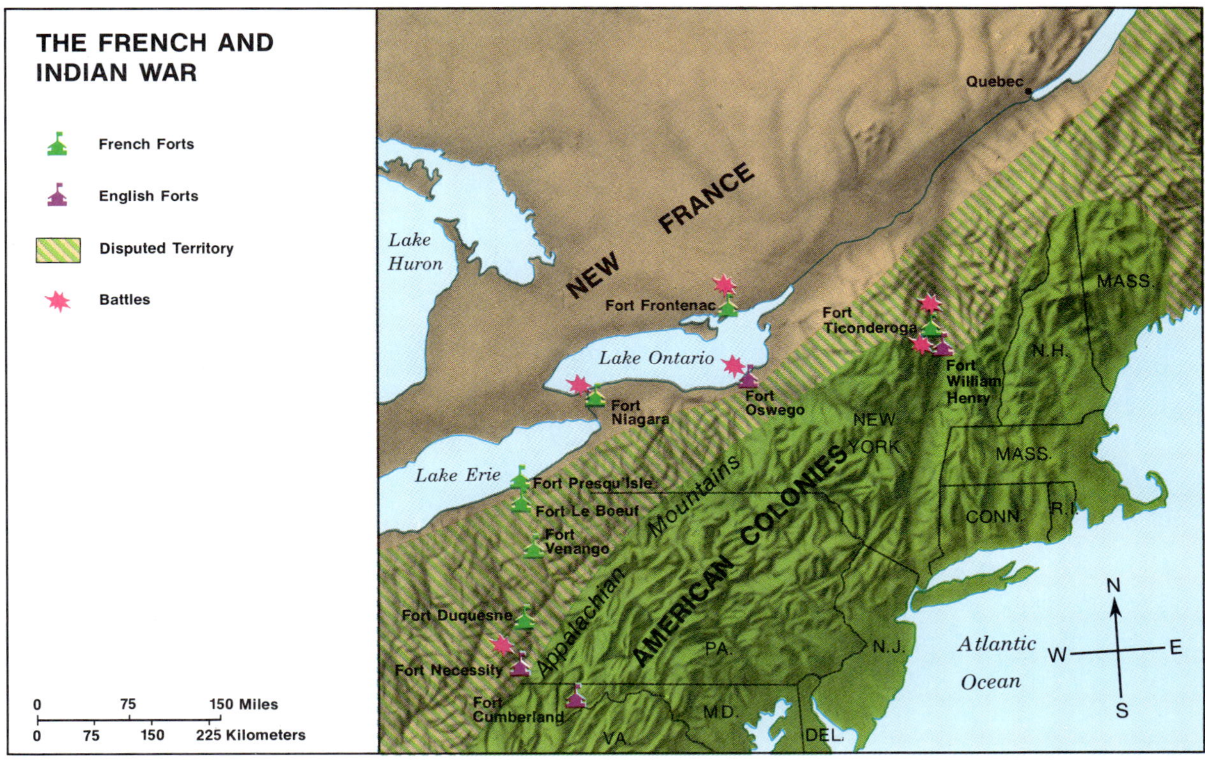

1. What reasons did France and England have for owning colonies in North America?
2. What reasons might a nation today have for owning colonies?

4 Tea and Revolution

The three years after the Boston Massacre were like the calm before a storm. The English Parliament had removed the taxes on all imported goods except tea. But the tea tax still angered the colonists. Quietly they worked together to fight against it. Many refused to buy tea. Committees of Correspondence published letters protesting Parliament's actions. Among the members of these groups were patriots like Sam Adams, Thomas Jefferson, and Patrick Henry.

To find out more about acting politically, try the investigation on page 98.

The Boston Tea Party

Tons of tea lay rotting in the warehouses of the East India Company, an English trading company in London. It seemed the company might go out of business. To keep this from happening, Parliament first cut the company's taxes. Then it said the East India Company could sell tea directly to the colonies. That meant the company could sell its tea for less than other tea merchants. This made colonial merchants very angry.

In December 1773 the first ship carrying the cheaper tea sailed into Boston Harbor. The colonists demanded that it return to England. The governor of Massachusetts said no.

The ship remained in the harbor with the tea in its hold. Finally a band of colonists acted. They boarded the ship and threw all the tea into the harbor. In one night they destroyed chests of tea valued at thousands of dollars. Nothing else on the ship was hurt.

Parliament was angered by the Boston Tea Party. It passed a series of laws to punish the people of Massachusetts. First it closed Boston Harbor to shipping. Then it said that officials who had been elected by the colonists would now be named by the King. The law also said the colonists could not hold town meetings. And it ordered the colonists to give soldiers food and shelter in private homes as well as public inns. For many people, life in the colonies became intolerable.

AN INVESTIGATION
into political action

There are many needs people cannot meet alone. There are sidewalks to be repaired, parks to be kept beautiful and safe, research to be done to cure diseases, cities to be renewed, and much more.

When a number of people have the same needs, they often work together. They work to get the money to pay the people who have the time and the skills to do something about that need. Very often there is a long waiting time between making the plan and getting money and people to do something about it.

In your community there are people who have already taken the first two steps. Look carefully in your local newspaper to find evidence of people working together.

1. Find the name of an organization formed by people to meet their needs. Perhaps this will be a police officers' association or a teachers' organization. What do they want? Whose help do they need? Do they need help from the government? Do they need help from other citizens?
2. What is their plan for meeting their needs?

Now find newspaper articles that tell about groups that have tried to get help, but have not been able to find solutions.

1. What action have they already taken? Have they held meetings, called a news conference, written to the government, gone to the courts, picketed the offices of those they think could help, or refused to work by going on strike? Why has nothing worked?
2. Can you tell from what they say and do how it feels to have to wait and wait to have needs met? Can you tell how people feel when a problem seems hopeless? Can you tell why other people do not help with the problem?
3. Try to describe in your own words what happens when there is a problem for which there does not seem to be a solution in the near future.

Patriots and Loyalists

Everywhere colonists talked about what they should do about Parliament's "Intolerable Acts." Even in England, people like William Pitt and Edmund Burke argued for the rights of the colonists. But few English people agreed with what they said.

The colonists themselves did not agree. Virginians were loyal to Virginia, New Yorkers to New York, and so on. About a third of the colonists were **Patriots.** They argued that the colonies should govern themselves. Another third were **Loyalists.** They did not agree with Parliament's laws, but they wanted to remain loyal to England and the King. The other third were not sure which side they agreed with. Both the Patriots and the Loyalists tried to win these people over to their side. At the same time, some Patriots were collecting guns. In small towns, local **militias** (mi • LISH • as), or citizens' armies, drilled openly. These "Minute Men," as they were called, were getting ready to fight.

In September 1774 representatives from twelve of the colonies met in Philadelphia for the First **Continental Congress.** There they wrote an answer to the Intolerable Acts. They demanded their rights as English citizens, especially the right to govern themselves. They asked people not to buy English goods until the Intolerable Acts were repealed.

Parliament received these demands in January 1775. It answered by putting more limits on trade in the colonies.

The Fighting Begins

In April 1775 Parliament ordered General Thomas Gage to attack the American rebels. Gage sent soldiers to destroy the colonists' military supplies at Concord, Massachusetts.

When Paul Revere and William Dawes learned of the English plan, they rode out at night to warn the countryside. By dawn, seventy armed Minute Men had gathered at Lexington to stop the English soldiers. The English commander got the colonial soldiers to step aside. But some of his soldiers fired anyway. When the shooting stopped, eighteen colonists and one English soldier had been hit.

PAUL REVERE, by N. C. Wyeth, Brandywine River Museum, Chadds Ford, Pennsylvania

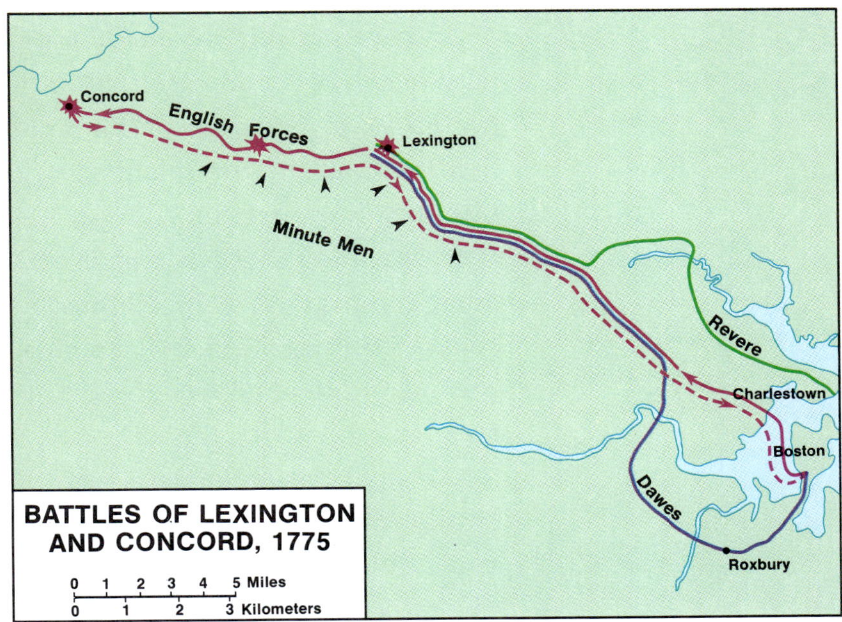

The English marched on to Concord and destroyed the supplies. But now there were Minute Men everywhere. They attacked the English soldiers all along the road back to Boston. By the end of the day, the English had lost 273 soldiers. This was almost three times more people than the colonists lost.

Another person who made a nighttime ride was sixteen-year-old Sybil Luddington. Sybil raced for forty miles on horseback to warn the militia under her father's command that the English army planned to destroy the supplies at Danbury, Connecticut.

Massachusetts began raising an army and asked the other colonists for help. Representatives from twelve of the colonies met again in Philadelphia in May 1775 for the Second Continental Congress. The Congress again demanded respect for the colonists' rights. It said the colonies would fight the unfair laws until Parliament ended them. Finally, the Congress created the Continental Army and sent soldiers to New England. George Washington was named commander-in-chief.

Rebellion Turns to Revolution

Even after the fighting in Massachusetts, many colonists still wanted to remain English subjects. They wanted only their rights. But Parliament would not listen. More and more colonists began to think about independence.

Events moved rapidly. In June 1775 General Gage attacked Minute Men on Breed's Hill and Bunker Hill in Boston. The English won the battle, but over a thousand of their soldiers were killed. That was more than twice as many soldiers as the colonists lost. In August, King George III rejected the demands of the Continental Congress. He declared the colonies in rebellion. Later in the year, the King closed the colonies to all trade.

By the summer of 1776, the idea of independence had spread throughout the colonies. Thomas Paine's pamphlet, *Common Sense,* had persuaded colonists everywhere of the need to fight. Massachusetts, South Carolina, and New Jersey rebelled against their English governors. North Carolina and Virginia told their representatives to the Second Continental Congress to vote for independence. In June a committee began to write a Declaration of Independence.

Thomas Jefferson, John Adams, and Benjamin Franklin were on that committee. On July 2, Congress voted for independence. Two days later they approved the Declaration of Independence. On July 4, 1776, the thirteen colonies became the thirteen states.

Fighting the War

The English and the colonists had been fighting since the battle of Lexington in April 1775. But with the Declaration of Independence, the fighting became more serious. No longer was it a colonial rebellion. It was now the War of Independence between the new United States and England.

England thought the war would be short. It had a large army and a powerful navy. It had money to buy supplies and to hire soldiers from other nations. The English thought the Loyalists living in America would help, too.

However, England was far away from America. The English knew little about the land where they would be fighting. But they did not take these problems seriously.

The colonists had problems, too. The Continental Army was poorly trained, and the navy was weak. There were not enough food, clothing, guns and powder, and medical supplies for the soldiers. A third of the people were Loyalists who opposed the war.

But the colonists had strengths, too. They were fighting on their own ground. They knew the land well. Their soldiers could shoot better than the English, too. Both men and women were willing to do whatever was necessary. As one woman said, "If I can't stand in the ranks, I can help forward with powder, balls, and supplies." Perhaps their greatest strength was their leader, George Washington.

Even so, it was a hard time for Americans. Washington withdrew to Valley Forge for the winter. His soldiers did not have enough food, clothing, or shelter. Congress had to leave Philadelphia when the English soldiers took it. "These are the times that try men's souls," wrote Thomas Paine in the first of his *Crisis* pamphlets. His words were read to the colonial soldiers in their camps.

The only good news came from Saratoga, New York. The supply line to English General John Burgoyne's (bur • GOINS) soldiers had been cut off. Burgoyne surrendered an army of 5,700 men. After the American victory at Saratoga, two important things happened. First, a representative from Parliament came to Benjamin Franklin in Paris with an offer of peace. Second, the French told Franklin they would send troops to help fight the war. Franklin told the English that the United States would accept nothing less than independence. In January 1778 he signed a treaty with France. The colonists' hopes of victory improved greatly.

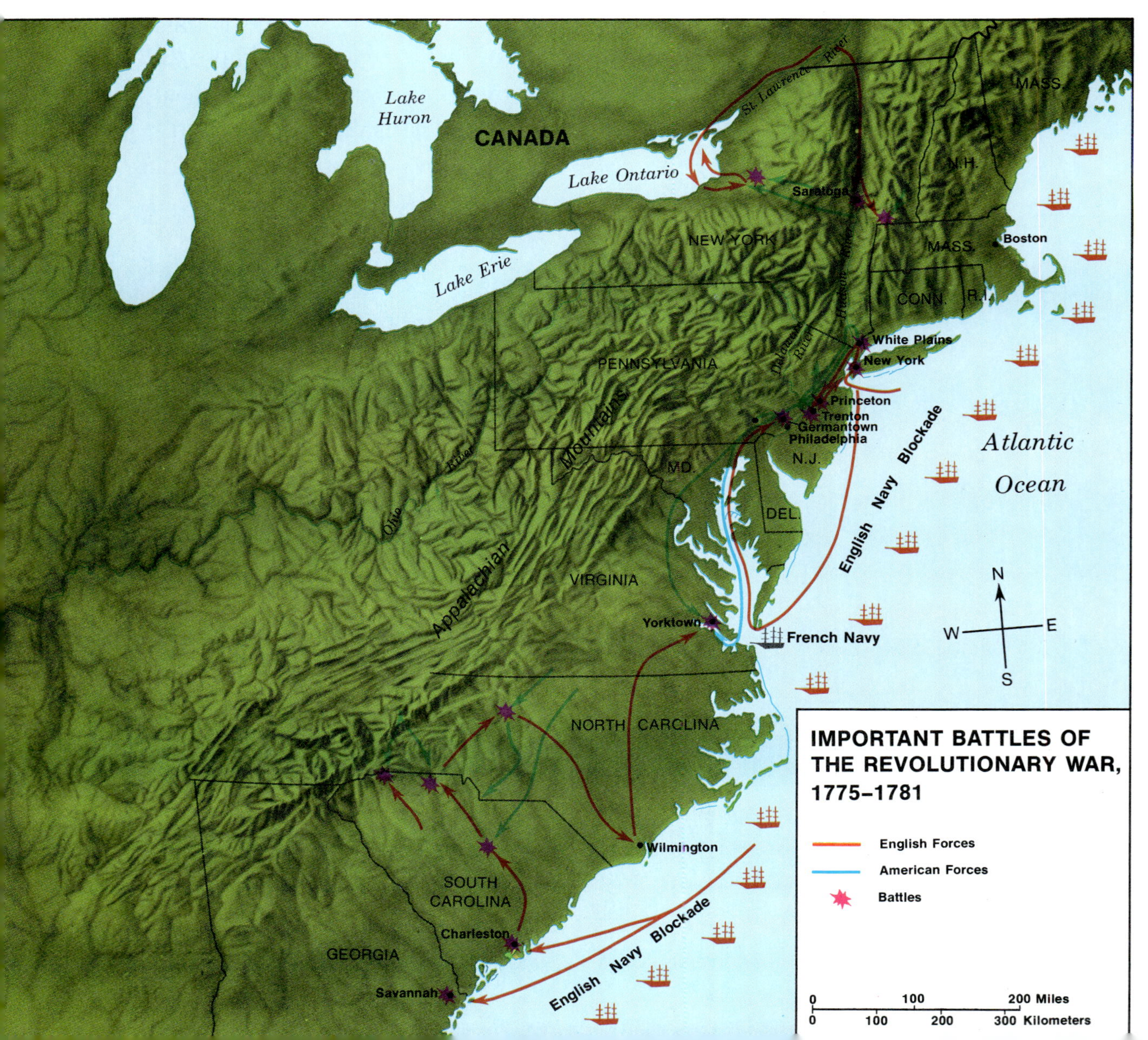

By 1781 the English had large forces of soldiers only in New York and Yorktown, Virginia, under General Cornwallis. Washington and his French allies pretended to move on New York. They marched on Yorktown instead. Then a French fleet took control of the sea off Yorktown. Cornwallis was trapped. On October 18, 1781, he surrendered his army of eight thousand men.

The Treaty of Paris

Yorktown was the last battle of the Revolutionary War. In 1782 Parliament agreed to make peace with the United States. Washington had won victory on the battlefield. Now it was up to Benjamin Franklin, John Adams, and John Jay in Paris to win peace. The result of their work was the Paris Treaty of 1783. The terms of the treaty greatly favored the United States. The new nation stretched west to the Mississippi, north to Canada, south to Florida, and northeast to Maine. Florida was given to Spain.

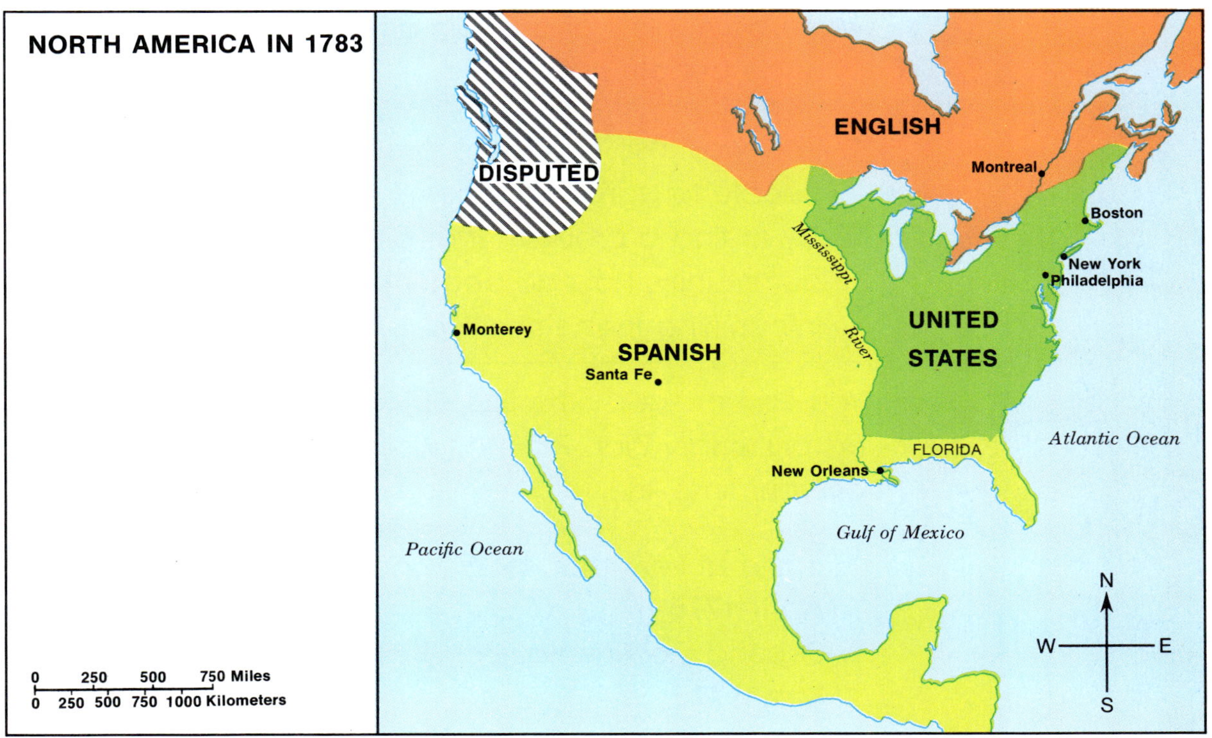

1. What was the Boston Tea Party?
2. How did Parliament punish the colonists for destroying the tea?
3. Who were the Loyalists? What did they think about English rule?
4. What happened at Lexington and Concord?
5. What was the message of Thomas Paine's *Common Sense*?
6. What strengths did the English have in the Revolutionary War?
7. What strengths did the Americans have? What weaknesses?
8. How did women help in the war?
9. Where was the last battle of the war fought?
10. Who won peace for the United States?

Even after the war began, both Patriots and Loyalists tried to talk more people into joining their sides. They wrote pamphlets and letters and gave speeches to change people's minds.

1. Why was it so important to each side to get other people to agree with them?
2. Try to find a problem that people talk about in your community. How do people today try to talk others into joining their sides?

You can make a time line of important events of the Revolutionary War. Put the following dates and events on your time line.

1. Battle at Lexington and Concord
   April 1775
2. Second Continental Congress begins
   May 1775

3. Battle of Bunker Hill
June 1775
4. The Declaration of Independence is signed
July 1776
5. Washington wins at Trenton
December 1776
6. Burgoyne surrenders at Saratoga
October 1777
7. France joins the war
February 1778
8. Cornwallis surrenders at Yorktown, Virginia
October 1781
9. The Treaty of Paris is signed
September 1783

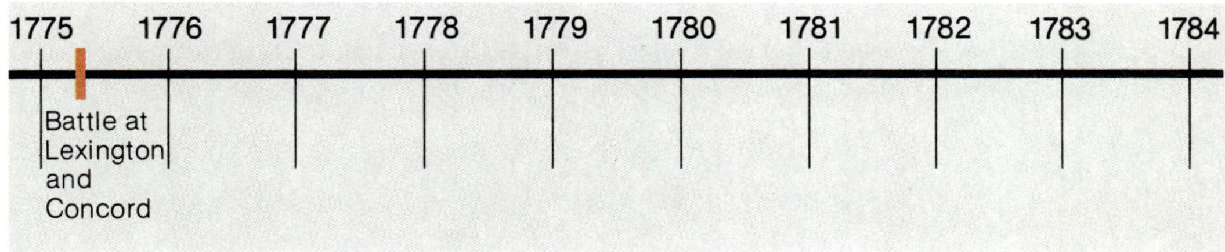

1. During the American Revolution, only about a third of the citizens were Patriots. Yet this minority brought about a great change. Can you think of other examples of how a minority has worked together to bring about an important change? How did they do so?
2. The Declaration of Independence says, in part, "We hold these truths to be self-evident: that all men are created equal. . . ." Today writers of a declaration would probably say ". . . that all people are created equal. . . ." Do the two statements mean the same thing? Why do you say so?

5 Filling out the Continent

In the Revolutionary War the American colonists had won the right to govern themselves. The treaty ending the war also gave the new nation all the territory from the Appalachian Mountains west to the Mississippi River.

The states themselves argued over some of this land. Other land was claimed by France and Spain. All of it was occupied by Native Americans. All of it offered to restless settlers the promise of new land and new opportunities.

In 1787 the Congress passed the Northwest Ordinance. This made one large Northwest Territory of all the new land east of the Mississippi River. Three to five states could be created when enough people settled in the area.

The Louisiana Purchase

Not long after the passage of the Northwest Ordinance, the nation faced another problem with land. France had given Spain the Louisiana Territory in 1762. But France got the territory back in 1800 in a secret treaty with Spain. Napoleon, the Emperor of France, wanted to build a French empire in North America. This worried many Americans. Western farmers had always moved their goods down the Mississippi River and shipped them from New Orleans. They feared the French would take away these rights.

To protect United States' interests, President Thomas Jefferson offered Napoleon $10 million for New Orleans in 1803. By then France was about to go to war with England, and Napoleon needed money. So he offered to sell all of the Louisiana Territory for $15 million. Jefferson accepted. The new territory doubled the size of the United States.

Exploring the New Lands

No one really knew how big the new territory was. Some people thought there might be an all-water route across the continent. If there were, perhaps it could be used for trade with India and China.

Settlers on the coast of California already were trading with the Spanish there and with Native Americans further north. These trappers and whalers traded skins at the Spanish ports of San Diego, Monterey, and San Francisco in California. Trappers also lived in the southwest country around Santa Fe and Taos in northern Mexico.

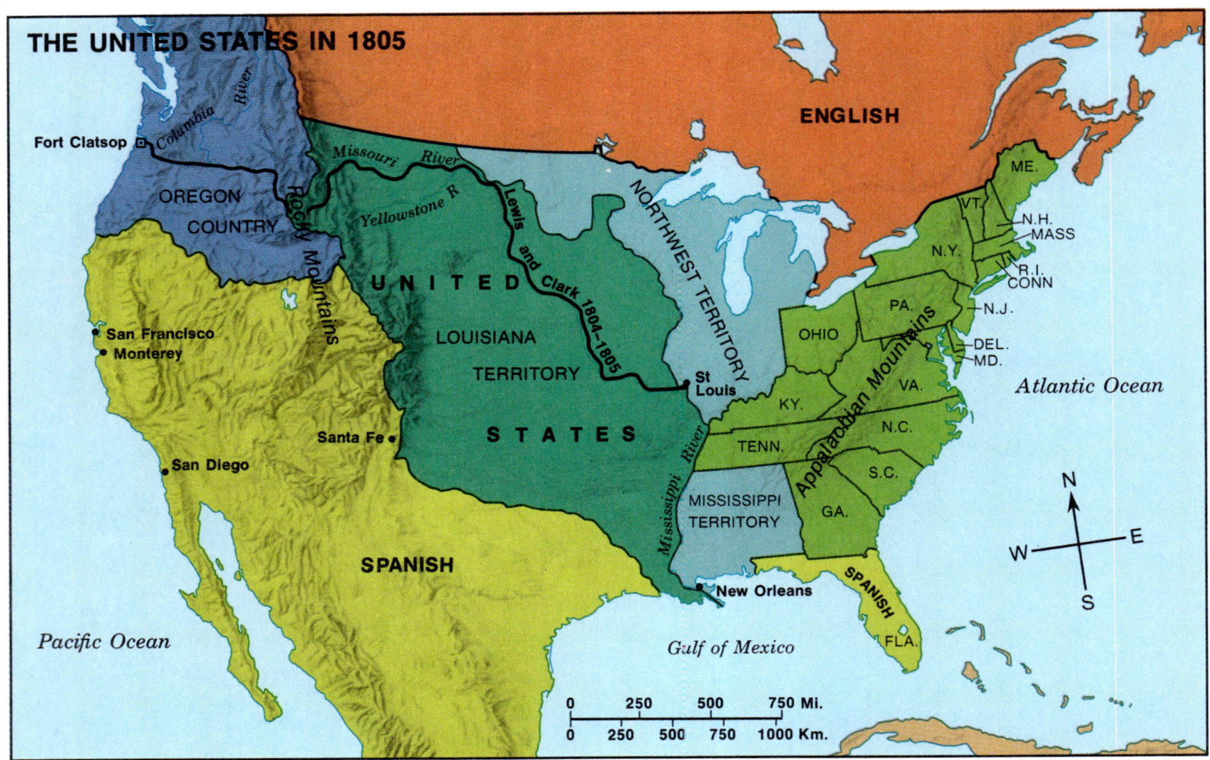

Jefferson knew about these traders, but he wanted scientific information and maps. In 1803 he asked Meriwether Lewis and William Clark to explore the northwest country. Lewis was interested in science, and Clark was skilled in drawing and mapping. They took with them twenty-three soldiers and three guides. One guide was a young Shoshone woman named Sacajawea (sak•ah•juh•WAY•ah).

Lewis and Clark left St. Louis in 1804. They headed west and north up the Missouri River. To the Native Americans and the few trappers who traded along the river, so many whites were a strange sight.

Lewis and Clark spent the winter of 1804–1805 with the Mandans of North Dakota. In the spring they continued west over the Rockies and down the Columbia River. In November 1805 they reached the mouth of the Columbia at the Pacific Ocean.

LEWIS AND CLARK ON THE LOWER COLUMBIA, by Charlie Russell, Courtesy of Amon Carter Museum, Fort Worth

They spent the winter there. Then they began the long journey back along the rivers and across the mountains. In September 1806 they arrived in St. Louis with maps, drawings, and detailed reports.

Wagon Trains West

Lewis and Clark's reports of the size and beauty of the Louisiana Territory started a new movement west. Drawn by the promise of free land, pioneers began the long, dangerous journey across the continent by wagon train. They crossed endless plains and parched deserts. They waded through rivers and streams and climbed mountain ranges. Rain and wind storms, snow, and heat added to the hardships. Many pioneers died on the way.

The journey usually began in Independence, Missouri. There the pioneers filled their wagons with supplies. Along the trail, many walked. They stopped to eat, feed and rest the horses, and camp overnight. In the desert, the heat often made it necessary to travel by night.

Despite the hardships and dangers, the pioneers came. First they came in a trickle, then in a steady flow, always going west, farther west. There was land. They claimed it and settled it. Often they fought the Native Americans who lived there. After the pioneers came tradespeople, sheriffs, and judges. When there were enough settlers in an area, they applied to Congress for statehood.

Trouble in Texas

At the same time, settlers moved into Texas. Texas was part of New Spain. In 1819 Spain tried to stop the American settlers from coming. The Spanish signed a treaty with the United States. Spain gave Florida to the United States. In return, the United States gave up all claims to Texas.

Both countries agreed that the Texas border would run along the Sabine, Red, and Arkansas rivers.

Two years later, the people in Mexico revolted against Spanish rule. The former Spanish colony became the Republic of Mexico. The Mexicans were not as strict about Americans moving into Texas. They granted farmers and ranchers large pieces of land. Many settlers from the United States moved into Texas to raise cattle and cotton. Some settlers brought their slaves.

As more Americans settled in Texas, they began to talk of making it an independent state. President Andrew Jackson tried to buy Texas from Mexico. His attempt caused Mexico's leaders to become alarmed. In 1830 Mexico closed Texas to Americans and made slavery illegal in Texas. The Americans in Texas were angry. Finally they revolted against Mexican rule.

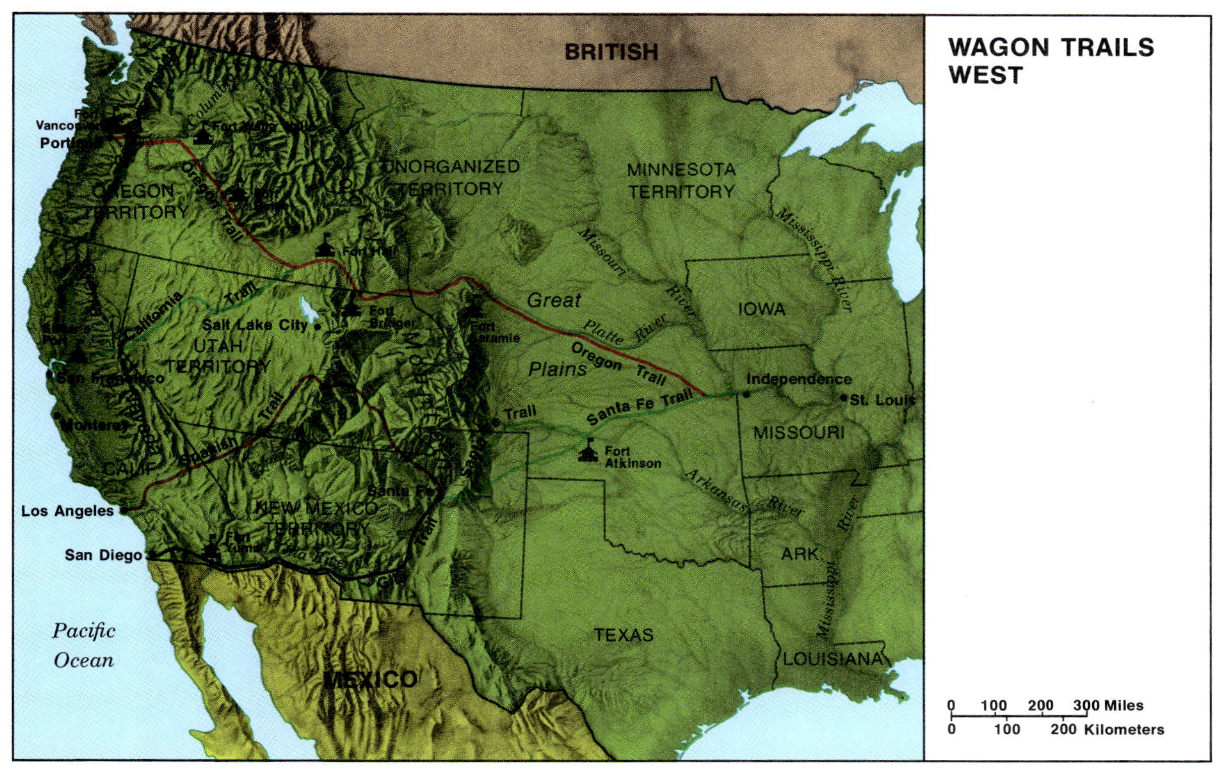

The Mexican leader, Santa Ana, and his soldiers marched against the American rebels in 1836. With three thousand soldiers, Santa Ana defeated 187 Americans at the Alamo, killing all of them. The United States government sent soldiers to help the rebels. Six weeks later Sam Houston defeated Santa Ana's army at San Jacinto (SAN juh·SIN·toh). Santa Ana was captured during the battle. He signed a treaty making Texas an independent state.

Texas now appealed to the United States. The Americans there wanted Texas to become part of the United States. Antislavery forces in Congress at first voted against statehood. But in 1845 Congress admitted Texas to the United States. Mexico broke off diplomatic relations with the United States. Both countries prepared for war.

War with Mexico

Most Americans did not want war. But now that Texas was part of the United States, they wanted California and New Mexico, too. President James Polk offered to buy California and New Mexico from Mexico. Mexico turned him down. Polk then sent soldiers to the Rio Grande.

In 1846 the Mexican soldiers attacked the Americans. Congress then declared war with Mexico.

The war went badly for Mexico. The United States won major battles at Monterrey and Buena Vista. The United States Navy blocked the Mexican ports in California. The army took all of California. Other American soldiers took the fortress at Vera Cruz in southeastern Mexico and captured Mexico City. This ended the war.

In 1848 the United States and Mexico signed the Treaty of Guadalupe Hidalgo (gwah•dah•LOO•pay e•DAHL•goh). Mexico gave the United States all its land north of the Rio Grande and west of Texas. This was two-fifths of all Mexico's land. In return, the United States paid Mexico $15 million. It also agreed to grant Mexicans in the new lands all the rights of United States citizens. The United States now stretched from the Atlantic to the Pacific Ocean.

The California Gold Rush

Before the war with Mexico, only about five hundred United States citizens lived in California. Most of them were traders and whalers. Some fished. A few had ranches in the valleys. Most of the people in California were Native Americans and Mexicans. Then, in 1848, gold was discovered at Sutter's Mill near Sacramento. Suddenly thousands of people rushed to California hoping to strike it rich.

The miners came from every part of the country. They even came from places as far away as Australia and China. By the end of 1849, 100,000 miners were digging and panning for gold in California. They came to be known as "forty-niners." Towns sprang up overnight. Suddenly California was the most populated area in the West. The people in California drew up a plan for statehood. In 1850 Congress made California the thirty-first state.

The United States had expanded to the western edge of the continent. Americans now turned to filling in the empty spaces. To find out how people thought of the West, try the investigation on the facing page.

AN INVESTIGATION into where is "the West"?

To a farmer in Jamestown in 1700, "the West" meant western Virginia. What do you think "the West" meant to each person below? An encyclopedia and some maps may help you. Write your answers on a piece of paper.

1. Thomas Jefferson
2. a cotton farmer in Georgia
3. Lewis and Clark
4. the pioneers in a wagon train leaving Independence, Missouri
5. a "forty-niner"
6. an American living in Texas in 1836
7. the Mandans of North Dakota
8. you

A Problem on Your Own

In 1800 part of the United States was called the Northwest Territory. Where was this territory? Why do you suppose it had that name?

1. What was the Northwest Ordinance of 1787?
2. What did President Jefferson try to buy from France?
3. Why did Napolean sell the Louisiana Territory to the United States?
4. What did Lewis and Clark do?
5. Where did the wagon trains usually begin their trip west?
6. What governments ruled Texas before 1836?
7. Why did the United States first refuse to admit Texas as a state?
8. What new lands did the United States get after the war with Mexico?
9. What happened in California in 1848?

Many of the pioneers who made the dangerous trip across country left behind homes, friends, and relatives. They could take only a few of their belongings with them. They knew little about the hardships they would face in their new homes.

1. Why do you think these families would risk everything to move west? What would they gain?
2. You may know a family that has moved to a faraway state or country. Why did they move?
3. What would it take to get your family to leave everything behind and move to a strange place?

In the eighty years between 1783, when the Revolutionary War ended, and 1853, the United States claimed all the land that now makes up the forty-eight continental states.

The map on page 117 shows when each area was added. Use the map to help you answer the following questions.

1. When was the Louisiana Territory added to the United States? Which river formed the eastern boundary of the Louisiana Territory?
2. When did Florida become part of the United States? From whom did the United States buy Florida?
3. When did Texas become a state? What river formed the southwest boundary of Texas?
4. Which states were once part of Mexico? When did this area become part of the United States?
5. When did Oregon Country become part of the United States? With whom did the United States sign a treaty for this land?
6. When was the last piece of land added to the continental United States? Where was this land?
7. Which parts of the United States shown on this map were bought from other countries?

After the Revolutionary War, more and more people in the eastern states moved west. They had "land fever." When they had used up one piece of land, they just picked up their belongings and moved to new land. It seemed to these people that there would always be more land.

1. What problems did this desire for land cause? Use the map on page 117 and what you have read to help you.
2. Today people can no longer move west to unsettled land. The United States is running out of unsettled land. What problems must people solve now that there is no more land to be settled? Think about things like food, resources, and space. What else do people need land for?

Reviewing Key Ideas

In this unit you have read about many different groups of people that live in North America. You have read about the many Native American groups that have lived on the North American continent for over fifty-thousand years. You have read about the many groups that came from Europe, Africa, and Asia to settle in North America, too.

In the years before European and African settlers came to North America, different groups of Native Americans lived across the continent. In the west, Shoshone lived in small bands, gathering roots and berries from their environment. They hunted small game. They roamed across North America, using the resources they found on the land. Farther south, the Pueblo lived a settled life in small cities. They seldom moved their homes. They used the land as a resource for growing their crops.

Each of the Native American groups had a different culture, or way of life. All of the groups used some of the same resources. But they each had some resources that were different from those of other groups. Thus, you can make this statement: The ways people use resources depend on their environment.

Different Ways, Different Values

Native American cultures differed. But most Native Americans used the land in similar ways. They changed the land very little. They cut only enough trees to have poles or supports for their homes. They cleared only small areas of land to plant their crops.

In these ways, the Native Americans showed how they felt about land and other natural resources. Most important, they showed that they were part of nature. They took only what they needed. They shared what they had. They acted in these ways because they cared about living in peace with nature.

The European settlers who came to North America felt different about resources, especially land. They valued the freedom of owning land. To them, there seemed to be no end to the land available in North America. They cut down trees to plant large fields of crops. They cut down trees to build houses. Eventually they built whole cities. They farmed the land until it wore out. Then they moved on to clear more

land. Thus you have also learned this about the idea of resources: The ways people use resources depend on what they care about.

Conflicts of Values

Throughout this unit you have read about how different groups of people have used land and resources in varying ways. When European settlers came to America, they took or bought land from Native American groups. Often, the Native Americans did not want the settlers to take their land. In their culture, land was for the use of all people. Fighting sometimes broke out between the settlers and the Native Americans.

During the middle of the 1700s, English colonists moved westward to build homes and farms. The French claimed this land as their own. One reason the French did not want settlers moving into the wilderness was because the area was a rich source of furs for their trappers. This conflict over the use of resources was one cause of the French and Indian War.

About eighty years later, some of the people living in Texas, California, and the United States wanted land that belonged to Mexico. After several years of conflict, war broke out. When the war ended, a large part of the Republic of Mexico became a part of the United States.

In each of these cases, different groups of people wanted to use the same resources in different ways. Thus, you can also make this statement about resources: Differences in the ways people want to use resources can lead to conflicts among groups.

Using Key Words

Use these key words to complete the sentences that follow.

boycott	militia
chartered	Parliament
Continental Congress	Patriots
indentured servants	persecuted
Loyalists	plantations

1. One way for early colonists to get to America was to form companies, such as the Plymouth Company. The king gave, or ____, land to these companies.
2. People who could not pay their own way often had their trip paid for by a master. They came to America as ____.
3. Many Quakers came to Pennsylvania. In England they had been punished, or ____, for their religious beliefs.
4. The large southern farms, where tobacco and other crops grew, were called ____.
5. The laws for the colonies were made by the English government, called ____.
6. The colonists did not like the Tea Act, so they did not buy English tea. When people refuse to buy goods, they ____ them.
7. Representatives from the colonies met to demand their rights as English citizens. They met in Philadelphia for the ____.
8. In towns in all the colonies, people formed citizens' armies called ____.
9. Colonists who wanted the colonies to be independent of England were called ____.
10. The colonists who wanted to remain part of England were called ____.

Focus on the Social Scientist

Have you ever asked yourself the question, "What if?" For example, what if you had been born to different parents? What if you had been a child movie star? How would your life be different now?

People are usually interested in what *did* happen, however. Historians like Dr. Oscar Handlin study the past. Dr. Handlin teaches history and has written books about the past.

In one book about American history, Dr. Handlin asks, "What if France had not offered to sell us the Louisiana Territory?" Dr. Handlin tells the story behind what happened.

In the 1800s France had a powerful ruler, Napoleon Bonaparte. He dreamed of making a kingdom of New France in North America. New France would be made up of islands in the West Indies and Louisiana. Napoleon planned to send ships and men to take New Orleans.

Napoleon organized ships and soldiers, but it took too long to get the supplies ready. The ships were about to sail when the weather got very cold. A rare thing happened—ice formed in the harbor! The ships were frozen fast until spring.

Meanwhile, Napoleon heard that his soldiers in the West Indies had yellow fever and many were dying. He decided to forget about New France and take more land in Europe instead.

But what if the French harbor had not frozen over? Would the United States still be a small nation? As you learn about history, you may like to ask, "What if things had been different? How would our lives be different?"

UNIT THREE

The United States and Its Government

The people of the United States built a new system of government when they wrote the Constitution. They believed the new government would help them live together in "a more perfect Union." But no one knew just how well the new government would work or how long it would last.

There were many differences among the states in 1787. The South was largely a land of farming. There was little industry. Many people were needed to work the huge cotton, tobacco, and rice plantations.

In the North there were factories and large ports for shipping. Most of the people were merchants—buying, selling, and shipping goods.

The interests of the two regions differed greatly. Northern states wanted laws to protect their trade. Southern states wanted laws to protect their farming.

Could the Union survive these differences? In this unit you will find out about the struggles the United States faced during the first ninety years of its history.

Union and Balance

In the early years, the United States was a country with two sections. The South had rich soil, wide rivers, good ocean ports, and a warm climate. Most of the people there were farmers. They used the rivers and harbors to ship their crops to markets.

The North had rocky soil and a cold climate. There were good ocean harbors, but few wide rivers. Fishing, manufacturing, and trade were the main ways to make a living.

Most Americans lived in one of these two environments. Once they had won independence, they had to choose leaders to make laws for everyone. But people living in such different ways often saw problems differently and wanted different solutions.

A Need for Order

"Every day brings forth some new crisis," the governor of Virginia wrote in 1786. In New York Alexander Hamilton said that the government was almost a failure. Many of the people in all thirteen states felt the same way.

It was hardly a "United" States. The nation was divided and confused. A merchant in New Hampshire had trouble trading with one in New York because the two states used different kinds of money. A merchant in Rhode Island had to pay one tax in Pennsylvania, another in South Carolina, and still another in Virginia. Planters in Georgia could not get their crops to the cities to sell. There were no roads.

Something had to be done. A strong national government was needed. It had to have the power to coin a single kind of money. It had to have the power to tax all citizens and to make the same laws for everyone.

To create a new government, fifty-five citizens from twelve states met in Philadelphia in 1787. Their meeting was called the Constitutional Convention. There they wrote the Constitution. Its purpose was described in the opening words, the Preamble:

> We, the people of the United States, in order to form a more perfect union, establish justice, insure domestic tranquility (trang•KWIL•uh•tee), provide for the common defense, promote the general welfare, and secure the blessings of liberty to ourselves and our posterity, do ordain and establish this Constitution for the United States of America.

Differences and Agreements

Creating a government was not easy. The people in the thirteen states had some things in common. They all wanted personal freedom and justice. They all wanted a chance to earn a living, to live peacefully, and to be protected from unfriendly nations. But there were many differences, too. Some of the states were large and some were small. Some were rich and some were poor. The main activity in the northeastern states was buying, selling, and shipping goods. In the southern states, it was farming. Some states allowed slavery, while other states had outlawed it. In every state people disagreed on what were the best ways to establish justice, secure liberty, and promote the general welfare.

The peaceful way to settle differences is to reach an agreement. If you cannot agree, you can **compromise** (KOM • pruh • myz). In a compromise you get some things you want and give up other things in return. The people who wrote the Constitution found they had to make many compromises in order to form a government that most of the people would accept.

The large states, for example, wanted the number of representatives in Congress to be based on population, or the number of people in each state. Under this plan, states with more people would have more representatives in Congress. The small states wanted each state to have the same number of representatives. Finally the states decided on a compromise. The number of representative in one part of Congress, the House of Representatives, would be based on population. In the other part, the Senate, each state would have just two representatives.

Disagreements over Slavery

Another disagreement arose over the issue of slavery. The first Black people in America had come with the Spanish. They had come first as explorers, then as laborers. Black people had planted and harvested the first wheat crop in America. In 1619 Black people came to Jamestown as

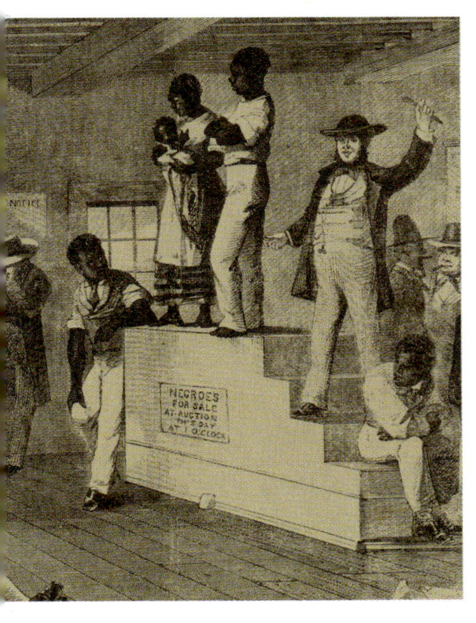

indentured servants. They had promised to work for someone to pay for their passage to America. They usually worked for four to seven years. Then they were free. But most of the Black people in the United States in 1787 had been brought from Africa as slaves.

Slavery itself was not new. There were slaves in ancient Egypt, Rome, and Greece. In a war the people who lost became slaves, and the people who won became slaveholders. The same was true in Africa. Slave traders would sail to Africa. There they would buy Black people who had been captured and made slaves by other Africans. Then the traders would sail back to America and sell the slaves.

In the beginning there was slavery in every state, north as well as south. In fact the slave trade was very important in the Northeast. New York was its biggest port. Selling slaves was a very profitable business. It was even more profitable than using slaves as laborers. As late as 1787 slavery was still legal in New York.

As they shaped the new government, the members of the Constitutional Convention had to decide what would become of the slave trade. They also had to decide how to count the slaves when deciding how many representatives a state could send to Congress. If all the slaves were counted, then a state with many slaves would have more representatives and thus more votes. How people looked at these questions depended on where they lived, as well as what they thought was right.

Finally the members compromised. For purposes of paying taxes and deciding how many representatives a state would have, a slave was to be counted as three-fifths of a free person. In return, it was agreed that the slave trade would end after twenty years. It was a question of interest, as one representative from South Carolina said. And it was in everyone's interest to compromise.

Rule by Law

Although the people who wrote the Constitution had to compromise on many issues, they all agreed on one thing: law, not people, should rule. They believed that most people could not be trusted with power. They thought that people were all naturally ambitious (am•BISH•uhs). People would act in their own interests instead of in the interest of all the people. This was not bad; it was human nature. "If men were angels, no government would be necessary," James Madison said.

The people who planned the government decided to let one ambition, or interest, compete against another. They set up a government in which one special interest would try to win votes over other special interests. That way, no one person or group could become too powerful. Selfish interests would lose out. Only those people willing to work together would win.

The planners of the Constitution decided to separate the powers of government and divide the government into three parts or branches. They gave different powers to each branch. The **legislative branch,** or Congress, would make laws. The **executive branch,** led by the President, would enforce, or carry out, the laws made by the Congress. The **judicial branch,** guided by the Supreme Court, would decide how the laws worked.

Separation of Powers

Each branch of government balances the others. This balance keeps any one branch from using too much power. Congress can make laws, but it cannot enforce them. It can vote for the government to spend money, but it cannot spend it. The President can carry out laws but not make them. He or she can spend money but not raise it. The Supreme Court can interpret laws, but it cannot make them or enforce them. This separation of powers is called a system of "checks and balances."

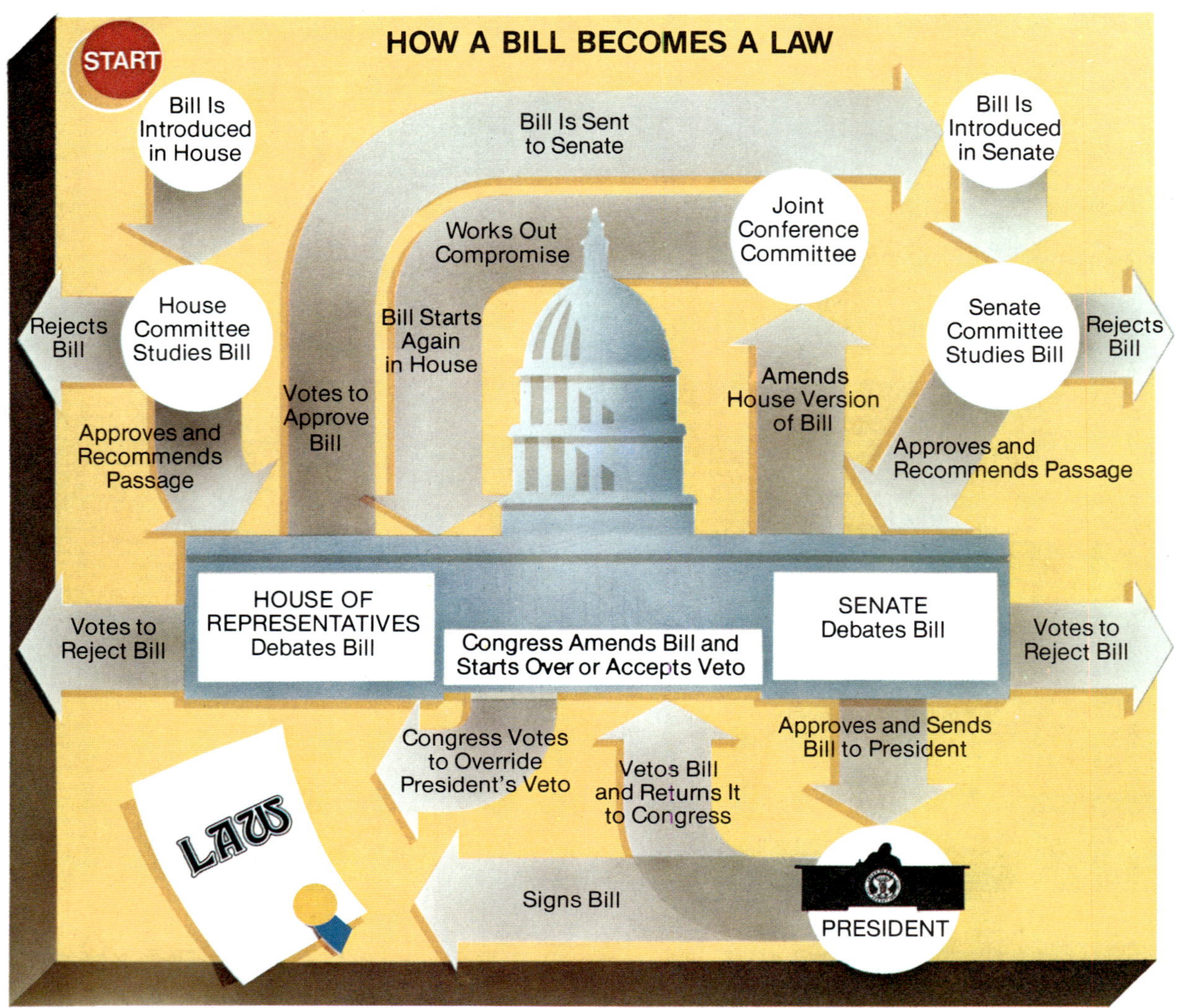

Each branch is independent. But just as a baseball team needs pitchers, hitters, and catchers to win, the government needs all three branches to govern. The justices of the Supreme Court interpret the law, but each justice is appointed by the President and approved by the Senate. The President makes treaties, but they cannot be carried out without the approval of the Senate. Congress passes bills, but the President must sign them before they can become law. If the President refuses to sign a bill, Congress can rewrite it.

Congress can also make the bill a law by **overriding** the President's veto. This takes a two-thirds vote of both the House and Senate.

Even with this system of checks and balances, many citizens opposed the Constitution. They wanted the Constitution to include a promise that the people and the states would be protected against too much power being used by the people in the national government. Eleven of the states agreed to accept the Constitution if it included a list of what the people in government could *not* do to other people. These ten additions, or **amendments,** to the Constitution are called the Bill of Rights. The Bill of Rights promises to all Americans such rights as freedom of speech and press, freedom of religion, and the right to a trial by a jury.

A Plan of Governing

The government of the whole United States is called the **federal government.** In a federal government, the states have some powers, and the national government has other powers. Under the United States federal system, each state has power over many of its own affairs. Other powers are shared by the national and state governments. These include the power to collect taxes and the power to have a court system.

The federal government, however, has power in matters that involve more than one state. The Constitution is "the supreme law of the land." All the states and all citizens must live by its rules.

Before the Constitution was written, a New Yorker was loyal to New York, a Virginian to Virginia, and so on. They still felt this way after the Constitution became the law of the land. But with the new federal government, people began to see themselves as part of something larger—the United States.

One Government, Different Life Styles

The citizens of the United States now began the great experiment to see if the people could really govern themselves. There were still many problems. The nation was rapidly growing larger. Differences in environment added to the many cultural differences among the people.

In the South the soil and the climate were good for growing many crops. Tobacco, rice, cotton, and sugar cane grew well. Farming was so successful that the larger farms needed many workers. Some of those farmers who could afford to kept slaves to work their large plantations.

In the South there were few cities, fewer banks, and no factories. The southern plantations were spread far apart. Each one was like a little community.

Each year the planters would sell their crops to merchants. The merchants would pay the planter and then decide when to sell the crops. If they thought there was too good a harvest, they would wait to sell. The planters and other farmers in the South depended upon the merchants. They did not build factories or start other businesses.

The owners of southern plantations were by far the most successful group in the United States. The taxes they paid helped support the government. Many of them had the time, the money, and the desire to go into government. Five of the first seven Presidents of the United States owned Virginia plantations. Many other national leaders came from the South.

Most of the southern farmers, however, were not plantation owners. They grew enough on their small farms to eat and made enough money to buy what they needed, but they did not make much profit.

In the Northeast the soil was rocky and the climate harsh. Large farms were not profitable. The Northeast did have swift rivers, however. Their water power could be used to turn wheels to run machines. This led people to build factories on the northern rivers. The towns and cities that grew up around the factories became the centers of business activity.

Conflict in Interests

In the 1780s regional differences in the United States were strong. The people in the Northeast and the South naturally had different interests. What was good for Northerners was often not good for the Southerners. Southern farmers wanted to sell their crops at a high price and buy their own supplies at a low price. Merchants in the Northeast, however, wanted to buy farm products at a low price and sell the finished goods at a high price. For example, merchants wished to buy cotton at a low price and make it into cloth, which they would sell at a high price. Merchants who could not use slaves themselves were more likely to be against slavery than the planters who depended on slaves to plant and harvest their crops.

Northerners and Southerners had gotten along fairly well as colonists when they had not needed each other. But once united, one region often needed help from the other. Northern merchants, for example, might want new taxes to pay for more port officers to control trade. They would have to get the Southern representatives to vote to help. But Southern farmers might not want to spend tax money in this way. The national government was set up to try to settle such regional disagreements in a way that was fair to every interest.

To find out more about how interest groups try to get the government to help them get what they want, try the investigation on page 142.

AN INVESTIGATION
into special interests

Every person and every family has "interests," things they want done to make life better for themselves. When people have "interests" that they cannot bring about by themselves or with others, they often turn to government. The government is made up of representatives. If the majority of the representatives agree that what people want should be done, they will vote to spend some of the money from taxes to get it done.

Find out about an "interest" some of the people in your community have. You can use the newspaper, or you can ask some of the neighbors you know well. What would they like the government to get done? Why do they think government should do it? How can they tell the government what they want?

Find out whether what they want is something the local or the state government can do. Is it something that the national, or federal, government would have to do?

Who would decide which government should consider the idea? Where would the money come from? Who would actually do the work? Who would make sure that what is done is what the people and the lawmakers want done?

Write a short report telling what you find out.

1. Why was the Constitutional Convention held? Where and when did it meet?
2. Why do people compromise sometimes?
3. Give two examples of compromise at the Constitutional Convention.
4. Why did the planners of the Constitution separate the powers of government?
5. What are the three branches of government? What does each one do?
6. What is the Bill of Rights?
7. How did the way of life in the South differ from that in the Northeast?

1. In the early years of the United States, each of the thirteen states tried to govern itself. What made the states decide to join together under one federal government?
2. Name at least two situations in which Americans today turn to the federal government for action.

Look at a copy of the Constitution of the United States. You can find one in an encyclopedia.

Read the first ten Amendments. What rights cannot be taken away by Congress? If one of these rights were taken away, what might happen?

In 1789 Rhode Island and Delaware had only enough citizens to give each state one vote in the House of Representatives. They knew that even with two votes in the Senate, they would not have as much power as bigger states, like Virginia and Pennsylvania.

1. What would these two small states have gained if they had not joined the Union?
2. What would they have lost?

Upsetting the Balance

The Constitution gave the people of the United States a plan for deciding the future. Still, there were many different views of what the future held. Thomas Jefferson believed that America's future was in farming. He did not trust cities. "Those who labor in the earth are the chosen people," he insisted. When he said this, more than ninety out every one hundred Americans lived on farms.

Alexander Hamilton disagreed with Jefferson. Hamilton believed that the nation's future was in industry and trade. These business activities were centered in the cities. Both Hamilton and Jefferson were important advisors to President Washington.

Hamilton wanted President Washington and Congress to pass laws that favored bankers and business people. Because the states with big cities had more votes, Congress passed Hamilton's bills.

When Jefferson saw what was happening, he left Washington's government. He started a new political party. People who agreed with his ideas joined it. In this way they could try to change the decisions of Congress that favored the bankers and business people. They could try to make the government pay more attention to their needs.

How Many People? How Many Votes?

Many people were coming from Europe to live in the United States. They had heard that the United States was a land of opportunity. Most of these immigrants settled in the cities of the Northeast, where there were factories and jobs. Soon the population of the Northeast was larger than that of the South.

Because there were now more people in the Northeast, the states in the Northeast were allowed to elect more members to the House of Representatives. With more representatives, they had more votes. After awhile they had enough votes in the House of Representatives to pass the laws they wanted.

The representatives of the people in the southern states were outnumbered. Laws that they wished to pass to help their people did not receive enough votes. They protested, and the differences between the Northeast and the South became more bitter.

The law that most angered the people of the South was a tax which Congress put on all goods imported into the country. This tax, or **tariff** (TAR • if), made foreign goods more expensive than the same goods made in the United States. For example, if a hat was made in London and sold in the United States, a tariff was added to the cost. An English hat that once cost only $3.00 might now sell for $4.50. A hat made in Boston might cost $4.00.

The tariff was good for the Northeast. If you owned a textile mill in New England, the tariff helped you sell more cloth. If you were a merchant, it helped you sell more goods.

The tariff was not good for the South, however. There were no factories for making goods in the South. There were farms and farmers. The farmers needed finished goods to work their farms. Farmers in the South now had to pay more for tools, supplies, and household goods. Southerners felt this was unfair.

After Congress passed a very high tariff in 1828, South Carolinians threatened to refuse to enforce it in their state. This threat was based on the ideas of Vice-President John C. Calhoun.

Calhoun believed that the individual states, not the federal government, were the final judge of their own rights and powers. Therefore a state could overrule any federal law. It could even **secede,** or withdraw, from the Union if necessary.

The dispute over the tariff was finally settled by compromise. The tariff was lowered, and South Carolina withdrew its threat to leave the Union. President Andrew Jackson spoke for most Americans when he offered a toast at a political dinner. "Our Federal Union," he said, "it must and shall be preserved." Calhoun followed Jackson with a toast of his own. "The Union, next to our liberty, most dear!" Then he added, "May we always remember that it can only be preserved by respecting the rights of the states. . . ."

The Cotton Gin

The gap between the Northeast and the South grew wider. In 1793 Eli Whitney invented the cotton gin. This simple machine could clean cotton. It also made it possible to grow a tougher kind of cotton that grew in soil where other cotton would not grow.

Cotton was needed world-wide. With the new cotton gins, southern farmers could now grow more cotton. To do so, however, they needed more workers for the huge fields. More Black Africans were brought to America as slaves. The cotton gin made growing cotton more profitable, but it also made slavery more profitable.

As time passed, even the many Southerners who did not like slavery needed more slaves. Because they needed the slave system, and at the same time they did not like it, they felt trapped. They felt that people in the Northeast did not try to understand their situation.

To find out more about how people who hold a minority viewpoint feel, try the investigation on the facing page.

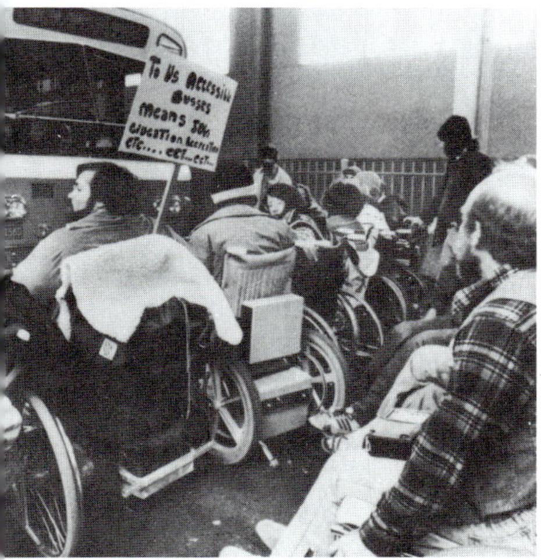

AN INVESTIGATION
into minority groups

Find one example of a group that is in the minority and feels it cannot have a fair chance because of majority rule. You can read newspapers or magazines or interview someone in your community. The group can be a racial group, a senior citizens' group, a women's group, a group of workers, or any other group that is in the minority on an issue. Try to find out the answers to these questions.

1. What opportunities do members of the group feel others have that they do not have?
2. What have they done to try to get those opportunities?
3. Do they think they need a new law? If so, what kind of a law?
4. Will they try to get a city, state, or national law? Why?
5. Who do they think might support such a law? Why might others vote to help them?

Free States and Slave States

Settlement of the western territories added to the problems between the South and the Northeast. From the earliest days of the United States, land and the promise of a fresh start drew pioneers westward.

The early pioneers came first to Kentucky and Tennessee and the Northwest Territory. Then they moved into the territory opened by the Louisiana Purchase. As they moved west, they took more land from the Native Americans who had lived on the land for thousands of years.

New roads and canals brought settlers in after the pioneers. They cleared the land for farms and built settlements, towns, and cities. They brought a few tools and goods and a lot of energy. Some of them brought slaves.

Most of the settlers with slaves settled in Tennessee, Kentucky, and the Louisiana Territory. The land there was good for growing tobacco and cotton. In the Northwest Territory the land was better for growing wheat and corn and for raising cattle and hogs. Farmers there usually did not own slaves.

The new territories were admitted into the Union as states. Those which had slavery were admitted as slave states; the others came in as free states. They were admitted in turn—one slave state, then one free state. This kept a balance in Congress between the North and the South.

In 1820 the Union stood balanced—eleven slave states and eleven free ones. The free states, with their larger populations, had more votes in the House. But the slave states had equal votes in the Senate. Then Missouri, where slavery was common, applied for statehood. The Senate said yes, but the House said no.

The problem was solved by the Missouri Compromise of 1821. It allowed Missouri to enter the Union as a slave state and Maine to enter as a free state. It also outlawed slavery in the rest of the Louisiana Territory north of the 36° 30′ parallel (36 degrees, 30 minutes north latitude).

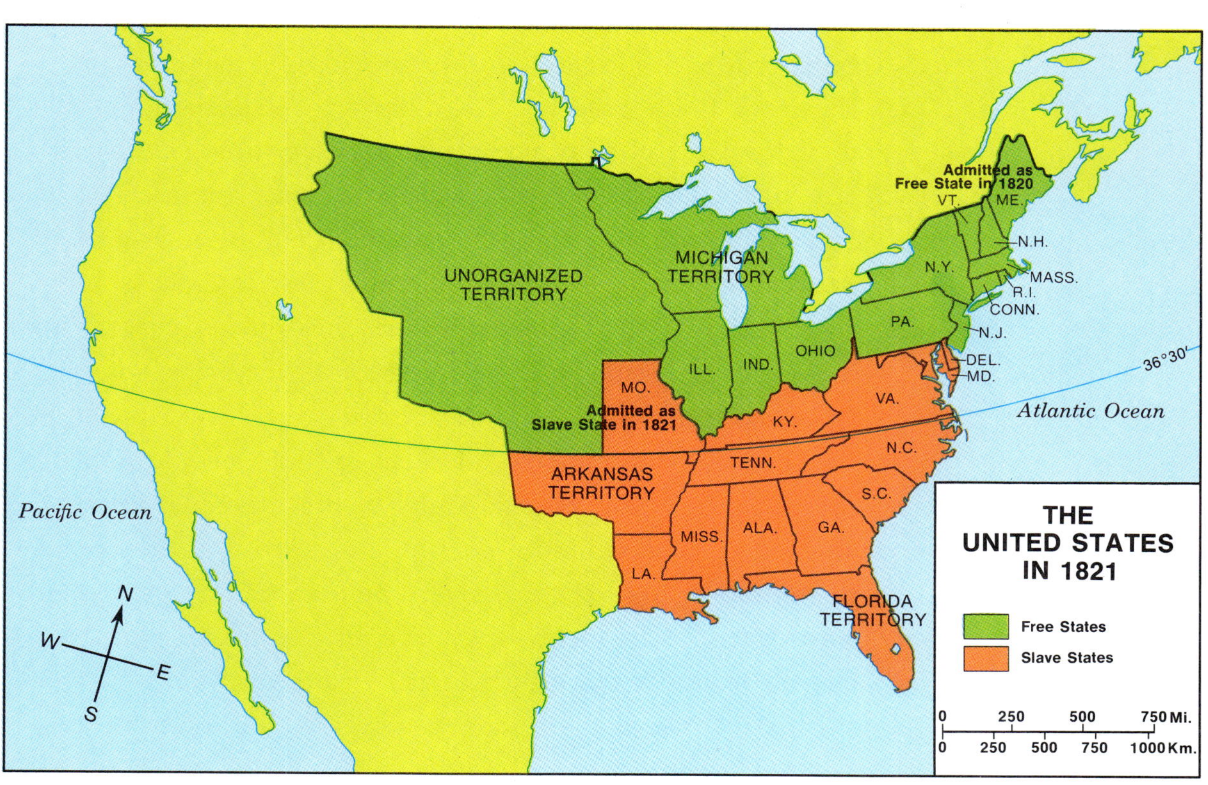

The balance between free and slave states had been kept, but not for long. Too many things were happening. Nat Turner, a Black preacher, led a slave revolt in Virginia that took the lives of sixty white people. **Abolitionists** (ab•uh•LISH•uhn•ists) in the Northeast demanded an immediate end to slavery. An "underground railroad" of antislavery people helped slaves escape to free states or Canada.

Abolitionist newspapers and speeches made many people think seriously about the problem of slavery. Frederick Douglass, once a slave himself, drew large crowds when he spoke about the injustices of slavery. More people joined the abolitionist movement. Many of these people did not agree that slavery should be ended at once. But they began to think that the national government should at least keep slavery from spreading. They wanted Congress to outlaw slavery in the western territories.

Most people in the South, however, had a different viewpoint. They felt that the only way to be sure that Southerners had equal rights was for the South to expand its way of life into more states. People from every region were moving farther west. Some were proslavery, others were antislavery. Usually they tried to bring their way of life with them. The question remained: when they applied for statehood, would they be free states or slave states?

Let the People Decide

Representatives from the free states wanted to pass a law to outlaw slavery in the western territories. Members of Congress from slave states believed that the federal government should protect the rights of slaveholders everywhere. They said that Congress had no right to pass a law against slavery. To do so would violate the Constitution and the states' rights, they said. They believed that the people of a new state had the right to choose whether or not they wanted slavery.

This idea was supported by the people of the Northwest Territory, now the states of Ohio, Indiana, Wisconsin, Michigan, and Illinois. There would be no need for arguments in Congress every time a new state wanted to be admitted to the Union. This idea of letting the people decide became known as **popular sovereignty** (sov•ruhn•tee).

Events moved rapidly. In 1848 gold was discovered in California. The gold rush that followed in 1849 brought thousands of "forty-niners" to the California hills in search of wealth. By 1850 the people of California applied for admission to the Union as a free state. Southern members of Congress opposed statehood for California. It would upset the balance of fifteen free states and fifteen slave states.

In an important debate, John C. Calhoun threatened that the South would secede from the Union if it did not get justice and "an equal right in the acquired territory." Daniel Webster spoke for "the preservation of the Union." Finally another compromise was reached.

California was admitted as a free state. The principle of popular sovereignty was applied to the rest of the western territories, and a strict Fugitive Slave Law was passed. No one was to help slaves go free. The law said a slave who escaped must be returned to the owner. Even the majority of Northerners thought that slaves should be treated as private property.

The Compromise of 1850 left both sides unhappy. It did not solve any of the big problems. The basic differences remained. The people of the Northeast were still merchants, bankers, clerks, mill hands, sales people, and shippers. In the South, the people were still farmers, committed to cotton and the slave system. Only one Southerner in ten owned slaves. But most of the Southerners with political power and money were among the slave owners. They wanted slaves to work on their large plantations.

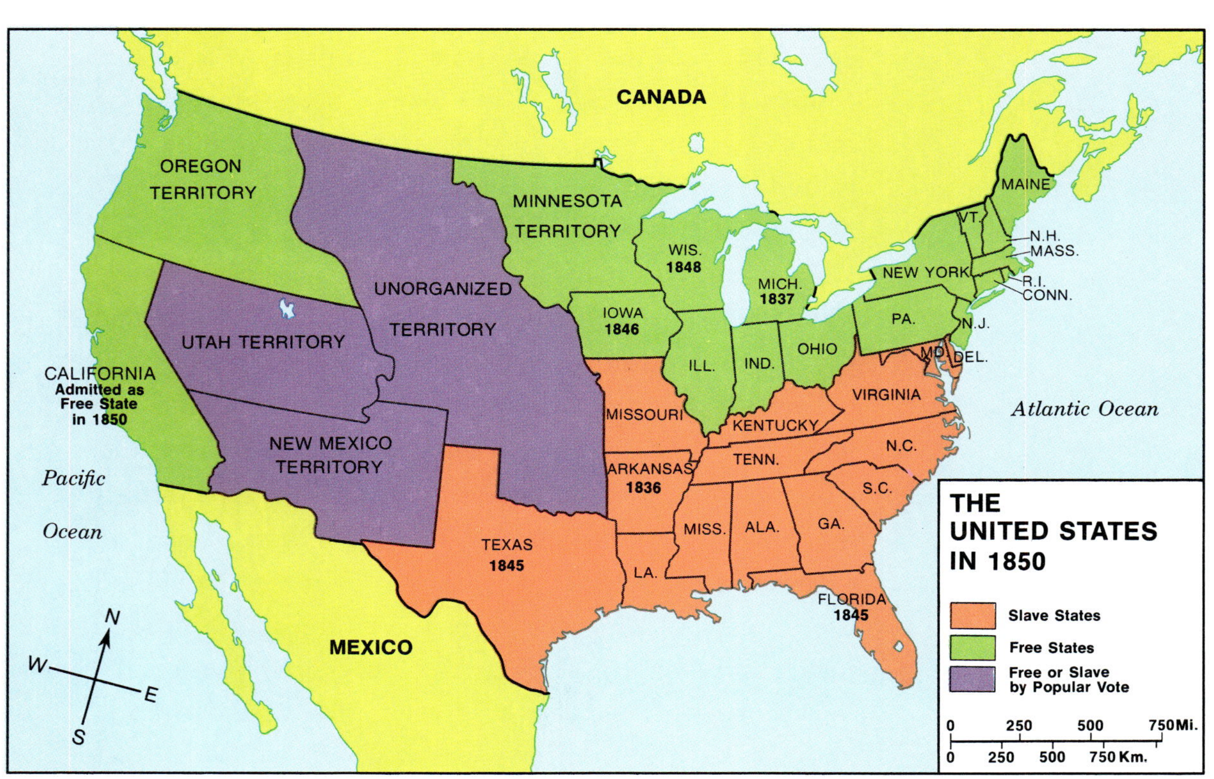

The Dred Scott Decision

Four years later, in 1854, Congress passed the Kansas-Nebraska Act. This law extended popular sovereignty to the territories above the 36° 30′ parallel. It therefore broke the Missouri Compromise of 1821. The majority in Congress had changed its mind. What could the people who opposed slavery do? What could free Black people and others affected by the Kansas-Nebraska Act do?

The Constitution states that if a citizen thinks a law is **unconstitutional,** or goes against the meaning of the Constitution, that citizen can sue the government in the Supreme Court to get the law repealed. Dred Scott, a Black man who had been taken into the Minnesota Territory by his master, sued the government to give him his freedom. But in 1857 the Supreme Court ruled that no Black man could be a citizen of the United States. Scott therefore had no right to sue for his freedom. The Supreme Court also said the Missouri Compromise was unconstitutional.

This decision caused strong feelings on both sides. Abolitionists did not accept the ruling that Blacks were not citizens. Slave owners did not like the ruling that the Missouri Compromise was no longer a law. Angry talk sometimes turned into violence. In Massachusetts mobs attacked Frederick Douglass, a former Black slave who had become an abolitionist. In Harpers Ferry, Virginia, John Brown, a white man, planned to steal weapons and lead a slave revolt. With money from abolitionists in New England and New York, Brown bought arms for about eighteen men. Brown was captured, found guilty of treason, and hanged. In Kansas groups of white settlers fought over the question of slavery in that territory.

Others worked against slavery in peaceful ways. In 1852 Harriet Beecher Stowe, a northern white woman, wrote a book called *Uncle Tom's Cabin.* In this book she told about the lives of slaves. The stories she heard from escaped slaves helped her write the book. It became very popular. Southerners were not allowed to read it, but many Northerners and Europeans did. Theater companies in the North gave performances of *Uncle Tom's Cabin* for more than fifty years.

Some abolitionists set up an "underground railroad" to help slaves escape to freedom in Canada. Blacks as well as whites worked in this movement. Harriet Tubman, herself an escaped slave, returned many times to the South to lead hundreds of slaves north. No danger would stop her. She became known as "the Moses of her people."

Disagreements between the Northeast and the South became more violent. Compromise no longer seemed possible. The nation was out of balance. In Illinois a man who wished to be elected to the Senate warned the voters, "A house divided against itself cannot stand." The man was Abraham Lincoln.

1. What tariff most angered the people of the South?
2. How did the cotton gin change farming in the South?
3. What did John C. Calhoun believe about states' rights?
4. What problem did the Missouri Compromise of 1821 solve? How long did it last?
5. What did the abolitionists want?
6. What was meant by popular sovereignty?
7. What did the Supreme Court decide in the Dred Scott case?

How did each of the following events change the balance between free states and slave states?

1. the arrival of many new immigrants
2. the taking of western lands from Mexico in 1848

Use the maps on pages 151 and 154 to help you answer these questions.

1. Which states were free states in 1821?
2. Which states were slave states in 1821?
3. Which states were admitted to the Union as free states between 1821 and 1850? Which were admitted as slave states?
4. In 1850 how many slave states were there? How many free states were there?

1. Draw a cartoon or write a letter showing what a Northern merchant might think upon hearing that Southerners were buying English cloth and clothing.
2. Draw a cartoon or write a letter showing how a Southern plantation owner might feel about paying higher prices for manufactured goods because of the high tariff on imported goods.

3 The System Breaks Down

The expansion of slavery into the western territories had become the biggest issue dividing the people of the United States. Behind this issue were deep economic and cultural differences between the Northeast and the South. But slavery was the issue everyone noticed and talked about.

Congress's attempt to settle this issue with the Kansas-Nebraska Act had failed. Kansas had become "bleeding Kansas." Proslavery and antislavery people were killing each other and burning each other's towns. People everywhere were angry and discouraged. Compromise seemed impossible. Southerners talked more and more about leaving the Union.

In Wisconsin a new political party was started. The people in the new party called themselves Republicans. The Republicans were people who generally opposed slavery. They especially opposed the expansion of slavery into the western territories. Abraham Lincoln was one of the new Republicans.

In the 1860 presidential election, Abraham Lincoln ran for President on the Republican ticket. Three men ran against him. Stephen A. Douglas of Illinois ran as a northern Democrat who favored popular sovereignty in the territories. John C. Breckinridge of Kentucky ran as a southern

Democrat. He demanded protection of slavery in the western territories. John Bell of Tennessee ran in the election as a Constitutional Unionist. He called for the preservation of the Union.

A New President

Less than half the people voted for Lincoln. This vote was larger than anyone else received, but it was still a minority. It was enough, however, to make Lincoln the winner.

Lincoln was a minority president—not the first and not the last. But far worse, in the eyes of Southerners, he was also a Northern President. Not a single southern or border state had voted for him. Southern leaders had long been prepared to leave the Union rather than be ruled by the North. Now they did it. Less than eight weeks after Lincoln's election, the people of South Carolina voted to secede from the Union. Georgia, Florida, Alabama, Mississippi, Louisiana, and Texas quickly followed.

In February 1861 delegates from these states met and formed their own government. They called it the Confederate States of America. Its Constitution was much like that of the United States. But it stressed the right of each state to decide most of its own laws. It also protected slavery wherever it existed. Jefferson Davis of Mississippi was elected president of the new Confederacy (kuhn•FED•uhr•uh•see).

The people in the eight remaining slave states waited to see what Lincoln would do. When Lincoln was **inaugurated** (in•AW•gyuh•raytd), or sworn into office, he told the people of the South that their rights would be protected. He said the government would not invade the South or try to end slavery in the states where it existed. "But," he added, "we cannot separate."

The Nation Is Tested

A few weeks later, the Confederacy tested Lincoln's words. South Carolina cut off supplies to the Union soldiers at Fort Sumter, just outside Charleston. Lincoln told South Carolina that he was sending an unarmed group to supply

the fort. South Carolina officials then demanded that the commander surrender the fort. When he refused, Confederate soldiers opened fire on the fort. The Northerners were forced to surrender. Two days later, on April 15, 1861, Lincoln called for 75,000 volunteers to put down the revolt in the South.

There has been much debate over "who fired the first shot." But the causes of the war were much deeper than the firing of a gun. Two ways of life existed in the United States. Calhoun had said that two ways of life could exist under one government only if both were protected.

Lincoln had no answer to the problem created by the Northern majority in Congress and the effect of its votes on the Southern way of life. Without an answer, the Southern states would not remain in the nation. Lincoln believed that once a state joined the nation it could not leave. How could a nation survive if a state could leave the Union whenever the voting went against it? The Civil War had begun.

To find out more about how war is declared, do the investigation on page 166.

To Preserve the Union

When Lincoln called for soldiers, the people of Virginia, North Carolina, Tennessee, and Arkansas voted to secede.

Not all of the people in the Confederate states favored slavery. Not all of them wanted to secede. But all of them had grown up with the culture and traditions of the South, and they were loyal to these traditions.

The Confederacy now numbered eleven states. Richmond, Virginia, was named its capital. Robert E. Lee was appointed commander of the Confederate forces.

The other slave states—Delaware, Maryland, Kentucky, and Missouri—stayed loyal to the Union. But the people in them remained divided over the question of secession, or whether a state could secede. Some people who believed in loyalty and laws found themselves on different sides of the war. Some people with different views on slavery and on secession found themselves on the same side.

Lincoln took command of the Union war effort. As Commander-in-Chief of the nation's armed forces, it was his constitutional duty to do so. Lincoln's plan was not to free the slaves or to end slavery. That would come later. The main purpose of the war, he said, was to restore the Union and prove that the national government could work.

Lincoln was most concerned with the ideas of representative government, compromise, and majority rule. He said, "We must settle this question now; whether, in a free government, the minority have the right to break up the government whenever they choose."

The war machine started up, slowly at first. The people of the free states did not expect a long war. Lincoln himself had set the first enlistments of soldiers at only ninety days. The people of the Confederacy were surprised that the Union fought at all. They had hoped the free states would let them go peacefully or perhaps meet Confederate demands. But there would be no peace. The next four years would bring instead death and destruction.

The Long War Begins

The Union had greater size and power. There were twenty-three million people in the Union. There were only nine million in the Confederacy, one-third of whom were Black slaves. More than nine-tenths of all industries and two-thirds of all railroads were in the Union. The Union had more of everything. It had more resources, weapons, supplies, money, ships, and soldiers, as well as industry and railroads. The Confederacy had two strengths. Its soldiers were skilled in shooting and riding, and they would be fighting on familiar ground, defending their own homes and land.

Why would the Confederacy risk such odds? There were a number of reasons. Southerners knew that all they had to do to win was to hold out. They did not have to conquer the Union.

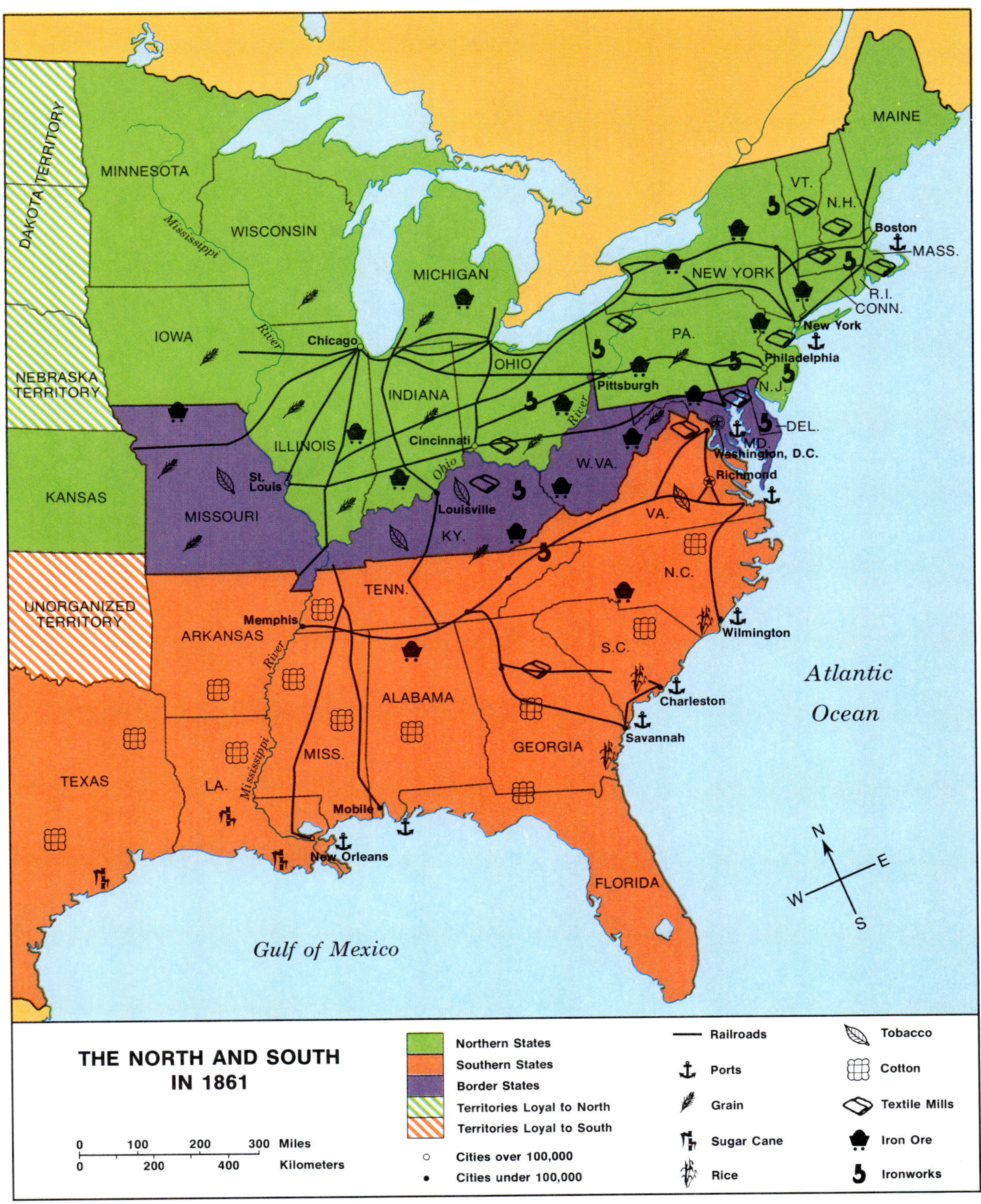
MAINE
VT.
N.H.
Boston
MASS.
R.I.
CONN.
NEW YORK
New York
PA.
Philadelphia
N.J.
DEL.
MD.
Washington, D.C.
Richmond
Pittsburgh
MINNESOTA
WISCONSIN
MICHIGAN
IOWA
Chicago
OHIO
INDIANA
ILLINOIS
Cincinnati
DAKOTA TERRITORY
NEBRASKA TERRITORY
KANSAS
MISSOURI
St. Louis
Louisville
W.VA.
VA.
KY.
TENN.
N.C.
Wilmington
S.C.
Charleston
Savannah
GEORGIA
ALABAMA
MISS.
Memphis
ARKANSAS
UNORGANIZED TERRITORY
TEXAS
LA.
Mobile
New Orleans
FLORIDA
Mississippi River
Ohio River
Atlantic Ocean
Gulf of Mexico
N
E
S
W
THE NORTH AND SOUTH IN 1861
0 100 200 300 Miles
0 200 400 Kilometers
Northern States
Southern States
Border States
Territories Loyal to North
Territories Loyal to South
Cities over 100,000
Cities under 100,000
Railroads
Ports
Grain
Sugar Cane
Rice
Tobacco
Cotton
Textile Mills
Iron Ore
Ironworks

AN INVESTIGATION
into who makes war decisions

Many dictators have gained and kept power by controlling the armed forces of their nation. The Constitution of the United States, however, prevents any single person from having the power to involve the nation in war. The chart on this page shows who must work together to make decisions about using the armed forces of the United States.

1. If the President declares war, what must he or she do next?
2. If Congress does not approve the President's action, what must happen?
3. How can Congress declare war?

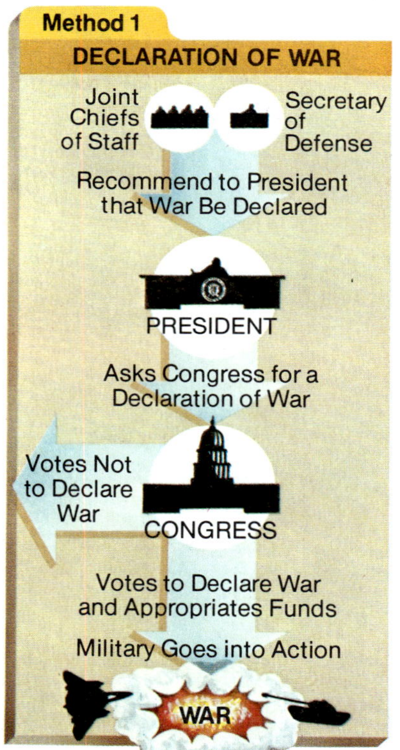

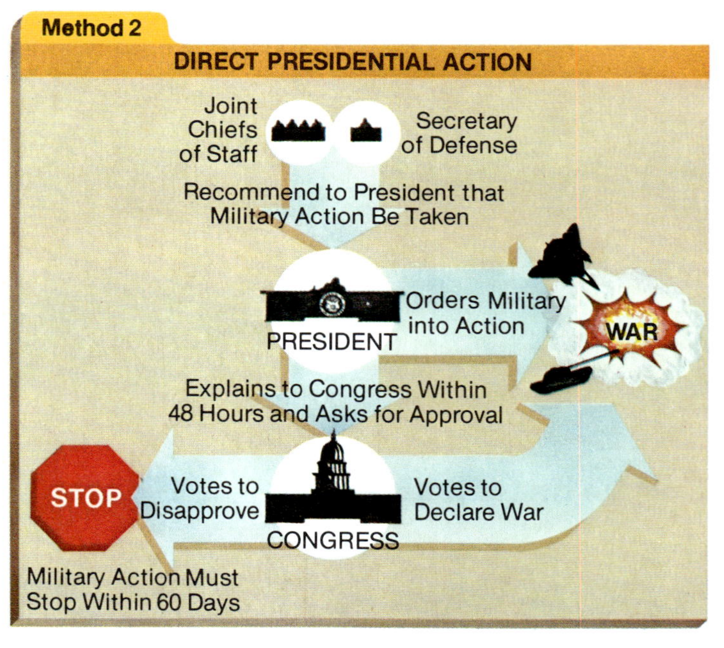

The Confederacy also had a great leader in Robert E. Lee. Lincoln had offered him the leadership of the Union army at the time of secession. Lee turned it down because he felt that his first loyalty was to his state of Virginia. With Lee as their leader, Southerners believed they could hold out until the people of the free states got tired of fighting and ended the war. But they misjudged the strength of the Union, and they misjudged Lincoln's leadership. Lincoln used every power at his command to make the war effort succeed.

Confederate leaders also believed that England or France would help them because both countries needed southern cotton for their mills. However, neither country offered aid.

The Union navy blocked Southern ports so tightly that the Confederacy could not ship its cotton to Europe or bring in the supplies it needed. For the people of the Confederacy, each year of the war brought greater hardships.

Most of the major battles of the war were fought on two fronts. One was the area around Richmond and Washington. Each side tried to take the other's capital. The other battleground was along the Mississippi River, where the Union tried to cut the Confederacy in half. Both sides suffered heavy losses in battle. Both sides had trouble getting soldiers, and both were hurt as thousands of soldiers deserted. But the Union, with its larger population, was hurt less.

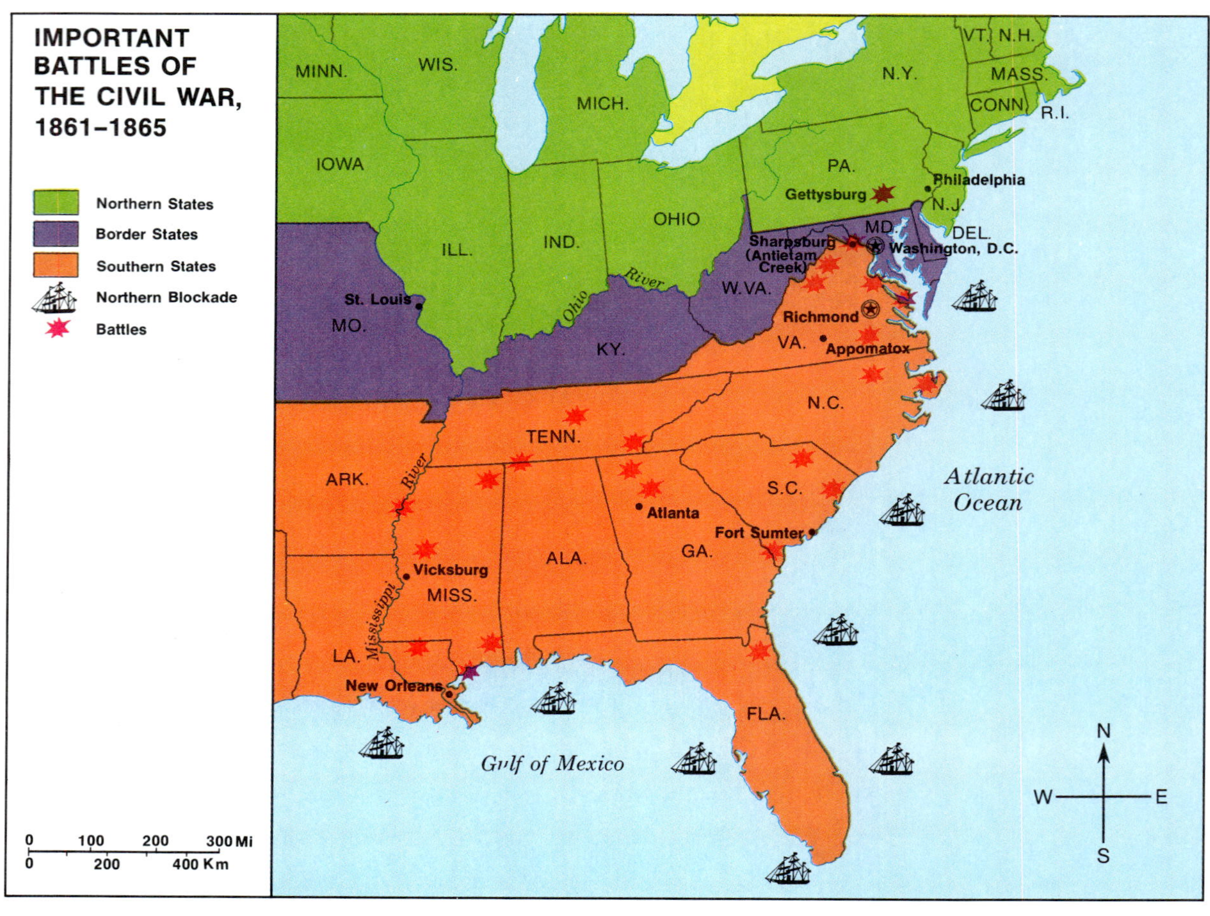

In the beginning, the Union forces fought raggedly. Their commanders handled them poorly. The Confederacy was holding its own, even threatening the Union. England and France watched carefully. They were prepared to offer help to the Confederacy as soon as the Union seemed to be losing. Then a few key battles turned the tide.

The first of these was at Antietam (an•TEE•tuhm) Creek, near Sharpsburg, Maryland, in September 1862. Union soldiers, under the command of General McClellan, stopped Lee's advance and forced him to retreat. Lee's defeat caused the English and French to decide not to send help to the Confederacy.

An End to Slavery

The victory at Antietam also encouraged Lincoln to issue his famous *Emancipation Proclamation* (i•man•suh•PAY•shun prok•luh•MAY•shun), which said that slaves were now free. He was very careful, however, to free only slaves in the Confederate states. Many people in the border states were in favor of slavery. Lincoln wanted to keep them loyal to the Union.

In fact, the Proclamation freed no slaves at all because the Union had no power over slaves in the Confederacy. The Proclamation was just the beginning of the end of slavery in America.

For more than two hundred years most Black people in America had been slaves. Some had been treated well, some had been treated badly. Either way, all had been denied their freedom. In most states it was against the law to teach slaves to read or write. Slaves could not take a day off, marry, or even keep their families together unless their owners let them. Often family members were sold to different plantations. "Volumes have been written in defense of slavery," Lincoln said, "but I have never heard of any of these authors wanting to be slaves themselves."

War and Destruction

The next two important battles were at Vicksburg, Mississippi, and Gettysburg, Pennsylvania. On July 4, 1863, Ulysses S. Grant, leader of the Union army, captured the Confederate fortress at Vicksburg. The victory came after six weeks of battle. The Confederate soldiers surrendered only after they were starving. The capture of Vicksburg split the Confederacy in half and gave the Union control of the Mississippi River. The Confederacy was now surrounded by Union forces.

At the same time, Union soldiers won a major battle at Gettysburg. This ended the last Confederate attempt to bring the fighting to the North. The victories at Vicksburg and Gettysburg also ended the last hopes of the Confederates for help from Europe. England and France now gave up the idea of even officially recognizing the Confederate government. Life in the South became even harder.

The end of the war came less than two years later in April 1865 at Appomattox (ap•uh•MAT•uhks) Court House, Virginia. In a tree-shaded farmhouse, Grant offered surrender terms to Lee. The Confederate leader accepted them, ending the bloodiest, costliest conflict in American history.

Three days later, Lee's soldiers surrendered their arms. They marched down the main street of Appomattox Court House between two lines of Union soldiers. They stacked their guns at the end of the lines and moved on, back to their homes and farms. No cannon saluted victory. No drums rolled defeat. Grant had forbidden it. There would be no celebration.

More than 620,000 Americans had died in four bloody years of war. Another 375,000 had been wounded. The South was in ruins. The North was exhausted. But the Union was restored, and slavery had ended.

1. What new political party was formed in Wisconsin? Who was its presidential candidate in 1860?
2. Why was Lincoln called a minority president?
3. How did the Constitution of the Confederate States differ from the United States Constitution?
4. Which states were part of the Confederacy?
5. Where were the first shots of the Civil War fired?
6. Who was the commander of the Confederate forces?
7. What was President Lincoln's main reason for going to war?
8. Most of the fighting in the Civil War took place in two main areas. Where were they?
9. Which slaves were declared free by the Emancipation Proclamation?
10. Why did President Lincoln not free all the slaves?
11. From which European countries did the South expect help?
12. Where did Lee's Confederate forces surrender to Grant?

Suppose that you and your neighbors want something that is not what most of the people in your community want. What can you do about it?

1. List the actions you can take.
2. Number the actions in the order in which you would take them.
3. Explain why you put the actions in that order.

Use the map on page 165 to help you answer these questions.

1. Which states in the South had supplies of iron ore?
2. Which states in the South had ironworks?
3. Which states in the North had ironworks?

4. Where were most of the ironworks?
5. Which cities in the South had populations of more than 100,000 people?
6. Which cities in the North had populations of more than 100,000 people?
7. Where were most of the big cities?
8. Where were most of the railroads?
9. Where were most of the textile mills?
10. How did supplies reach the troops in the North and the South?

President Lincoln once asked; "[Can] any government, not *too* strong for the liberties of its people . . . be strong enough to maintain its existence in great emergencies?"

1. How might a government be "too strong" for the liberties of its people?
2. Why might a weak government not last?
3. How strong should a government be?

In the speech he gave when he became President, Lincoln talked about the government of the United States. He reminded the nation that a representative democracy cannot survive if a minority of the people refuse to accept the decisions of the majority.

4. What majority decision was President Lincoln talking about in his speech?
5. How did the South show it would not accept the decision of the majority?
6. Can Americans who have a minority opinion say what they think in public?
7. Do they have to obey the law even if they disagree with it?

Reviewing Key Ideas

The United States Constitution is a plan for government. When the first thirteen states agreed to form a new government under the Constitution, no one knew how well it would work. It had to be tried and perhaps changed.

In 1789 the people in North America shared many ideas about government. They cared about many of the same things. These ideas and values are written into the Preamble, the Constitution, and the Bill of Rights. In studying the making of the Union and its plan for government, you have learned this about governments: One reason people organize governments is to protect what they care about.

Conflict and Compromise

The American people hoped the new government would be strong enough to protect their liberties and way of life. But they did not agree about how strong the government should be. Many thought a strong central government was necessary. But many others said a strong central government could threaten the interests of individual states. They wanted states to be able to govern themselves. One conflict, then, concerned the federal system itself.

There were other conflicts, too. Recall the conflicts over slavery in the territories. Congress at first resolved these conflicts by compromise. Even though they disagreed, people in free and slave states were willing to compromise. They valued the Union and their system of government. They were satisfied that this system worked to protect their interests. In studying how conflicts were resolved, you also have learned this about governments: In order to last, a government must protect the interests of most of the people.

Recall the growing differences between ways of life in the North and the South. There were changes in the economy of the North. There were changes in the economy of the South. As

the conflict over slavery grew, the South gradually lost influence in the central government. By 1860 many southern political leaders believed that the power of the central government threatened their interests. In studying the events that led to the Civil War, perhaps you have learned this understanding: People do not value a system of government that does not protect their interests.

There is a difference between a plan for government and the way that government works in the life of a nation. The difference is in the ways the people use their government. In this unit, you have studied some of the ways American people used their plan for government to serve changing needs. You have learned, then, that people take part in their government and adopt that government to their changing needs and values.

Using Key Words

Use these key words to complete the sentences that follow.

amendment	judicial branch
compromise	legislative branch
executive branch	overriding
federal	tariff
inaugurated	unconstitutional

1. The government of the United States is called the ____ government.
2. The people who wrote the Constitution had to give up some things in order to form a government that all the states would accept. When people give up some things in order to get others, they ____.
3. The part of the federal government that makes the laws is called the ____.
4. The part of the government that carries out the laws is the ____.
5. The branch of the government that decides how laws work is the ____.
6. If the Supreme Court decides that a law goes against the meaning of the Constitution, the law is declared ____.
7. An addition to the Constitution, such as the Bill of Rights, is called an ____.
8. Every four years, the person who is elected President of the United States is sworn into office, or ____.
9. If the President does not sign a bill, Congress can still make it a law by ____ the President's veto.
10. A tax Congress puts on goods imported into the country is called a ____.

Focus on the Social Scientist

Historians tell what happened in the past. To do this, they gather and study facts. Then they try to interpret their meaning. That is, they use the facts they have gathered to try to explain how and why changes have occurred and what the changes mean.

Sometimes new facts are discovered about the past. Historians then have to make new explanations and interpretations. For example, for many years, American history books did not discuss the many roles Black Americans played in building the United States. In the past few years, since the Civil Rights Act was passed, historians have begun to study the roles of Black Americans in the past. Other social scientists are studying the roles of Blacks today.

John Hope Franklin is a Black historian who has written many books about the history of Black people in America. One book is *From Slavery to Freedom: A History of Negro Americans.* In this book he describes the African backgrounds of Black Americans and traces their history from their arrival in America until the present. He examines the role of white people in the South, especially after the Civil War.

Professor Franklin also interpreted his findings. "The history of the Negro in America is essentially the story of the strivings of the nameless millions who have sought adjustment in a new and sometimes hostile world. . . . They have been the nation's constant reminders of the imperfection of its social order. . . ." Do you think Dr. Franklin's interpretation will change someday? If so, how?

A New View of Government

An unpainted, wooden fence surrounded the playground at Butler Oaks School. Ever since Karen had begun going to the school, she had disliked the fence. It was, she thought, really ugly. One day as she arrived at school, she wondered if she could paint the fence with beautiful designs and pictures. How could she start the project?

Karen talked with some of her classmates. Together they went to the teacher to ask if they could paint pictures on the playground fence. The teacher could not give them permission, but she was willing to ask the principal. Because the town council decides how school property is used, the principal had to get permission from them.

The town council was willing to discuss the children's request. Several council members liked the idea and were willing to approve the project. Some people on the council were doubtful that young children could do good work. Another group on the council didn't oppose the idea, but they thought that other people in the community might object to it. Before they made a final decision, the council asked to see a sketch from the children.

The principal told Karen and her friends what the town council had asked. Then she suggested that Karen and her teacher form a committee to help get the sketch drawn. This was a big responsibility. Karen wanted to be sure that she was going to get a good sketch. She knew she would need to ask for help from teachers and other students in her school.

Several children who were interested in the project formed a committee. They had to make two important decisions. First they had to decide what was going to be painted. Then they had to decide who would do the painting. They thought of several ways to solve these problems. For instance, everyone in the school could participate in deciding and drawing. Or Karen and the committee could do the job alone, since they had been interested in the project first. The work might also be done by the oldest children, or the best artists, or even by the teachers.

Karen and the committee talked with the other classes to find out their ideas. Finally the committee decided to ask every class to submit drawings. These entries would be judged by the committee and the teachers. The winning drawing would be painted on the wall. Each class could choose who they would like to do the painting for their class.

The winning sketch was shown to the town council. Most of the council members were impressed by the idea and the sketch. They finally gave their approval for the painting.

The way Karen's idea to paint the fence got accepted is similar to the way in which a law is passed in the federal government. Trace the steps that were necessary. List them in order.

A Community Project

In Burlingame, California, all three hundred children in the Washington School painted their school area. First the children voted to select twelve favorite subjects to paint. Then each child helped paint one of the subjects.

The people in Burlingame liked the painting so much that they were glad to display more children's art in the community. There are now permanent exhibits in the town hall, post office, fire station, and other buildings. The town sells post cards which show these projects. Everyone in the community is proud of the work which the children have done.

1. Some communities have strict rules about how buildings can be built and decorated. Do you think government officials should be allowed to tell people how to decorate their private property?

2. The project in Burlingame was organized differently than the one at Karen's school. If your school were doing such a project, which way would you choose? Why? Which way do you think is the fairest? Which way do you think is the simplest? Which way do you think would create the finest painting?

UNIT FOUR

Opportunity in the United States

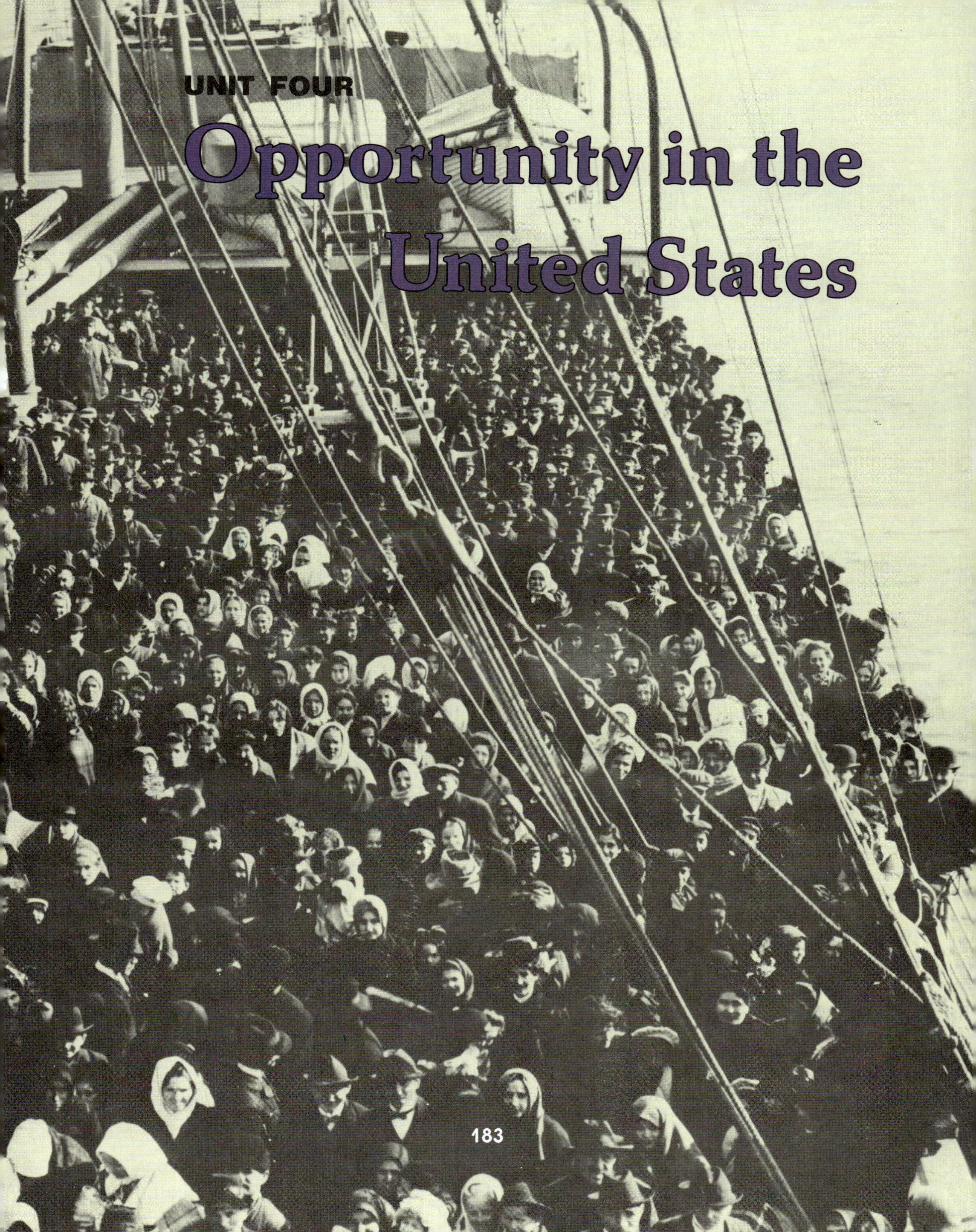

Between the Atlantic and the Pacific, the young nation stretched. Its people saw different things in this land of plains, mountains, and deserts.

To Native Americans the land and its people were one. An old tribal song tells the Native American way:

In a sacred manner
I live.
To the heavens
I gazed.
In a sacred manner I live.
My horses
Are many.

In the growing cities, other Americans worked and played. They invented new ideas, new machines, and new ways to do things. Carl Sandburg described his city, Chicago:

Hog Butcher for the World,
Tool Maker, Stacker of Wheat,
Player with Railroads and the
  Nation's Freight Handler;
Stormy, husky, brawling,
City of the Big Shoulders.

People from many countries came to the new nation looking for opportunity. Their goal was success, and their measure was progress.

A Nation of Invention and Opportunity

For centuries Native Americans lived undisturbed in North America. The land and the animals on it gave them all they needed. When either was used up, they moved to a new area. There was plenty of space, especially in the center of the country, the Great Plains.

Each plains tribe had its own culture. But all of them lived in peace with their environment. With the coming of the European settlers, however, plains life changed. The settlers brought new inventions to the plains that changed the lives of the Native Americans. They also changed the shape and uses of the land itself.

Inventions Change the West

The first great change came with the horse. The Spanish explorer Coronado brought horses to the Great Plains in 1541. The people he met had never seen a horse before. In their culture horses had not been necessary. For food some grew small crops of corn, beans, and squash. Others got most of the other things they needed from the buffalo they hunted. They covered their tepees and made clothes and ropes from buffalo skins. From the sinews (SIN • yoos) of the buffalo they made thread. From the bones they shaped tools. Most of the other Native American tribes on the plains also hunted buffalo.

The buffalo roamed the plains in huge herds. A hunter might stand for hours while a single herd trotted past. After the Spaniards came, Native Americans saw how useful the horse would be for hunting. As they got more horses, life for the plains tribes changed. Most tribes gave up farming. They became nomadic (noh•MAD•ik) hunters, following the buffalo herds.

In the early 1800s settlers from the east moved into the Great Plains. The settlers came to work the land, to own it, to fence it in. But the Native Americans fought to keep the plains open for hunting. In their culture, land was to be used by all people and not owned by anyone. They used horses to fight the settlers. Native Americans on horseback could shoot arrows faster than the settlers could fire their guns. For many years, the plains were too dangerous for settlers to live there.

Then in 1835 Samuel Colt invented a new revolver that could shoot faster than the bow and arrow. In 1860 Oliver Winchester's new repeating rifle could shoot even farther than the Colt .45. Fifteen years later, barbed wire made it cheap and easy to fence in the land. With fences, cattle could graze for miles on the rich prairie grass and still be controlled.

In 1869 the first cross-country railroad was completed. Railroads themselves were not new. The eastern states had been connected by rail since the 1840s. But a railroad across the continent opened the West to settlement.

While wagon trains took five months to cross the prairies and deserts, trains took less than a week. The cross-country railroad brought more settlers to the West. The railroad shipped the farmers' cattle and crops east and the merchants' goods west. The nation's economy grew.

New towns sprang up along the rail lines. Within ten years, five cross-country railroads had been completed.

The Native Americans saw their way of life being destroyed. They could not fight off the great numbers of settlers who came. The railroad lines split the buffalo herds apart. Hunters killed buffalo for the price of their hides. As many as three million buffalo were killed a year. Ranchers fenced in the open ranges. Farmers plowed the fields. Without the buffalo, the plains culture could not last. Tribe after tribe was defeated and forced to move.

More and more settlers moved West. In 1890 the United States Census Bureau announced that the West was no longer a frontier. To find out more about the railroads and the frontier, try the investigation on the facing page.

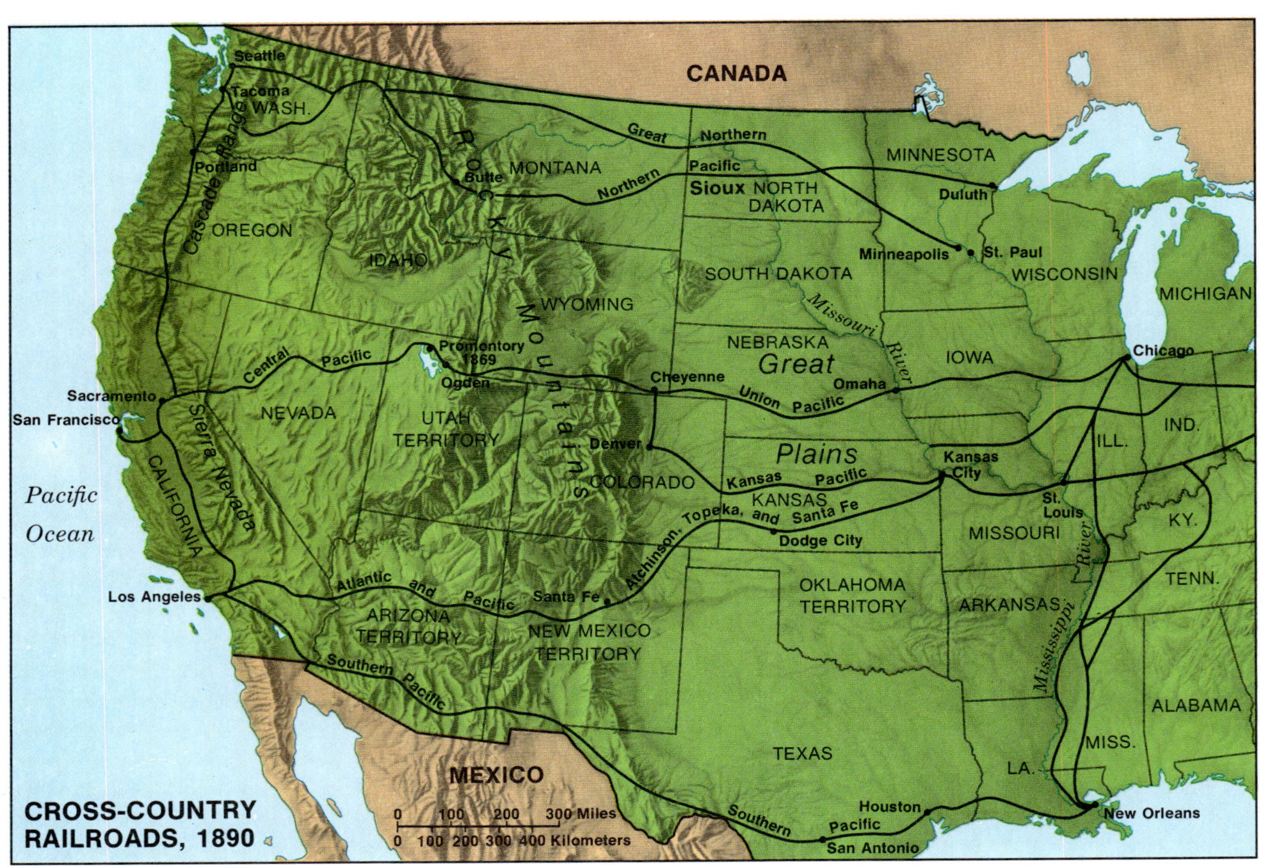

CROSS-COUNTRY RAILROADS, 1890

AN INVESTIGATION
into railroads

The first cross-country railroad was completed in 1869, just four years after the end of the Civil War. People still had hard feelings about the war. But many Americans said the new railroad would help to bring the nation back together.

1. How do railroads help bring the people of a nation together?
2. Look at the map on page 165. What regions of the country were not connected by rail to another part in 1860?
3. Now study the railroad map on the facing page. In what parts of the country were railroads built after the Civil War? Were there any parts of the country which were not connected by railroads now?
4. For the price of a railroad ticket, a Virginian could become a Californian. What effect might railroads have on the way people interact?
5. What effect might railroads have on regional differences? Why?

A Problem on Your Own

Today people do not often travel long distances by railroad. Can you name two ways of transportation that have partly taken the place of railroads for long-distance travel? Have these new ways also helped to bring the people of America together? How?

Connecting the Nation

While some Americans sought new opportunities in the West, others looked for new ways to do things. Their inventions and new ideas changed industry. They also changed the way Americans lived.

The railroad opened the Great Plains to settlement. It also connected different sections of the nation. The journey from the Atlantic to the Pacific coast by railroad took about a week. This encouraged more trade between distant sections of the country.

Railroads began in England in 1826 when John Stevens invented the locomotive. Four years later his son, Robert, invented the T-rail. By 1850 the United States had three times more track than all of Europe.

With railroads, cities like Chicago, Pittsburgh, Atlanta, and St. Louis grew quickly. The railroads brought food to the many people living in the cities. They also brought the

raw materials needed to manufacture goods. Then they carried the finished goods from the cities to every part of the country to be sold.

New ways of communicating (kuh•MYOO•nuh•kayt•ing) over long distances were also connecting the country. Samuel F.B. Morse invented the telegraph in 1844. It quickly became an important link between the old states and the new western lands. Messages could be sent from coast to coast almost instantly. When the last spike was driven in to finish the cross-country railroad, the telegraph sent the news to every corner of the country.

Thirty-one years later, Alexander Graham Bell invented the telephone. By 1900 there were more than one million telephones in use, mostly in the cities. Railroads and telegraph and telephone lines connected one city to another. The cities became the centers of business, industry, art, and entertainment.

New Developments in Industry

The growth of industry was changing American life as well. Until the 1870s most Americans lived in rural areas. They were mainly farmers or small shopkeepers. But after the Civil War, America rapidly became an industrialized (in•DUS•tree•uh•lyzd) nation. At its heart were the cities with their railroad yards, their factories and office buildings, and their workers. Many of these workers were new immigrants from Europe and Asia.

The cities grew because of the discovery of new machines and new sources of power to run factories. By the 1860s kerosene (KER•uh•seen) had replaced whale oil as fuel for lamps. In 1882 Thomas Edison built the first electric power plant in New York City. Steam-powered electric plants were soon built in other cities across the nation.

Old industries grew and new industries sprang up. One of the most important new industries was steel. Steel was used to build railroads, bridges, machines, and factories. Between 1870 and 1900 the amount of steel produced in the United States increased more than a thousand times.

New factories with modern machinery to make cloth, foods, cars, and products of all kinds were built. Coal production doubled. New deposits of iron ore, gold, and silver were mined.

As factories and businesses grew, owners needed faster and cheaper ways to produce large quantities of goods. The automobile industry was a good example. Henry Ford did not invent the automobile, but he made it possible for many families to own one.

Ford borrowed an idea from Eli Whitney, the inventor of the cotton gin. In 1800 Whitney had worked out a new way to make guns. Instead of making each gun part by hand, Whitney invented machines that made the same parts for every gun. Then workers could put many guns together quickly.

Ford did the same with automobiles. Using standard automobile parts, workers put the automobiles together on a moving conveyor belt. In this way, Ford could produce more cars at a lower cost. In 1900 there were only eight thousand cars in the United States. In 1908 Ford introduced his Model T. Four years later there were one million cars. Other industries soon began using Ford's **assembly line** to increase the amount of goods they could produce.

It took a lot of money to build factories and develop modern machinery. Before 1880 most businesses were owned by one person or a family. But as businesses grew, owners needed to raise more money. They also needed ways to share costs. Many of them formed partnerships of two or three people. Others formed large **corporations.** A corporation sells **stock,** or shares of its business. In this way, it raises money to run its business. The people who buy the stock share in the ownership of the corporation and get part of the profits.

Corporations were not new. Some European voyages to America had been paid for in this way. Now corporations helped business and industry to grow. Production costs went down. Profits went up.

Captions of Industry

The people who ran corporations became wealthy and powerful. These "captains of industry" worked hard to get all the business in their industry. Four of these men rose above all others to control great business empires. They were Andrew Carnegie in the steel industry, Cornelius Vanderbilt in railroads, J. P. Morgan in banking, and John D. Rockefeller in oil.

Oil was discovered in Pennsylvania in 1859. Rockefeller quickly saw how important oil was. In 1865 he sold his grocery business and bought an oil company. He then persuaded the railroad that shipped his oil to return a part of his shipping costs to him. This cut his costs, so he was able to sell oil cheaper than anyone else. The refinery

grew. In 1870 Rockefeller and his partners formed a corporation, the Standard Oil Company of Ohio.

Rockefeller combined Standard Oil with other oil companies to form a **trust.** The companies shared their resources. Then they lowered their prices. Smaller companies could not afford to sell oil as cheaply. One by one they went out of business. With no competition, Standard Oil had a **monopoly.** A company has a monopoly when it is the only seller of a good or service.

Other industries did the same. There was a beef trust, a steel trust, a sugar trust, a lead trust, a cotton-oil trust, and so on. In each industry a few companies banded together to share their resources. With increased profits they bought control of an entire industry—raw materials, production, distribution, and sales. Smaller companies went out of business. Then the trusts could raise prices.

The trusts grew so powerful that people demanded they be broken up. In 1890 Congress passed the Sherman Antitrust Act. But the government did not begin to control the trusts until the early 1900s, when President Theodore Roosevelt was President.

1. How did the Native Americans' view of the Great Plains differ from the settlers' view?
2. How did the plains people use the buffalo to get the things they needed to live?
3. How did the horse change the way of life of the plains tribes?
4. How did the building of railroads help to end the plains culture?
5. Name three inventions that helped link different sections of the country.
6. How did Ford's assembly line change industry?
7. Why did business owners form corporations?
8. Who were the four biggest "captains of industry"? How did they build their business empires?

America changed rapidly between the end of the Civil War and World War I. New inventions in transportation, communications, industry, and business changed the United States from a rural into an industrialized nation.

1. If you had lived in a growing city in the United States during this time, how might your life have changed?
2. People are often opposed to change. What changes might people have opposed during this time? Why do you think they might feel this way?

The **Gross National Product,** or GNP, is the value in dollars of all the goods and services produced in the United States in a year. The first graph shows the GNP of the United States from 1870 to 1910. The second graph shows how many people lived in the United States in the same years. Use the graphs to help you answer the questions on the facing page.

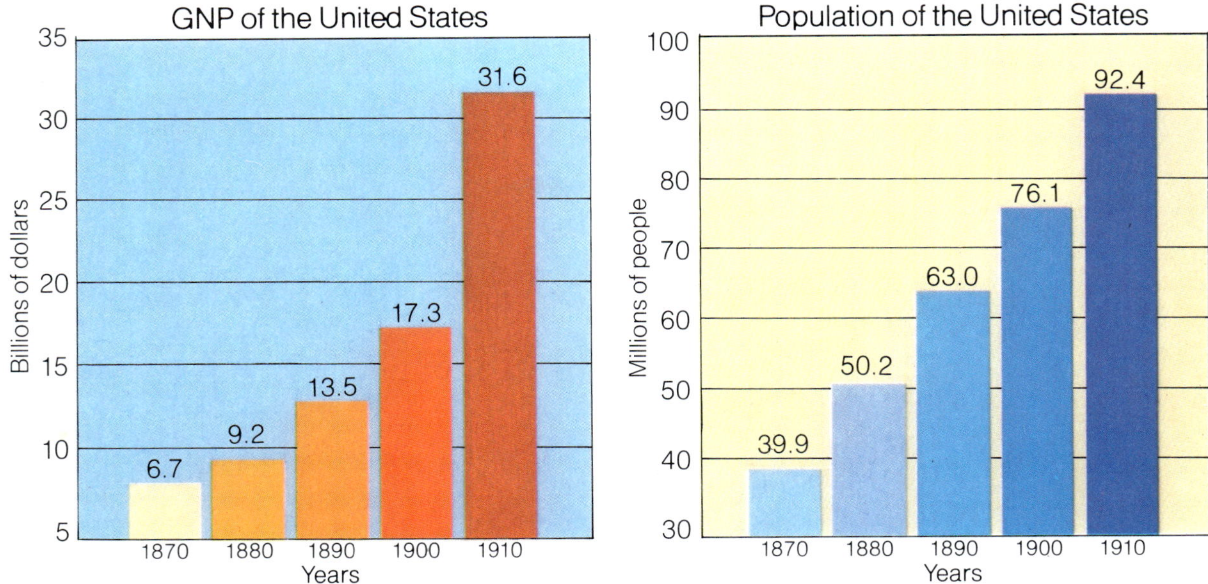

1. What was the GNP of the United States in 1870? in 1890? in 1910?
2. How many people lived in the United States in 1870? in 1880? in 1910?
3. What effect do you think the growing number of people in the nation had on the GNP? Why?

Railroads and barbed-wire fencing changed life on the Great Plains. Henry Ford's assembly-line cars changed the way goods were produced and the way people traveled.

Two inventions that might change life in your area are a cheap method for changing sea water into fresh water and a cheap method for getting energy from the sun.

1. Which of these inventions would have the greatest effect on your area? Why do you think so?
2. What are some changes it might make in people's lives?

The Search for a Better Life

As Americans pushed westward in their search for new land, Europeans searching for a better life left their homelands and came to the United States. Most of the immigrants in the early 1800s came from England, Scotland, Ireland, Germany, and Scandinavia. Many of them moved westward looking for farmland. Some settled in the Northwest and Louisiana territories. Later they settled in the Oregon Country and in Florida, Texas, and California. They built farming communities throughout the United States.

After the Civil War, immigrants still came from countries in Northern Europe. But now these immigrants were joined by great numbers of southern and eastern Europeans. Between 1870 and 1900, eleven million immigrants landed in New York. Most of them came from Italy, Greece, Hungary, Poland, Rumania, and Russia. On the West coast, thousands of Chinese immigrants arrived in California. They came to work the mines and to build the cross-country railroad.

Some immigrants did not blend easily into American life. They had different customs. They worshipped differently, and they spoke different languages. Life in the new country was hard for them.

Looking for Work in the Cities

Although many immigrants went west with the wagon trains, many more remained in the eastern cities. The jobs were there, especially for workers without skills. New York, Boston, Philadelphia, and smaller cities along the east coast grew rapidly. So did Chicago, St. Louis, and Cincinnati in the Midwest, and San Francisco on the west coast. The United States became known around the world as the "land of opportunity."

The cities were busy. Everywhere new houses and new factories were built and new businesses opened. Streets were paved, subways were dug, and tracks were laid. Railroads and canals were built to connect the cities. Companies wanted cheap labor to do all these jobs. To encourage people to immigrate, they put advertisements in European newspapers.

Millions of immigrants came to work. Many families moved to the new country in stages. The husband came alone and found a job. After he had saved enough money, he sent for his family. Together in their new home, they worked hard and saved their money. Most hoped to start their own shop or business.

People from one country tended to stay together. In the big cities, there were Italian, Polish, German, Chinese, and Slavic neighborhoods. Here the old language and culture survived. These neighborhoods made the immigrants feel at home. The people were familiar, and the ways were their own. But often the neighborhoods were run-down and overcrowded. Sometimes whole families lived in one room.

The struggle for a better life was hard. In most immigrant families, everyone worked, even the children. Wages were low, and families needed every penny. Women and children worked twelve-hour shifts in factories called

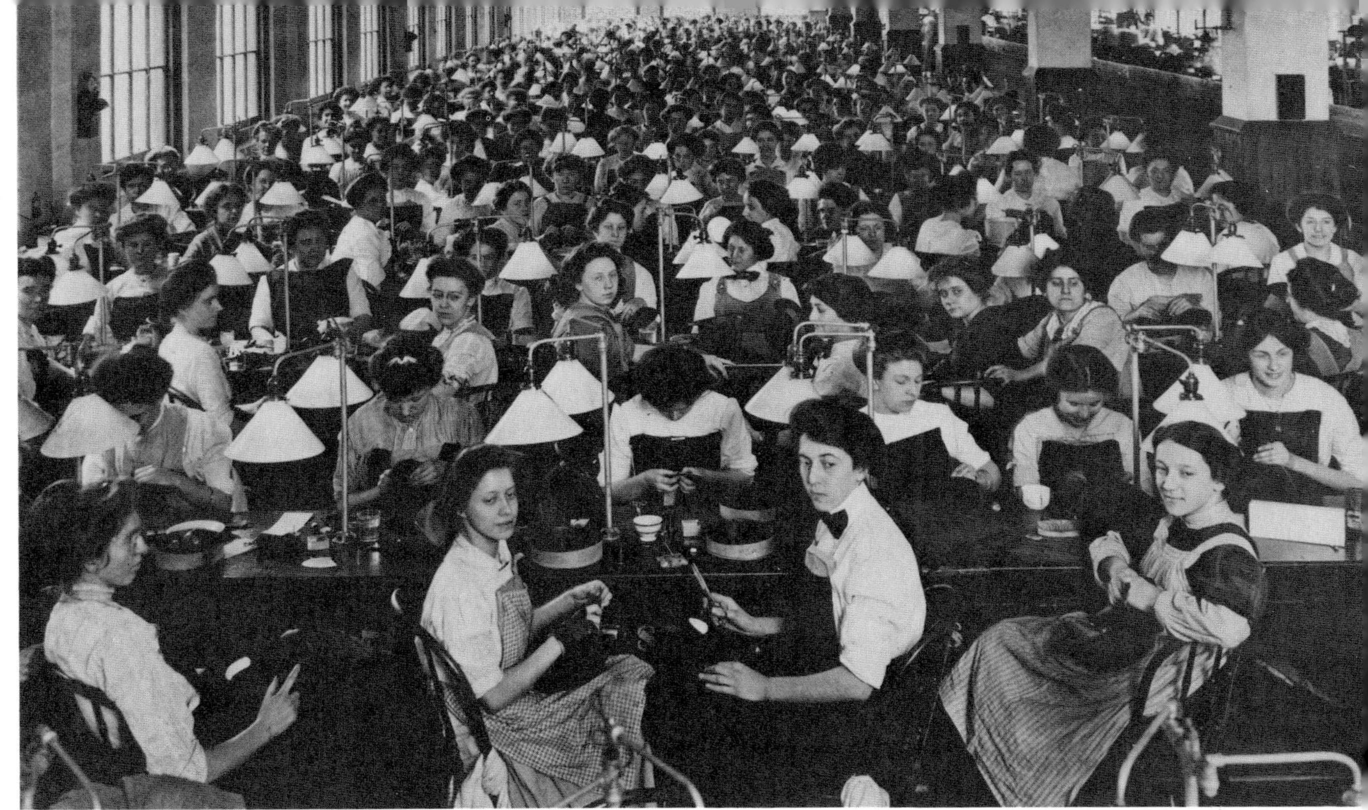

"sweatshops." The owners gave little thought to workers' safety or to factory fires.

Some workers tried to form unions. Together they might have some power to bargain with the factory owners. But immigrant workers were more divided than united. Most wanted to succeed on their own. They feared that if they joined a union they would lose their jobs. There were not many jobs for immigrants. Many of them were competing against each other for the same jobs.

American workers did not like the immigrants because they worked for lower wages. Immigrants who had lived in the United States for awhile disliked the newer immigrants because they worked for even lower wages. Hatred for Chinese immigrant laborers grew so strong that Congress passed a law against them in 1882. The law said no more immigrants from China could come to the United States. That law was not changed until 1943.

The Farmers Organize

The nation's population was growing, especially in the cities. With more people, there was more demand for farm crops. To get their crops to the distant cities, farmers depended on the railroads.

The railroads touched everyone's lives, but none more directly than the farmers'. The cost of shipping farm products to market often meant the difference between profit and loss for farmers. If the cost was too high, farmers would lose money. To protect themselves, farmers joined together in groups that would speak for them. The first of these was called the National Grange.

The Grange tried to get farmers to work together. It also worked to limit the railroads' power. By getting laws passed, the Grange could force railroads to charge less to ship farm crops.

Illinois created the first Railroad Commission in 1871. It could set rates for railroad freight. Shortly afterward, several other midwestern states formed similar commissions. The Grange had helped to make this happen.

The farmers had other problems, however. One was the problem of getting a fair price for their crops. New machinery was helping farmers produce more food. But as the crops got bigger, farmers were paid less money for them. In almost every year after 1870, farm profits went down.

Farmers also had problems with banks. Many farmers had to borrow money each year to buy seed and equipment. If their harvests were poor, they would not make enough money to repay the bank loans. Then the banks might take their farms. Farmers lived knowing they could lose everything with a change in the weather.

In 1886 there was a bad dry spell. It lasted for ten years. Many farmers lost their farms to the banks. Those who could keep their farms started cooperatives and farm associations. These groups worked for laws that would help farmers get a fair share of the nation's progress.

By 1892 farmers' groups were powerful enough to help start a new political party. It was known as the Populist Party. Populists wanted the government to help farmers and poor people in many ways. They wanted the government to take over the railroads, telephones, and telegraphs. They asked the government to coin more money so that farmers could get loans more easily. They also wanted the government to tax people according to their income. Under this plan, the people who made the most money would pay the highest taxes.

The Populists' candidate for President lost the election. But other Populists candidates were elected to Congress and the state governments. Many of their ideas later became laws. The farmers had shown that organizing into groups gave people more power to improve their lives.

The Workers Organize

While the farmers were organizing, workers in the cities were beginning to do the same. Skilled trades workers, such as hatters, cigar makers, machinists, and blacksmiths, had organized themselves before the Civil War. After the war, unskilled workers began to do the same.

The labor movement began slowly. In 1866 the first National Labor Union was formed to try to give workers an eight-hour workday. A year later the first union of unskilled laborers was started in the shoe industry. Although a few states adopted an eight-hour day, the laws were not carried out.

Other unions came and went. Companies usually fought the unions. Workers continued to face long hours, low wages, and bad working conditions. When business slowed down, many workers lost their jobs. Most workers felt they needed more protection.

In the summer of 1877 railroad workers on the Baltimore & Ohio Railroad went on strike to protest lower wages. Soon workers on other railroad lines stopped working, too. There had been strikes before, but this was the first general strike against the nation's railroads.

Workers went on strike in more than a dozen cities. In some places state and federal soldiers were called to battle with striking workers. Several people died in the fighting. After this some states passed laws making strikes illegal.

The labor movement continued to grow, however. In 1886 the American Federation of Labor (A.F. of L.) was formed to organize workers by trade. Each trade had representatives on a national council. Under Samuel Gompers, the A.F. of L. became the most important labor union.

Workers succeeded in winning some rights and benefits. States began to pass laws to protect workers. The workday was limited to eight hours. Factories were made to improve dangerous working conditions, and children were not allowed to work. Life for workers in the United States was beginning to improve by the 1890s.

1. From what countries had most immigrants come before the Civil War?
2. How did immigration change after the Civil War?
3. What were some of the reasons why immigrants came to the United States?
4. Where did most immigrants settle? Why?
5. What made immigrant neighborhoods comfortable for people who were used to the ways of their old countries?
6. How did the railroads affect the farmer?
7. Why did farmers and workers organize?
8. What did the Grange help to bring about?
9. Why did farmers want the government to coin more money?
10. What were some of the ideas of the Populist Party?
11. Which union became the nation's most important labor union? Who was its leader?
12. What were two benefits won by labor unions for workers?

Immigrants came to the United States seeking a better life. Often the whole family had to work long hours for low wages. They might live in one room. Life was hard. Yet most of them stayed, and many became successful.

1. Why do you think they wanted to stay despite the hardships? What might they have been proud of? What might they have hoped for?
2. Often immigrants lived in neighborhoods with others from their home country. Why do you think they wanted to live together? How might they have felt living with people from other cultures?

There have been labor, or trade, unions in the United States since the nation began. But after the Civil War, labor unions became more powerful. Each of the following people were important leaders of the labor movement in the late 1800s.

William Sylvis
Uriah Stephens
Terence Powderly
Rose Schneiderman
Leona O'Reilly
Eugene V. Debs

Choose one person. Find out the answers to the questions below. Then write a short report or draw a series of pictures to show what the person believed in and what he or she did.

1. What union did he or she lead?
2. When was the union started?
3. For what reasons was the union begun?
4. What did the union want to do for workers?
5. What changes did the union bring about?

Farmers in the late 1800s organized themselves into granges. At the same time workers formed unions. Both groups found it was important to organize in order to make their lives better.

1. There may be groups in your neighborhood or community that are organized for some purpose. What are they? What do they want? What are they doing about it?
2. Why do you think people have a better chance to get what they want when they organize? Why might some people not want to organize?

3 The Nation Becomes a World Power

By the 1840s the United States stretched from the Atlantic to the Pacific Ocean. Many Americans now felt that the nation had grown as far as it could. But half a century later, they once again began to look beyond their boundaries. America's rapidly growing farms and industries needed new markets for their products. Before long the United States would push beyond the edges of the continent.

More Land for the United States

In 1867 the United States bought Alaska from Russia for $7,200,000. This is about half the price it had paid for the Louisiana Territory in 1803. Many people thought it was a costly mistake. The land was cold, mountainous, and far from any settlements. For years it remained forgotten. The only people who lived in Alaska were the native Eskimos, some other Native Americans, and a few trappers.

Life in Alaska changed in 1896, however. Gold was discovered in the Klondike region in the nearby Yukon Territory. Another gold rush, like the one in California, began. Miners came to the cities of Skagway and St. Michael on their way to the Yukon. In 1898 other miners headed for Nome, where more gold had been discovered. Shortly afterward, a territorial government was set up in Alaska.

THE KLONDIKE NEWS

VOL. I — DAWSON, N.W.T. APRIL 1ST 1898 — NO. 1

OUTPUT FOR 1898 $40,000,000.

With the discovery of gold, Americans saw that Alaska was a valuable area. In the 1900s Alaska became an important source of fish, gold, and other minerals for the United States. Alaska's importance as a storehouse of natural resources was proven again when huge oil deposits were discovered on the far northern shores.

Until the airplane was invented, people could not get to many places in Alaska. But airplanes could bring food and supplies to communities in the rugged mountains and frozen wilderness. Today the airplane is the major way of transportation in Alaska. Radio also helped to connect faraway communities and build a communications network in Alaska. With the radio and the airplane, more people were willing to come to Alaska to develop the land and settle there. Finally, in 1959, Alaska was admitted to the Union as the forty-ninth state.

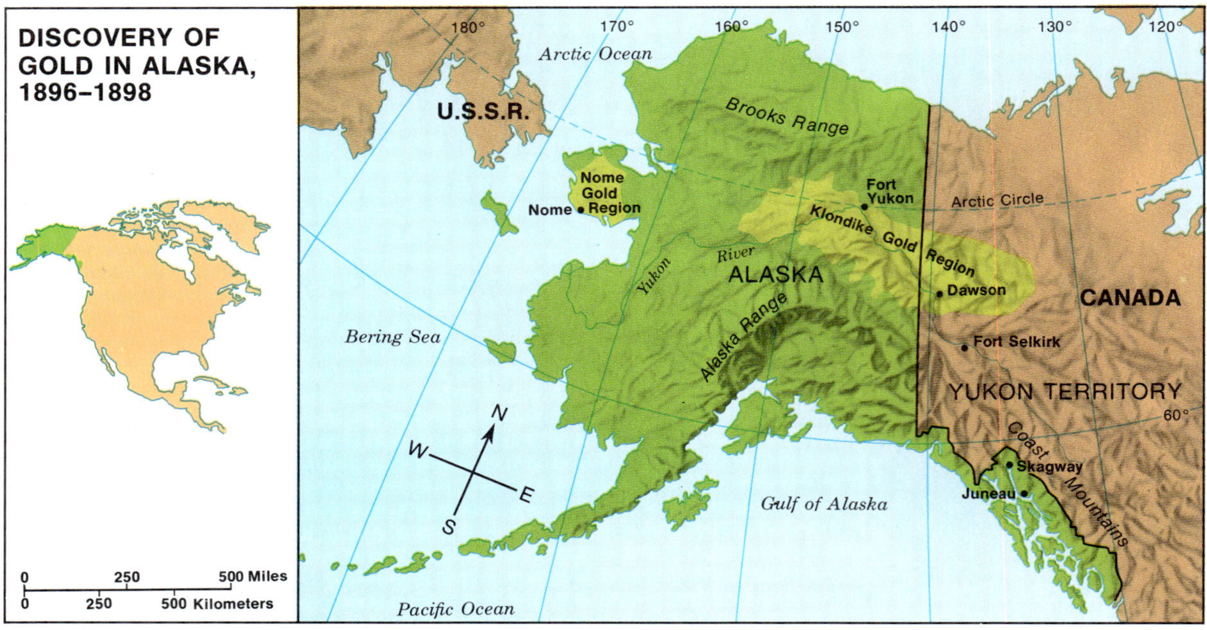

The islands of Hawaii are even further from the continental United States than Alaska. Americans had long been attracted to these warm islands in the Pacific. Beginning in the late 1700s, European and American ships had stopped in the islands for fresh water and food. Traders had stopped there as early as 1810. Missionaries and planters soon followed. In the islands they found people whose ancestors had probably sailed to Hawaii from other islands in the Pacific hundreds of years earlier.

In 1876 the United States signed a trade treaty with the king of Hawaii. Hawaii promised not to sell land to other countries. Eleven years later, a new treaty said the United States could build a navy base at Pearl Harbor.

Sugar cane and pineapples were Hawaii's largest crops. Most of the big planters were Americans. These planters wanted Hawaii to become part of the United States. Then they could get payments from the government for their sugar cane. Other Americans wanted Hawaii to become a territory of the United States, too. Hawaii would give the

United States a port in the Pacific for shipping. In 1898 Congress approved a treaty making Hawaii part of the United States. Two years later Hawaii became a territory. But, like Alaska, Hawaii had to wait until 1959 before it became a state. The two states are the only ones not sharing a common border with any of the other states.

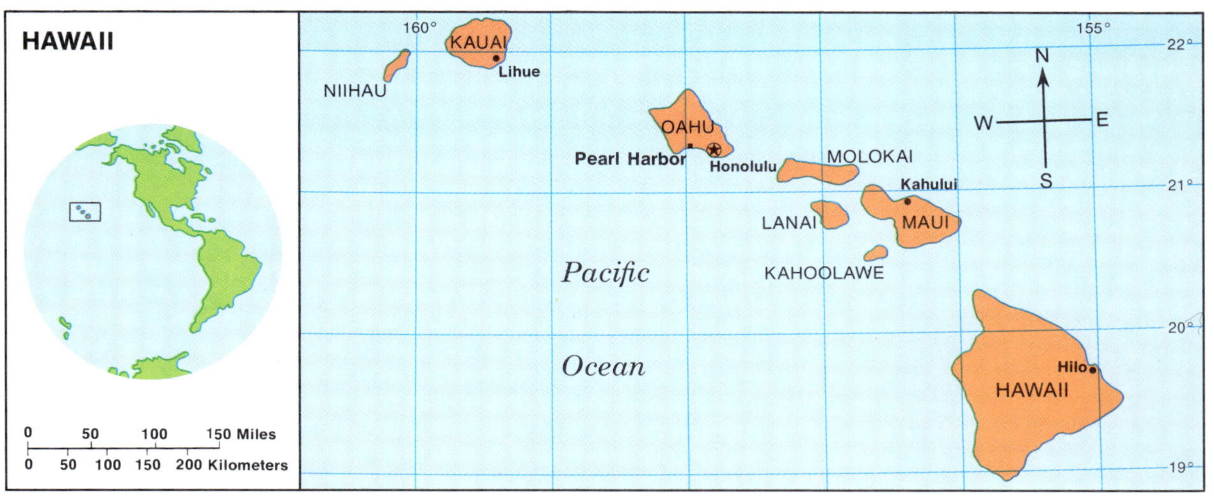

The Spanish-American War

The United States began to expand its power in the east, too. Only 150 kilometers from the tip of Florida lies the island of Cuba. A little farther south is Puerto Rico. These islands in the Caribbean (kar•uh•BEE•uhn) Sea were the last of Spain's territory in the Americas. United States businesses had invested money in the Cuban sugar industry. Because it was so close to the mainland, many Americans thought Cuba was important to the safety of the United States, too. Some wanted to make it part of the United States. Others wanted only to make sure that it did not threaten the United States.

In 1895 the Cubans revolted against Spanish rule. A war broke out on the island. The Cubans destroyed American-owned sugar mills and plantations. The war stopped trade and threatened American businesses in Cuba. The Spanish stopped the rebellion and put rebels in prison camps.

In 1898 Cubans began rioting again in Havana. President McKinley sent the battleship *Maine* to Havana Harbor to protect Americans living in Cuba. Shortly after it had arrived, the *Maine* blew up and sank. The cause of the blow-up has never been learned, but most Americans thought it was a mine set by the Spanish. Many Americans called for war. President McKinley did not want war. But before long Congress drew up a war resolution demanding Cuban independence. Spain broke off diplomatic relations with the United States. The United States Navy blocked Cuban ports. Spain then declared war on the United States.

Theodore Roosevelt was assistant secretary of the navy. He had prepared the navy for battle. When Spain declared war, American ships sailed to Cuba. They also sailed to the Philippine (FIL•uh•peen) Islands. The Philippines were Spain's most important navy base in the Pacific Ocean. In the Battle of Manila Bay, in the Philippines, the American navy destroyed all of the ships in the Spanish fleet. The

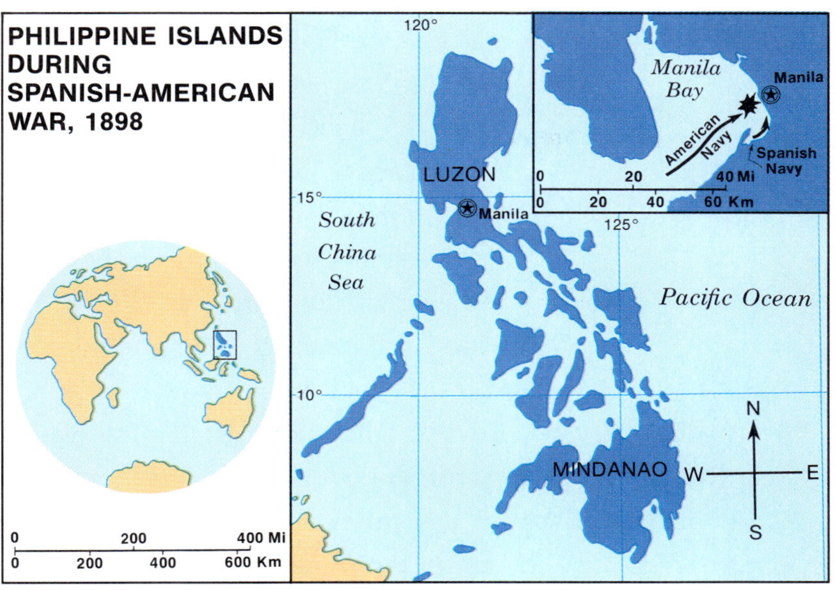

American ships then blocked Manila Harbor. Spain surrendered Manila fourteen weeks later.

In Cuba the war continued. Roosevelt himself led a charge of soldiers up San Juan Hill. This victory put the Spanish ships in Santiago Harbor under American control.

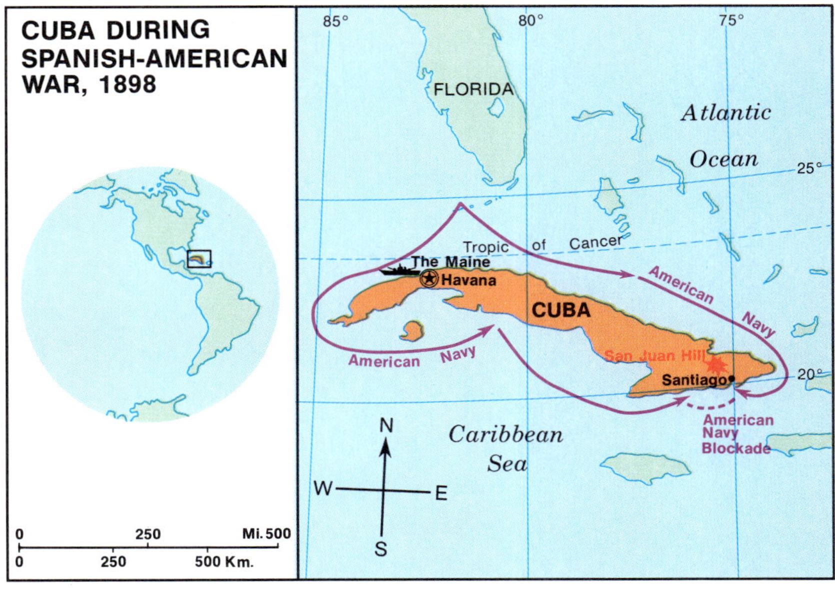

When the Spanish ships tried to escape, the entire fleet was destroyed. Three weeks later, Spain asked for peace.

The Spanish-American War had lasted less than four months. Under the Treaty of Paris, Spain granted Cuba independence. Spain also gave Puerto Rico, Guam, and the Philippines to the United States. In return for the Philippines, the United States paid Spain $20 million. The United States had become a world power with territories in both the Caribbean and the Pacific.

Roosevelt, Reform, and Expansion

In 1901 President McKinley was killed in office. Vice-President Theodore Roosevelt became President. Roosevelt had many interests. He was a historian, an athlete, and a conservationist (kon•suhr•VAY•shuhn•ist). His life could have come right out of a story book. As a child he was sickly and shy. By exercising and learning to box, ride, and hunt, he made himself strong. As a young man he spent several years in the Dakota Badlands, where he raised cattle. He was also a sheriff. During the Spanish-American War, he became a war hero. Even after he became President, he wrestled and took judo lessons.

Theodore Roosevelt was an active President. His "Square Deal" promised to regulate business and increase every worker's share in the nation's wealth. He carried out the Sherman Antitrust Act to break up the giant trusts. He worked with Congress to pass laws to regulate the railroads and the food and drug industries. He worked to conserve the nation's forests and to irrigate desert lands. Because of his work, Congress created many national parks.

After the Spanish-American War, America's influence grew in both the Caribbean and the Pacific. By 1900 Hawaii, Guam, the Philippines, Wake Island, and part of Samoa in the Pacific were all territories of the United States. In the Caribbean, the United States had made

Puerto Rico, the Panama Canal Zone, and by 1917, the Virgin Islands American territories. Cuba, the Dominican Republic, and Haiti had become American **protectorates** (pruh • TEK • tuhr • its). That meant the United States agreed to protect each island. In return the United States had some control over each country.

President Roosevelt wanted to see American influence and power spread. Under President McKinley he had built up the navy. As President he made the United States the "police officer" of the Western Hemisphere. With American influence and interests increasing around the world, Roosevelt also decided that the navy needed a way to move quickly from the Atlantic Ocean to the Pacific Ocean. For this purpose, a canal was needed somewhere across Central America.

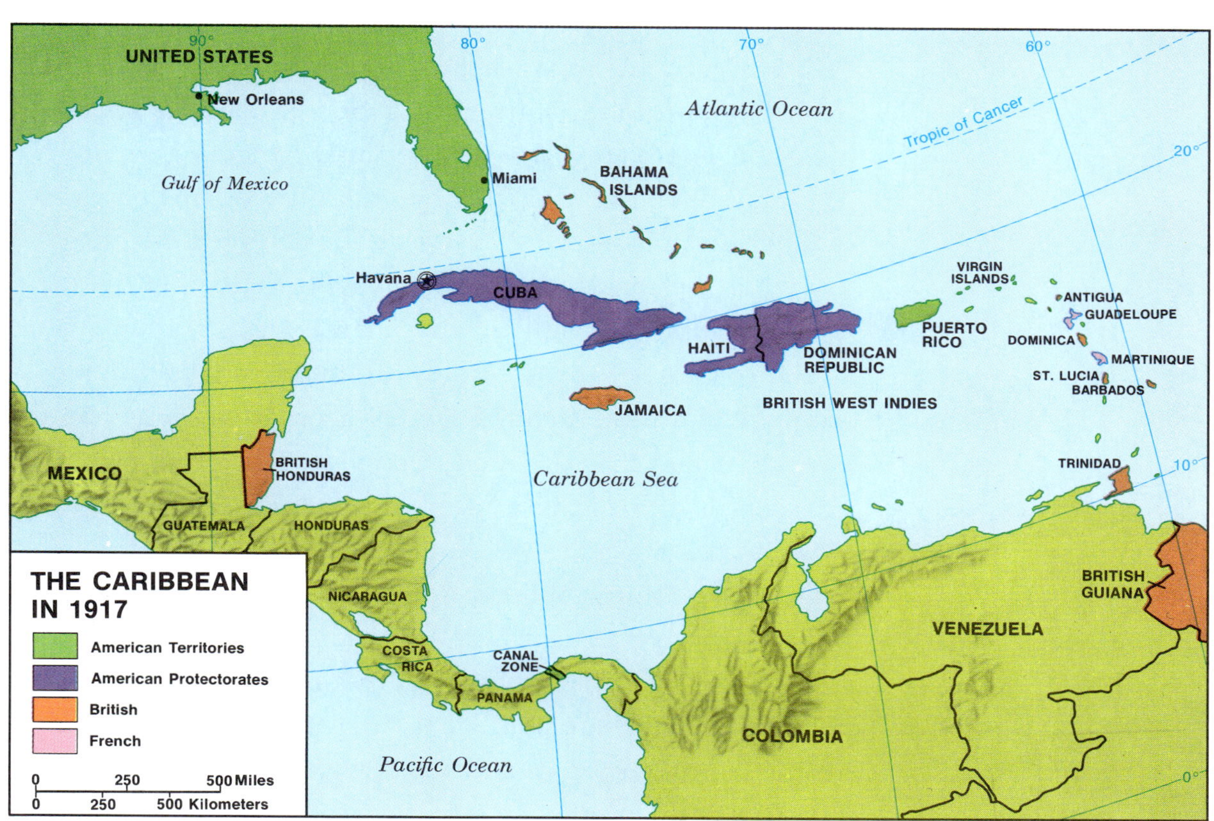

The Panama Canal

People had long dreamed of cutting a canal across the Central American land bridge that connects North and South America. Ships could then pass quickly from the Atlantic to the Pacific Ocean. They could avoid the slow and dangerous journey around South America.

Americans first became interested in a canal when California became part of the United States in 1848. England was interested, too. The two nations agreed that neither would have complete control of any canal. But neither country tried to build one.

In 1901 President Roosevelt decided to get a canal built. First he wrote a new treaty with England. This treaty gave the United States complete control over any canal. Then Roosevelt offered Colombia $10 million, plus $250,000 a year in rent, for the right to build a canal. The Colombians turned down the offer. They wanted $25 million. Roosevelt sent a warship to Panama as a show of force.

Shortly afterward, a group of people in Panama revolted against Colombian rule. They declared Panama a republic. Two days later the United States recognized Panama as an independent nation. The new republic accepted American terms for the canal. Eighteen years later the United States paid Colombia $25 million for Panama.

The canal itself took ten years to build. It is 80 kilometers long and more than 12 meters deep. Mountains had to be leveled and the jungle cleared away. Doctors designed a program to control the tropical mosquitoes (muh•SKEE•tohz). In this way, the yellow fever and malaria which had stopped the French builders were controlled. Engineers built a series of locks. These locks raise and lower ships from the sections of the canal in the lowland jungles to the sections in high mountain lakes. In 1914 a ship made the first trip through the canal locks. It now took only eight hours to sail from the Atlantic to the Pacific Ocean.

World War I

The year that the Panama Canal opened also marked the beginning of World War I in Europe. In the summer of 1914 an Austrian prince was killed. It seemed like a small event at the time. But it stirred up old feelings between European nations.

For more than one hundred years, European nations had been fighting wars over boundary lines. To protect themselves, nations often made alliances (uh•LY•uhn•ses), or treaties, with other nations. The wars were usually between nations in different alliances. World War I began as a war between the Central Powers, headed by Germany, Austria-Hungary, and the Ottoman Empire, and the Allies, headed by England, France, Belgium, Russia, Serbia, and Japan. In all, twenty-three countries fought in the war.

World War I was the most destructive war the world had seen. On the ground, soldiers dug long, winding trenches to protect themselves from attack. Enemy cannon fire hit the trenches for days and weeks on end. For the first time, airplanes armed with machine guns looped and buzzed through the skies. Silently beneath the sea, another new weapon—the submarine—searched out enemy ships and sank them.

After three years of fighting, the war stalled. Neither side could defeat the other's forces. On land, soldiers in trenches faced each other across row after row of barbed wire fences. At sea, the British navy blocked German ports. German submarines sank every Allied ship they found.

The United States tried to stay out of the war. But most Americans favored the Allies. American ships carried passengers and supplies to England. German submarines attacked American and British ships, killing American passengers. Wilson warned Germany against further attacks. But Germany said it would sink any ship its submarines found in the Atlantic. Then in February 1917 a note from

Germany to Mexico was discovered. The note said that if the United States entered the war, Germany would help Mexico attack the United States and regain the territory it lost in 1848. The United States entered the war on the side of the Allies. President Wilson said, "The world must be made safe for democracy."

More than two million American soldiers went to Europe to fight. Another 500,000 sailors helped to block the German Navy. More than 100,000 Americans died in the war.

Entering the war was the nation's most forceful step in its new role as a world power. Although World War I lasted only eighteen months longer, Americans felt its effects for many years after. American soldiers who came back from Europe were changed people.

In the four years of World War I, thirty nations had become involved in the war. More than 16,000,000 lives were lost. Half of the dead were not in the armed forces.

1. When did the United States buy Alaska?
2. How did Hawaii become part of the United States?
3. When did Alaska and Hawaii become states?
4. Why were Americans interested in Cuba?
5. What part did the battleship *Maine* play in the Spanish-American War?
6. What were some of the reforms that Theodore Roosevelt supported?
7. In what two areas of the world did United States influence spread after the end of the Spanish-American War?
8. What is a protectorate?
9. Why was Theodore Roosevelt interested in a canal across Central America?
10. When and why did World War I begin?
11. When and why did the United States finally enter the war?

When the United States paid $7,200,000 for Alaska, it was paying about two cents an acre. Even at this price, many people thought Alaska was not worth it. They thought the sea voyage to get there took too long. Once there, they found it was almost impossible to get from one place to another.

1. What inventions and discoveries made people change their minds about the value of Alaska?
2. How much money do you think the United States would be willing to pay for Alaska if it were being bought today?
3. Suppose someone were selling land on the moon. Would people be willing to pay two cents an acre? What inventions and discoveries might make the land there worth buying?

The map on page 215 shows the territory the United States controlled in the Caribbean by 1917.

1. Which countries were part of the United States?
2. Which countries were American protectorates?
3. What other nations had territory in the Caribbean Sea?

In 1904 President Theodore Roosevelt declared that only the United States, and not any European country, should become involved in the affairs of Latin American countries. Before this, the United States had sent ships to Cuba and Panama. It had sent strong messages to England warning it to stay out of Venezuela. Between 1900 and 1920 American military forces landed in the Dominican Republic, Haiti, Nicaragua, and Honduras.

1. If you had lived at this time, what reasons might you give for the United States' right to become involved in the affairs of other countries in the Western Hemisphere?
2. What reasons could you give for why the United States should not get involved in the affairs of these countries?
3. Might there be situations in the world today in which the United States should become involved in another country's affairs? Why or why not?
4. In 1977 President Carter signed a treaty with Panama. The treaty said that Panama would have complete control of the canal by 2000 A.D. Now the United States controls the canal. Many Americans agreed that Panama should control the canal. But many others disagreed. What arguments might each side have given to support their position?

4 Americans in a Smaller World

The defeat of Germany ended World War I, but a peace treaty had to be worked out. Representatives from England, France, Italy, and the United States met in Paris to prepare the terms they would present to Germany. President Woodrow Wilson went to Paris to speak for the United States.

Wilson felt that peace would last only if the nations of the world worked together. He drew up a plan for a league of nations. England, France, and Italy accepted his idea. In the next few years, sixty nations joined the League of Nations. But many Americans opposed the League. They were tired of wars. They wanted only to be left alone. The Senate voted against joining the League of Nations. Americans turned their attention to their own affairs.

The Roaring Twenties

Many Americans began the 1920s hoping to return to the old ways of hard work, thrift, and simple, orderly lives. But that way of life was being threatened. Since the 1870s Americans had been on the move. Many people had moved from farms and small towns to the cities. By 1920 more than half the people lived in cities. In the fifty years between 1870 and 1920, the United States had changed from a rural to an urban nation.

The move to the cities brought many changes. There were many conflicts between old, rural ways and the new city life. Some people did not like the changes. Congress responded by passing laws to support the old ways. One such law was the Prohibition (proh•uh•BISH•uhn) law of 1920. It made it illegal to sell liquor.

Women began changing their ways, too. The Nineteenth Amendment, adopted in 1920, gave women the right to vote. In business, in politics, and in the professions, women began to work beside men. More women went to work in offices and stores. Women worked for civic and political changes through such new groups as the League of Women Voters. Women also changed the way they dressed and the way they acted. Not everyone liked the changes. Laws were passed in some places saying women could not wear short dresses and swimsuits.

Business and industry also changed. There was money to pay for new inventions and new industries. Natural gas and electricity provided the energy to power new machines in factories and in homes. Refrigerators, irons, vacuum cleaners, and telephones became common in American homes. Most Americans lived better than ever. One out of every nine workers owned an automobile. The automobile industry was the largest industry in the country.

New inventions also changed the habits of the American people. The first radio station, KDKA, began broadcasting in 1920 in Pittsburgh. Within a few years there were radio stations in every big city and radios in almost every American home. Listening to the radio became a favorite way to spend the evening.

People also began going to the movies. Soon movies were the nation's fourth largest industry. Actors, actresses, and singers on the screen and on radio were seen and heard by millions. There were new heroes to follow. New

ways of dressing and acting seen in the movies began to shape the dreams of men and women everywhere.

New inventions made the world seem smaller. Telephone service connected people to each other. Radio and movies connected them to faraway places. For travel to Europe and Asia, there were swift new steamships. Charles Lindbergh flew his airplane, *Spirit of St. Louis,* nonstop from New York to Paris in 1927.

As the twenties came to a close, it seemed that anything was possible. Babe Ruth of the New York Yankees hit sixty home runs in one season. This was a new world record. The prices of corporation stocks kept going up, and some people got rich. With higher wages, workers, too, had more money to spend. Many used all their savings to buy stocks. Soon stocks were selling for much more than they were worth. They did not represent the real value of a company. By 1929 the nation's economy rested on a bubble of air.

The Great Depression

In October 1929 the air began to leak out of the bubble. Stock prices dropped sharply, and people began to worry. On October 29, "black Thursday," the stock market crashed. Many people rushed to sell their stocks before it was too late. As everyone tried to sell, prices dropped further. Some people lost all their money. The nation sank into a serious economic **depression.**

The Great Depression touched everyone. Businesses failed, banks closed, and farmers lost their land. Thousands of workers lost their jobs. Factories produced fewer and fewer goods because people could afford to buy less and less. People who were lucky enough to have jobs generally had to work for less pay. Some people earned as little as fifty cents an hour. Children often worked fifty hours a week for $1.00. By 1932 one out of three of the nation's workers did not have jobs.

In 1931 the depression spread to Europe. In one country after another businesses closed and people lost their jobs. The world had been getting smaller. What affected one country now affected all others.

The New Deal

President Herbert Hoover tried to fight the depression. The federal government loaned money to business and industry. Hoover hoped that by loaning money to businesses, the government could make them successful again. Successful businesses would employ more workers. People with jobs could, in turn, buy more goods.

Within six months the federal government had loaned over $1 billion to businesses. But many people were still hungry and without jobs. They protested. Some of them marched to show their protest.

In 1932 there was a presidential election. Hoover ran for reelection on the Republican ticket. Franklin D. Roosevelt ran as the Democratic candidate. Roosevelt told the voters that the government should give more aid to the people. He promised "a new deal for the American people."

Roosevelt won the election by many votes. In the first hundred days, the government started many new programs. The New Deal had begun.

To give jobs to young workers, the federal government started the Civilian Conservation Corps (CCC). CCC workers built roads, worked on national parks and dams, and helped fight soil erosion. Another federal agency, the Works Progress Administration (WPA), put people to work building highways, schools, and water and sewer plants. The WPA even had work for painters, writers, musicians, and dancers. In their first two years, the CCC and WPA put over four million Americans to work and paid more than $6 billion in wages.

The government also paid more than $3 billion in welfare benefits to workers without jobs. Farmers were paid if they did not plant part of their land. The government hoped that this would cut down the size of crops and push farm prices up.

The New Deal put people to work and helped the nation's businesses. It also changed the role of the government greatly. Government now became a partner in shaping the nation's economy.

War in Europe

The Great Depression affected the nations of Europe, too. Many European nations were badly damaged during World War I. Industry and farming in some nations did not recover fully during the 1920s. The world-wide depression added to their problems in the 1930s.

Some European countries turned to strong leaders for help. Benito Mussolini (buh•NEE•toh moo•suh•LEE•nee) took power in Italy. Adolf Hitler and the Nazi party took power in Germany. In return for the promise of a better life and better government, these leaders took away many of the people's freedoms. They became **dictators.**

Meanwhile, in Japan, Emperor Hirohito (heer•oh•HEE•toh) was taking control of much of Asia. Some Americans watched these developments carefully. Quietly the United States built up its navy. But most people in the United States wanted nothing to do with these power struggles in other parts of the world.

In the late 1930s, Italy, Germany, and Japan began to invade other countries. Italian soldiers marched into Ethiopia in 1936. Japan invaded China in 1937. Two years later German soldiers invaded Poland without warning. Immediately after this invasion, Poland's allies—England and France—declared war on Germany. World War II had begun. The war soon spread across all of Europe.

Within a year all of central Europe, including France, had fallen under German control. In June 1941, German forces invaded the Soviet Union. Germany now controlled all of Europe. The Russians were withdrawing, and England alone was left to fight Germany. At this time the United States would go only so far as to supply England and the Soviet Union with war materials.

WORLD WAR II IN EUROPE, 1942–1945

The United States Enters World War II

On December 7, 1941, Japanese airplanes bombed the United States Navy base at Pearl Harbor in Hawaii. American bases on Guam, Midway Island, and the Philippines were also attacked. More than nineteen United States Navy ships were sunk or damaged. About 3,500 Americans were killed or wounded. The next day the United States declared war on Japan. Germany and Italy then declared war against the United States. The war was now truly world-wide.

Japan's attack on Pearl Harbor united Americans behind the war. Men and women joined the armed forces or took jobs on assembly lines making war goods. Factories produced guns, tanks, and airplanes for all the Allied forces. Warships and cargo ships were built by the hundreds.

In Europe, English, American, and Soviet forces fought together. In January 1942 the English stopped the German forces at El Alamein in North Africa. In November 1942 the Soviet Union stopped the Germans at Stalingrad. The tide had turned.

The Soviet Union pushed the German forces back toward Poland in 1943. English and American soldiers invaded Italy. Italy was forced to surrender. In 1944 an American and English force under General Dwight D. Eisenhower invaded France from the north and south. The two armies marched toward Germany, pushing the German forces back as they went. As the end neared, Mussolini was killed, and Hitler killed himself. On May 8, 1944, Germany surrendered. The war in Europe ended.

As dictator of Germany, Hitler had blamed his nation's problems on the Jews. During the 1930s and early 1940s, Nazi police arrested German Jews. They sent them to prison camps. In these camps, Jews were tortured and starved. Many thousands were killed in gas chambers. By the end of the war, Nazis had murdered more than six million Jewish men, women, and children.

The War in the Pacific

In the Pacific, the United States pushed the Japanese forces back, island by island. The battle of Guadalcanal (gwahd•uhl•kuh•NAL) in 1943 was the first of many victories. In 1944 Americans took over the Philippines. In 1945 American forces took Okinawa (oh•kuh•NAH•wuh).

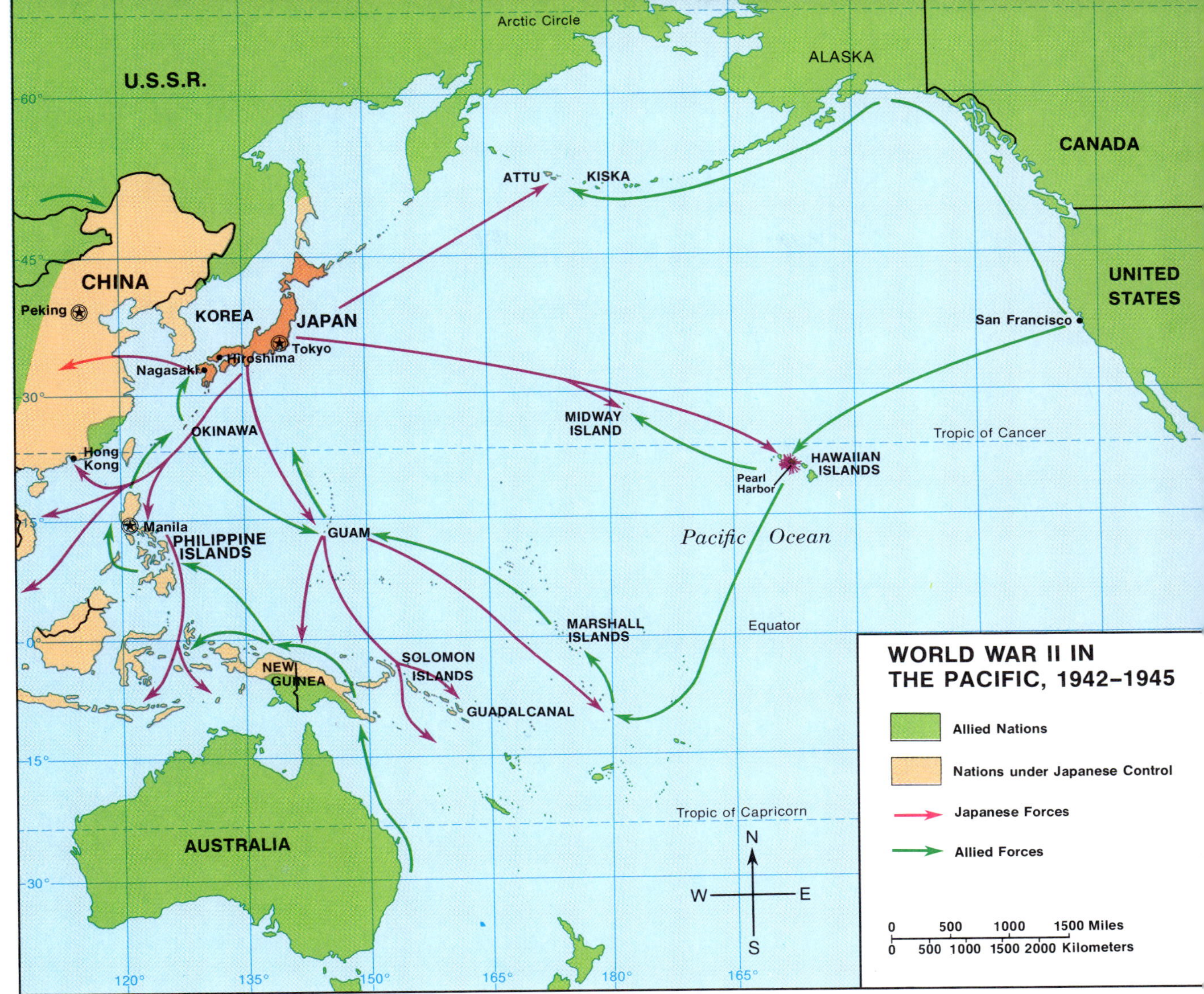

The United States demanded that Japan surrender as Germany had. When the Japanese refused, the United States dropped an atomic bomb on Hiroshima (heer•oh•SHEE•muh). The first atomic bomb destroyed the city and killed more than 160,000 people. The Japanese still would not surrender. The United States then dropped a second atomic bomb on Nagasaki (nah•guh•SAH•kee). Japan surrendered the next day.

World War II ended on August 15, 1945. The United States was now the most powerful nation in the world.

1. Why did many Americans oppose joining the League of Nations?
2. Why were values and ways of living changing after World War I?
3. How did some people try to keep older values?
4. How did movies and radio change people's lives and desires?
5. What was "black Thursday"? Why did it happen?
6. What happened during the Great Depression?
7. What was President Hoover's plan for ending the depression?
8. Describe two programs of Roosevelt's New Deal.
9. How did the depression affect Germany and Italy?
10. What happened on December 7, 1941?
11. What forced Japan to surrender?

Franklin Roosevelt's New Deal greatly increased the role of government in the United States. Since then, the government has continued to grow. Today more people have jobs with the government than with any other industry.

1. Make a list of some ways that the government affects your life. Think of everything that you and your family do and need that is run by local, state, or federal branches of government.
2. Make a second list of all the people you know who are employed by any government agencies.

The graph shows the number of people who were without jobs between 1929 and 1940. Use the graph to help you answer the following questions.

1. How many people did not have jobs in 1929? How many were jobless in 1930?

2. In which year of the depression did the largest number of people not have jobs?
3. Roosevelt became president in 1933. How did the number of people without jobs change in the years after 1933?

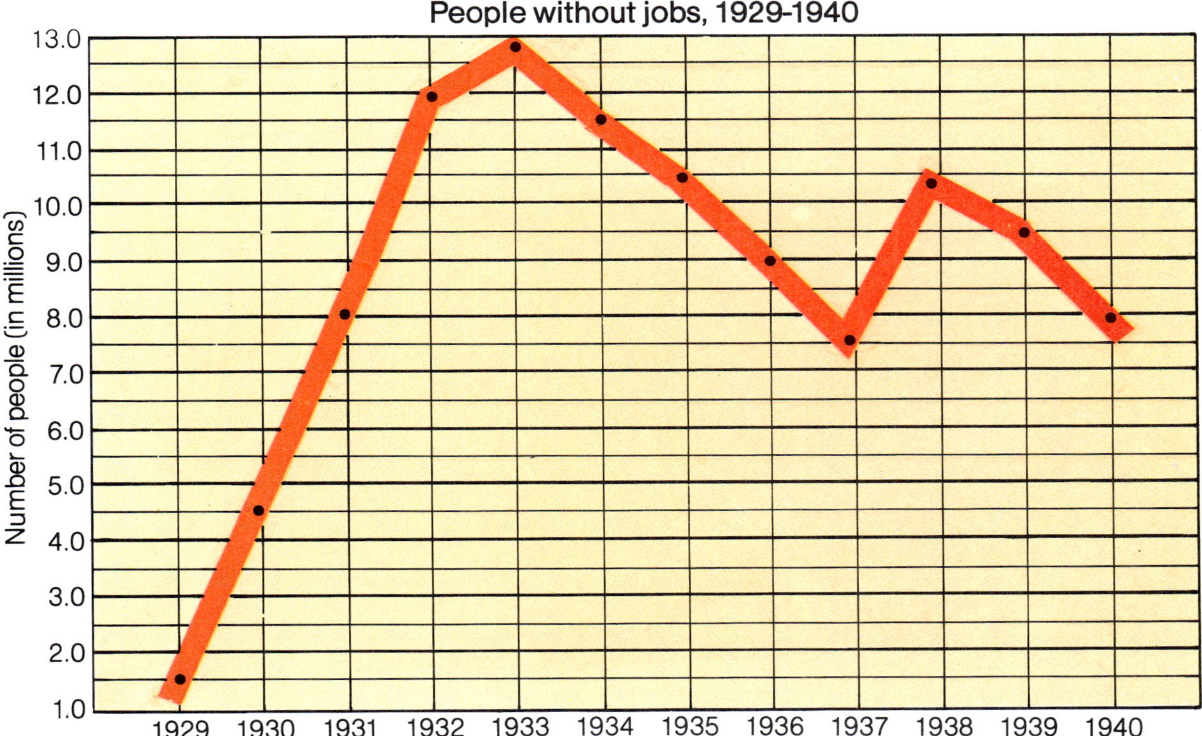

In the 1920s radio and movies introduced the American people to new places, new ideas, and new ways of dressing, acting, and thinking. Never before had so much information been available to so many people. Since the late 1940s television has become a part of almost every American's life. What is shown and said on television affects nearly everyone.

1. Who do you think should be responsible for what is shown on television?
2. Do you think there should be any control over what is shown? Give reasons for your answers.

Toward Full Rights for All Americans

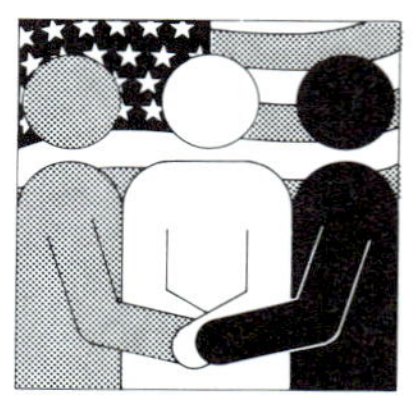

When World War II ended, the task of rebuilding for peace began. The heads of the three big powers—England, the Soviet Union, and the United States—had met at Yalta in 1945 to make a plan for peace. Out of this meeting a new world organization, the United Nations (UN), was formed. The United States was one of the first members.

Each nation began to rebuild its cities and clear its countryside. Industries began to produce once again. The United States had only a little rebuilding to do. During the war no bombs fell on the United States mainland. No battles were fought on the continent. The factories of every other nation in the war had been damaged or destroyed. But American factories and cities had not been harmed. Railroads and highways were better than ever.

During the war Americans had not been able to buy many products. Now they could buy whatever they needed. New automobiles poured out of Detroit. Television sets, cameras, refrigerators, and record players rolled off the assembly lines. Frozen foods and TV dinners changed the nation's eating habits. Prices on the stock market rose. Industry produced more and more products and American people bought more of everything.

The Space Age

England, the United States, and the Soviet Union had fought together during the war to defeat Germany and Italy. After the war, these allies split apart. The United States became the leader of a new western alliance, which included the countries of western Europe and most of the rest of the western hemisphere. The Soviet Union led an eastern alliance, which included the Communist countries of eastern Europe and China. These two groups became involved in what was called a "cold war." No shots were fired, but each side struggled to gain power.

The cold war was carried into space, too. In 1957 the Soviet Union shot the first satellite, *Sputnik I,* into orbit around the earth. A few months later the United States sent up its first satellite. The space age had begun.

Space became the new frontier. The United States spent billions of dollars to explore it. In 1961 John Glenn became the first American to orbit the earth. Seven years later the *Apollo 8* spaceship, with people aboard, orbited the moon.

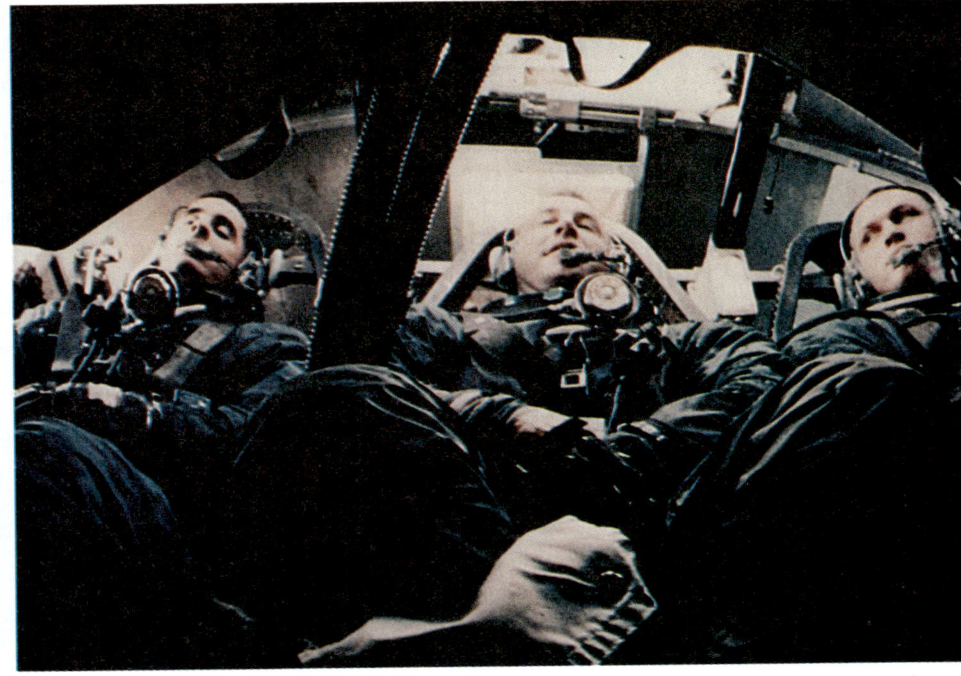

And on July 16, 1969, astronauts (AS•truh•nawts) Neil Armstrong and Edwin Aldrin walked on the moon. They were the first humans to do so.

Other satellites also orbit the earth and the moon. They send important information back to earth. They help to send television signals between continents. Spaceships have also been sent to Mars, Venus, Jupiter, and Uranus.

Space flight began as a race between the United States and the Soviet Union. The result has been more information about the earth than people have ever had before.

The Struggle of Blacks for Equality

The growing wealth in the United States in the years after the war was not shared by all Americans. Some missed out because they lived in areas of deep poverty. Others lacked basic jobs skills. Still others were left out because they were members of minority groups. Nearly one hundred years after the Civil War, many Black Americans still did not have the basic rights of Americans.

The Fourteenth and Fifteenth Amendments had made Black Americans full citizens and guaranteed them "the

equal protection of the laws." Since then Black people had done what they could to become equal Americans. Booker T. Washington in 1895 told Black Americans to learn skills. Then they could prove themselves through hard work. Washington believed that no group of people could succeed until it learned that plowing a field was equal to writing a poem.

W. E. B. Du Bois thought differently. He demanded the right to vote, equal treatment by police and the courts, and equal educational opportunities for Black people. He did not believe any people had to earn these rights.

Some white people also tried to help bring about change. In 1910 a few joined Du Bois and other Black leaders to form the National Association for the Advancement of Colored People (NAACP). The NAACP was the first group formed to give Black people a stronger voice in the community and in the nation. A year later, another group of Black and white Americans started the Urban League. It studied the economic and social problems of Black people in the cities. It also tried to help them find jobs.

Thirty years later, the Congress of Racial Equality, or CORE, was started. In 1942 a group of Black and white friends from CORE walked into a coffee shop in a southern city and sat down together. The owner of the shop would not serve the Black people unless they sat in a separate, or segregated, section. But the friends refused to sit apart. They remained seated until the owner agreed to serve them where they were. After this successful "sit-in," the owner agreed to **integrate** (IN•tuh•grayt) his coffee shop. He would serve Black people wherever they sat.

Other civil rights groups were formed to help fight racial inequality. With these groups, Black people found new ways of acting to win their rights and their share of opportunities. They demonstrated for better education, more jobs, and an integrated society. Slowly the efforts of the civil rights group began to pay off.

The Executive Responds

In 1948 a committee advised President Harry Truman to end segregation in the armed forces. But Truman decided not to include a plan for integration in his yearly message to Congress. Black leaders then called for Black people to refuse to serve in the armed forces until they were integrated. They might have to go to jail, but their action would call people's attention to the injustice of segregation. A few months later President Truman ordered the armed forces to be integrated. One branch of the government had begun to respond to the changes in society.

In 1950 a new war put Black and white soldiers side by side on the battlefield. In Korea, a country in East Asia, Soviet and American interests clashed in the "cold war." The Soviet Union supported the Communist government of North Korea. The United States supported the anti-Communist government of South Korea. Each government wanted to control all of Korea.

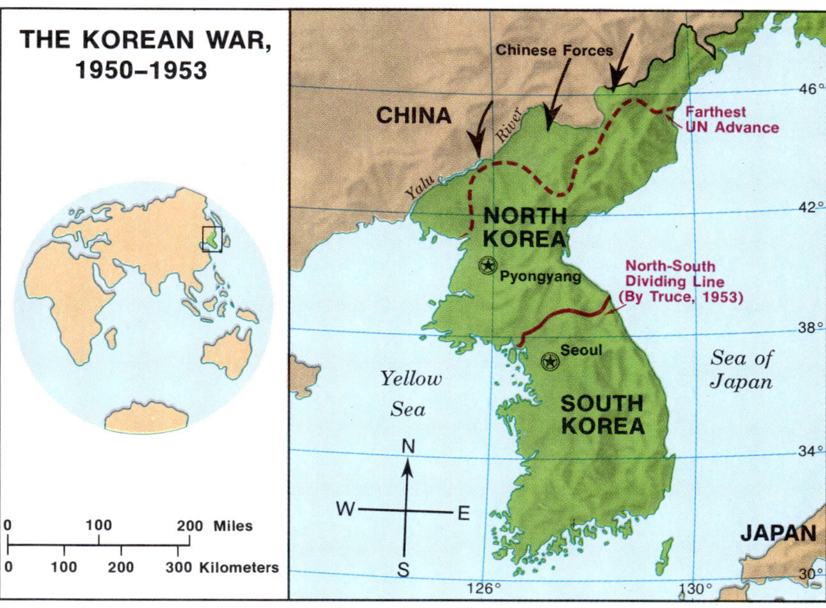

In June 1950 North Korean forces invaded South Korea. The United Nations asked member nations to help push back the North Korean soldiers. President Truman sent a United States air and navy "police force" to South Korea. American and UN soldiers drove the North Koreans toward the border with China. Then Chinese soldiers came to help the North Koreans. Together they drove the UN forces back near the first north-south dividing line. There a **truce,** or an end to the fighting, was declared.

Many Americans were unhappy with the truce. They wanted to drive the Communists out of Korea. But all Americans agreed that the newly integrated American forces had fought well.

The Courts Respond

The segregation of Black people in the South was based on the idea of "separate but equal," which was stated by the Supreme Court in 1896. If schools, parks, and swimming pools for Black people were equal to those for white people, segregation was legal.

In 1954 the NAACP challenged this principle. Lawyers for the NAACP argued that segregated schools were unconstitutional. The Supreme Court agreed. In *Brown versus the Board of Education of Topeka,* it ruled that under segregation Black people were not getting "the equal protection of the law." The Court ordered schools to be integrated.

For many people, it was a difficult ruling to accept. They had become used to their ways of doing things. They did not want to change them. Many schools in the rest of the country were also segregated. But segregation in those schools was by custom rather than by law. This was called "de facto" segregation. It was the result of Black and white people living in separate neighborhoods.

The 1954 Supreme Court ruling did not apply to "de facto" segregation. That problem remained, and it became worse. Many public schools in the North and the West were as segregated as the schools in the South had been.

In the 1970s the Supreme Court began to deal with this problem. It finally agreed that "de facto" segregation was also unconstitutional.

The integration of southern schools in 1954 was the start of major changes in the United States. In 1956 Dr. Martin Luther King, Jr., a young Baptist minister, asked people to boycott, or not use, the buses in Montgomery, Alabama, because they were segregated. It was the first of many nonviolent protests by Black and white people against segregation in restaurants, theaters, buses, and all public places. Martin Luther King, Jr., called it "massive noncooperation" (non•koh•op•uh•RAY•shuhn). He asked people to use words, not force. He said, "We will only say to the people: 'Let your conscience be your guide'."

Slowly the nation responded. Congress passed five civil rights acts between 1957 and 1968. These laws further strengthened voting rights for Black Americans. It was made illegal to refuse Blacks and people of other minority groups jobs, housing, or entry to public places because of their race.

To find out how another group of Americans worked to win its rights, try the investigation on page 244.

AN INVESTIGATION into the rights of Native Americans

When Europeans first came to America, they found that the people who already lived here were peaceful and friendly. But by 1868 white people had signed nearly four hundred treaties with the Native Americans and had broken nearly every one. As more whites arrived, some tribes were forced to move farther west five or six times.

The Bureau of Indian Affairs was set up in 1824 as part of the War Department. Soldiers were sent to force Native Americans to move to lands called reservations. When the Bureau became part of the Department of the Interior in 1849, it tried to change the culture of the

Native Americans. Native American children were sent away to schools and made to speak English. They could not see their families or learn about their culture.

Until 1848 Native Americans could not vote in several states. Most Native Americans still live on homelands. Many of them are poor and unable to find work. They have not been given equal opportunities to participate fully in American society.

In the past years groups of Native Americans have been working to win their rights. They have held protests and marches. In 1978 a group of Native Americans walked from the West Coast to Washington, D.C., to bring their fight to the attention of the government and the people. Native Americans have also gone to court to get back the land that was taken from them by the treaties.

1. In what ways are the problems of Native Americans like those of Black Americans?
2. Besides legal rights, what else do people need in order to feel equal with others?

A Problem on Your Own

What are Native Americans in your state or region doing to win their rights? Write a report or make a bulletin board display.

Vietnam and Protest

In the 1960s a war was going on in Vietnam, a country in Southeast Asia, that would soon involve Americans. The war was between the government of South Vietnam in Saigon (SY•GON) and Vietcong rebels supported by the Communist government of North Vietnam in Hanoi (hah•NOI). President Kennedy sent military supplies and advisers to South Vietnam in 1961 to support the war effort of the Saigon government.

For the first few years, only a few thousand Americans went to Vietnam. They acted as military advisers only. But in 1964 President Lyndon Johnson sent more soldiers and supplies to help South Vietnam. Most Americans supported this limited role in Vietnam.

Johnson won the 1964 presidential election by a large number of votes. But in Vietnam, more Americans were

being killed. Two American Navy ships were attacked in the Gulf of Tonkin, off North Vietnam. Johnson ordered the American forces to strike back. Congress gave the president authority to "take all necessary measures" to protect American forces in Vietnam.

In 1965 the war got bigger. American forces were increased from 23,300 to 184,300 people. In March President Johnson said American soldiers would fight with the South Vietnamese forces. He also ordered North Vietnamese bases bombed.

The President had hoped that the American forces could slow the drive of Vietcong soldiers into South Vietnam. He hoped the government of North Vietnam would then accept a peace settlement. But the North Vietnamese said they would not talk about peace until all American soldiers were withdrawn from Vietnam.

In the next three years, the number of Americans in Vietnam rose to 536,100. Over 100,000 were killed or seriously wounded. American planes dropped three million tons of bombs on Vietnam. That was more than they had dropped in all of World War II.

As the war in Vietnam grew, some Americans at home began to oppose the war. They did not like the bombing and the growing number of American deaths. They asked why the United States was spending so much money and so many lives on this war. Students and others organized marches and "sit-ins" to protest the war.

In March 1968, with American protests rising, Johnson ordered a limit on the bombing of North Vietnam. He also told the American people that he would not run again for president in November. The war had already divided the people of the United States. Now it cut short the career of a President.

The Hanoi government agreed to begin peace talks. They opened in Paris in May 1968. Richard Nixon was elected President that November. During 1969 and 1970, nothing was agreed to at the peace talks. The war went on. In the spring of 1970 American and South Vietnamese soldiers went into Cambodia to cut Vietcong supply lines. They withdrew to Vietnam in June. The invasion of Cambodia caused further protests in the United States.

Bombing continued through December 1972. But President Nixon slowly withdrew American soldiers. In January 1973 an agreement to end the fighting was signed in Paris. The last of the American soldiers came home that spring. Fighting continued, however, between North and South Vietnamese forces.

There had never been a declaration of war against North Vietnam. Yet the Vietnam War was the longest war in American history. The total cost of the war was over $137 billion. That is more than half the total budget of the federal government in 1973. Like the Korean War, the Vietnam War ended without a clear victory for either side. It also once again made Americans want to stay out of the affairs of other countries.

Women Organize for Their Rights

In the 1960s women began to demand a change in their role in American society. Since World War II, a growing number of women were working. But only low-paying jobs were open to most women. Better jobs went to men. Women who held the same jobs as men were generally paid less money for the same work.

Many women had worked in the civil rights movement. They had seen that protests could bring about change. Women began to work together in groups such as the National Organization for Women (NOW). They held meetings and demonstrations to bring the unequal roles of women to the attention of all Americans, men and women. They worked to get Congress and the state governments to pass laws to give women equal rights. One common goal that all women's groups worked for was enforcement of the Civil Rights Acts of 1964. This law made job discrimination against women and minorities illegal.

Women had fought for equal rights in politics and education since the 1800s. In 1848 Lucretia Mott and Elizabeth Cady Stanton called the first women's rights meeting in the United States. It was held at Seneca Falls, New York. The women agreed on a women's bill of rights. It stated, in part: "We hold these truths to be self-evident: that all men *and women* are created equal."

In 1920 the government responded to women's demands. The Nineteenth Amendment gave women the right to vote. Many women were now satisfied. Slowly women were accepted in more jobs. A few women became doctors, lawyers, and businesswomen. But progress was slow. A women's place was still considered to be in the home.

In the 1960s a new group of women began fighting against these ideas. They wanted to be independent and equal people. They also wanted equal job opportunities and equal pay in those jobs. They wanted their full rights as human beings. Some called these goals and demands "women's liberation."

Congress began to respond to women's demands for these rights. In 1974 it passed an amendment to the Constitution to protect these rights by law. State governments were slow to accept the amendment, however. Women political leaders got $5 million for a series of women's conferences, or meetings, throughout the nation. These were first held in individual states. Then in 1977, 20,000 women came together at a national meeting in Houston, Texas, to plan further ways to win their rights. They came in answer to a call from Congress to "identify barriers that prevent women from participating fully and equally in all aspects of national life." Out of the meeting came a National Plan of Action. Once again millions of Americans were working together and using the many ways guaranteed by the Constitution to gain their full rights.

1. In what way was the United States after World War II different from the other countries that had been at war?
2. What was the cold war and who took part in it?
3. How did the space age begin?
4. How did W. E. B. Du Bois's ideas differ from Booker T. Washington's ideas?
5. When were the armed forces integrated?
6. Explain the meaning of the phrase "separate but equal."
7. What did the Supreme Court decide about segregation in 1954? in the 1970s?
8. What did President Johnson hope to do by sending American troops to fight in Vietnam?
9. Name two ways in which Congress has responded to women's demands for equal rights.

Great changes have taken place in the United States since World War II. Spaceships have opened new frontiers in space. Computers have taken over many jobs once done by people. Protest movements by women and minorities have caused schools, businesses, and governments to think and act differently.

1. Which of these developments has caused the greatest change in your community? Why?
2. Which will have the greatest effect in the future? Why do you think so?

The graph on the facing page tells you the mean income of four groups of American workers in 1975. *Mean* income means that half the people in the group made more money and half the people made less money than the amount shown. Use the graph to help you answer the questions on the facing page.

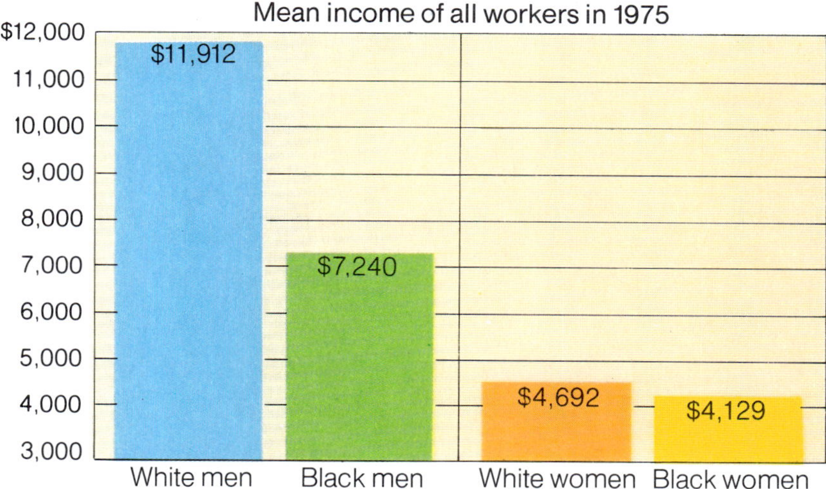

1. Did Black men make more or less than white men?
2. Did Black women make as much as Black men?
3. Did white women make more or less than white men?
4. Which group had the highest income?
5. Which group had the lowest income?
6. What can you say about the income of women as compared to men?
7. What can you say about the income of Blacks as compared to whites?

In 1968 Congress passed the Fair Housing Law. This law says that a property owner cannot refuse to rent or sell housing to someone because of that person's race or color.

1. How did this law help to end "de facto" segregation in the United States?
2. How might the law affect a community that has been segregated by custom for many years? How might people have to change their ideas and values?

Reviewing Key Ideas

Before European explorers came to America, the cultures of the Native American people were well established. In the Southwest, the Navahos farmed and hunted to meet their needs. On the Great Plains, Native American groups hunted the buffalo that roamed the plains. Each Native American group usually lived in one place.

In the 1500s, when Spanish explorers brought horses to North America, life on the Great Plains started to change. Horses made it easier for Native American groups to follow the herds of buffalo. They became nomadic, leaving their farms behind. Their culture changed as they depended more on the buffalo. Thus, you have come to this understanding: Inventions and different ways of doing things change the environment and cultures of people.

Later, railroads were built across America. People and goods could be moved easily over long distances. Opportunities increased. Industries grew. Large numbers of people came to America to find work. As opportunities increased, so did the size of companies. Many businesses became very large. The workers in factories were not always treated fairly by the business owners. But the companies were so big that individual workers could not change their working conditions. The workers banded together and formed unions. By working together, workers were able to get businesses to improve working conditions. Thus you can see that the continuing opportunity for growth and change required that people develop new ways of working in groups.

Equal Rights New opportunities in the United States brought other changes, too. Women began to protest for the right to vote. Elizabeth Cady Stanton, Susan B. Anthony, and others organized groups to get political rights for women. More and more people began to want to protect the rights of women. This led to new laws. Thus you have learned something more about government: Groups can work to cause the government to protect their rights and interests.

You have also read how Black Americans organized to gain their rights as United States citi-

zens. Such leaders as Martin Luther King, Jr., and W. E. B. Du Bois gathered groups of people together to work for full rights for Black Americans. Coretta King, wife of Martin Luther King, Jr., carried on her husband's work after he was killed. In time, the government passed new laws to make sure that all Americans had full rights.

In the last three units, you have seen how the United States government was formed under the Constitution. You have also seen how it was tested and sometimes changed. But the people who wrote the United States Constitution planned so well that the government can serve the needs of the people of a changing nation. Thus you have also learned this about government: People can take part in government and adapt it to their changing needs.

Using Key Words

Use these key words to complete the sentences that follow.

corporation	monopoly
depression	protectorates
dictator	stocks
Gross National Product	truce
integrate	trust

1. A business that sells shares in the ownership of the company is called a ____.
2. The shares that the business sells are ____.
3. When companies in the same industry joined together to share resources, they formed a ____.
4. The new, larger company often drove smaller companies out of business. With no competition, the company had a ____.
5. The value of all goods and services produced in a nation in one year is the ____.
6. In 1929 businesses failed and thousands of people lost their jobs. A period when production and employment go down is called a ____.
7. The United States gave military protection to some smaller countries in return for some economic and political control over them. These countries became ____.
8. A leader, such as Hitler, who takes away people's freedoms is called a ____.
9. People are working to give all people in our society equal education and job opportunities. They are working to ____ the society.
10. An end to fighting, such as in a war, is called a ____.

Focus on the Social Scientist

Imagine moving with your family to another country, where the language, culture, and customs are all different from your own. How would you make friends? How would you go to school? How would your family get the things it needs?

These problems and many others are faced by people moving to the United States from the Philippines. Everything may seem strange—the climate, the language, and the way of life.

Lillian Bucton is a social scientist who helps people from the Philippines adapt to the culture of the United States. As a social worker, she is exploring the reasons why Filipinos move to the United States. She also studies the problems they have in adapting to American society.

The first group of people Ms. Bucton worked with was pre-school Filipino children. These children needed to learn to speak English before they started kindergarten. While the children learned American ways, their teachers and parents also wanted them to remember some of the ways of their Filipino culture. For example, the children learned about American games like kickball. But they also played *pantintero,* a Filipino circle game.

Ms. Bucton has also worked with handicapped Filipino people. These people have special problems that make it difficult for them to learn. They need some help in getting job training and English lessons.

In working with both of these groups, Ms. Bucton says this about her job: "The most enjoyable part of my job as a social worker has been seeing that some people's lives have changed for the better because of my efforts."

UNIT FIVE

Using Resources

All over the world, people use the resources of their environment. They use them to live. People in different parts of the world use their resources in different ways.

Earlier you studied three people who live on the continent of North America—the Hopi, the Eskimo, and the people of Tepetongo. As you have seen, they use their resources in different ways. But they all use their resources to meet their needs. What they use depends on what resources they have in their environment. It also depends on their tools, knowledge, and values.

North America is a continent of many different environments. Until recently it has also been a land of space and plenty. There has almost always been enough room to grow—places to move to when the old places became crowded or worn out.

Next you will read about ways people use what they have wisely and about some ways that are not so wise.

A Mountain Farm

Italy is an old nation in Europe. Many people live in its cities and valleys and on its hills. In Italy there is enough rain to water the good soil and enough warm sunshine to make crops grow quickly. The climate is a valuable resource.

For hundreds of years people have farmed the land in Italy. The land is another valuable resource. But Italy is a small country. Much of the land surface is hilly or mountainous. Over the years the number of people has grown larger. They have had to use their resources carefully.

The picture on the next page shows an Italian farm. It may be only ten acres of land, or five, or two. People who are used to hundred-acre or thousand-acre farms might think that such a farm is too small to work. But to an Italian farmer, land is valuable. All of it must be used.

Farming the Mountainside

Like other farmers, Italian farmers like to farm level land best. It is easy to plow and to care for. As the population grew, however, there was not enough level land for everyone. Some people had to farm the hillsides.

To farm the hillsides in Italy took much work. Farmers had to prevent and stop **erosion** (i•ROH•zhuhn), the wearing away of the soil by water or wind.

Running water is a resource, but it causes erosion of another resource, the soil. Hill farmers have seen water run down a hillside, carrying soil with it toward the bottom of the hill. They have noticed that level places on a hillside have less erosion than steep places. A level place on a hillside is a **terrace** (TER•uhs). Farmers have noticed that water stops running when it comes to a terrace. It does not wash away the soil. Instead it soaks into the soil and goes to the roots of plants on the terrace.

For years, Italian farmers have built terraces to stop erosion. They cut away parts of a slope to make it level. They use the soil that is cut away to build land out from the slope. They often make walls to hold up the steep slope. Some of the mountains are terraced from the foot almost to the top. In this way Italian farmers have changed their hilly environment so they can use soil and water resources on hillsides, as well as on level ground.

Mountain Zones and Climates

If you ever climb a mountain, you will probably find that the weather gets colder as you go higher. There may be more wind. If you go high enough, you may find snow.

The kind of weather a place has over a long time is its **climate.** Climates at different heights on a mountain are called **climate zones.**

Winter weather comes first to the highest zone and stays there longest. Some mountain tops are so high that the climate is cold all year long. There is always some snow on these mountain peaks.

At the foot of the mountains in Italy, near sea level, the weather is warm most of the year. The soil is good for farming. But higher up the mountain the soil is poorer, and there are many rocks. Running water has carried the good soil down the mountain.

Poor soil does not hold water well. The soil in higher zones—even with terraces—is usually drier than the soil in lower zones. The zones on a mountain differ in climates, kinds of soil, and amount of water. In each zone, then, people must live and work in different ways.

You can make a model of the different zones. The investigation on pages 264–265 will show you how.

AN INVESTIGATION
into relief maps

Here is a map of Italy. The green part in the middle is shown on the colored map below. Each color on the map shows a climate zone. The colors match those on the color key. The numbers show heights above sea level.

Where would you be most likely to find each of these?

rocky soil	warm weather
good soil	cold weather and snow

A Problem on Your Own

You may want to make your own relief map showing height above sea level. Use some cardboard from grocery boxes if you can get it. Cut a different piece of cardboard for each height zone. Then paint each piece in a different color for each zone. Make a key for each color.

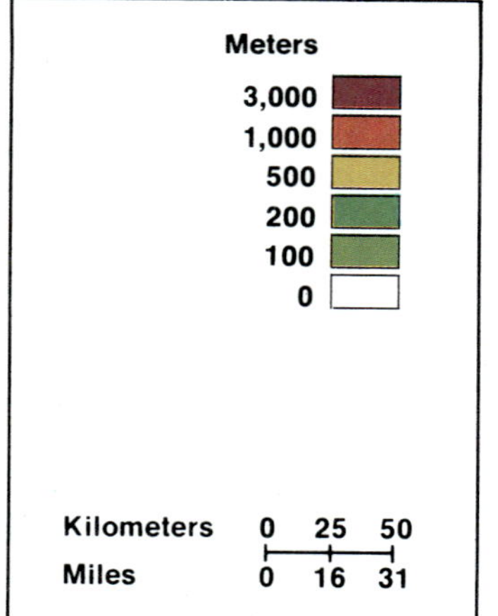

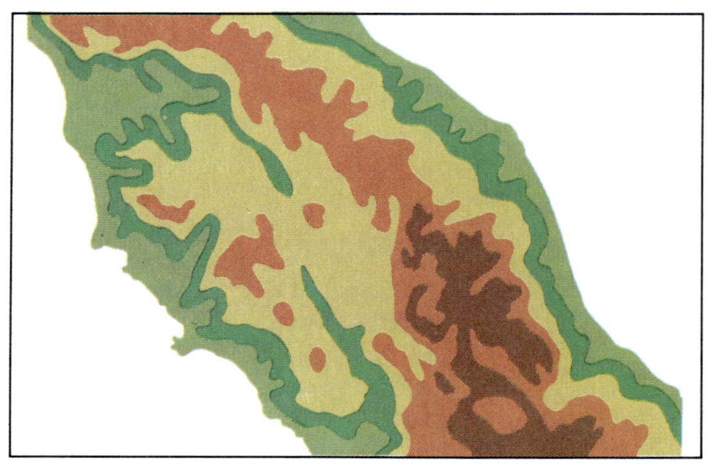

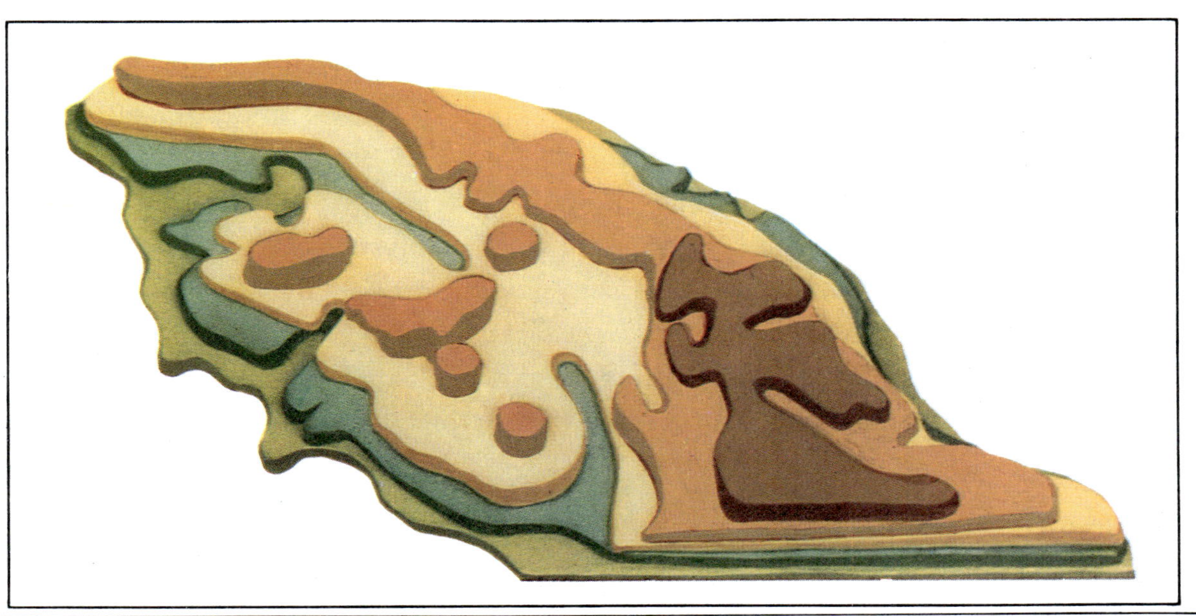

Planting the Zones

Different plants grow best in different soils. Some plants grow better in one climate zone than in another. Italian farmers have found that each of these five crops has its own best mountain zone:

Forests and pastures grow wild and are not usually farmed. They may be cut down or plowed under for other crops. Forest trees are cut for wood. Sheep and goats graze in rough mountain pastures. Forests and grasses can grow where the climate is too cold for most crops.

Oranges, lemons, and grapefruit ripen at different times on their trees. They are picked through the fall and winter. But they cannot ripen in climates with a cold fall and winter. They need a long, warm growing season and a good water supply.

Olives also grow on trees. Olives ripen at the same time and then are ready to pick. The trees need warm summers and little water. After the harvest the trees will not be hurt by cold weather.

Chestnut trees grow on high, steep slopes. Their long roots go very deep into the earth to find water that other plants cannot find. The nuts are ripe in October.

Grapes need hot weather to ripen. But most grapevines are not harmed by cold winters. Grapes grow best in deep, rich soil.

Farmers often plant two crops on a terrace—grape vines between rows of olive trees, for example. Still, one crop is most important in each mountain zone.

Each of these crops grows best in a different climate zone in Italy. Suppose an Italian mountain has five zones. Zone one is the lowest and zone five is the highest. Italian farmers usually raise sheep in zone five. Chestnut trees grow best in zone four and grapevines in zone three. Olive trees are planted in zone two; and oranges, lemons, and grapefruit grow well in zone one, the lowest climate zone.

Adapting and Changing

The picture above shows how Italian farmers might use a hillside to grow the five crops. All five zones probably would not be found on one farm. Many small farms would be found up and down the hillsides. Some farms might be in just one zone. Others might be big enough to be in two or three zones.

Suppose that farmers at the bottom of the hill earn a good living selling the oranges they grow. Some farmers farther up the hill might wish to earn more by growing oranges. But they would be taking a bigger chance. A cold spell could ruin their crops.

Soil, water, and climate are all part of the environment. In each zone these resources are right for some crops. They are not good for other crops. The environment limits what a farmer can grow. Freezing weather, for example, limits the farmer to crops that are not hurt by cold. Very hot weather might require an extra water supply.

Italian farmers have learned how to change their environment by terracing. Terracing improves the resources of hillside farms. Soil and water are saved or improved by terracing. But terraces cannot change the climate. Making and caring for the terraces also use up important **human resources.** If Italian farmers did not have to spend time terracing, they might be able to grow more crops.

Italian farmers must adapt to their environment. They adapt to it by planting crops that grow easily in the mountain zones where they are planted. By making terraces on hillsides, farmers change the environment. In this way they improve the resources used for growing the crops they will eat and sell.

1. What is erosion?
2. What is climate?
3. What have Italian farmers done to stop erosion on their hillside farms?
4. Name two differences between zone five and zone one of an Italian hillside.
5. Why can Italian farmers not grow the same crops in every mountain zone?

Italian farmers have changed their environment to improve their resources. People everywhere do this.

1. Describe two ways that people near you have changed their environment to improve resources.
2. Have you ever seen plants growing in a greenhouse with glass sides and a glass roof? A greenhouse is heated inside. How does this change in the environment improve resources?

Use the relief map of the United States on pages 356–357 to help you find the following places.

1. Five states with very high mountains
2. Five states that appear to have no mountains at all

Look once again at the way Italian farmers grow different crops in different zones.

1. Could adding fertilizer change the zone where a crop grows best? That is, could you grow oranges in the chestnut zone by adding fertilizer? Why or why not?
2. Suppose you could pump water to the top zone. Would you then be able to grow oranges there? Why or why not?

2 Using Water Wisely

The great Central Valley of California lies between two long mountain ranges—the high, snow-capped Sierra Nevada (see•AIR•uh nuh•VAH•duh) on the east and the lower Coast Range to the west. This valley is more than 640 kilometers long and almost 80 kilometers wide. Today it is an important valley for farming.

Several rivers flow into the Central Valley, mostly from these two mountain ranges. Over thousands of years the rivers have carried much topsoil down from the mountains. The topsoil has been deposited on the floor of the valley in deep, rich layers. Topsoil is the very best kind of soil for planting and growing food crops.

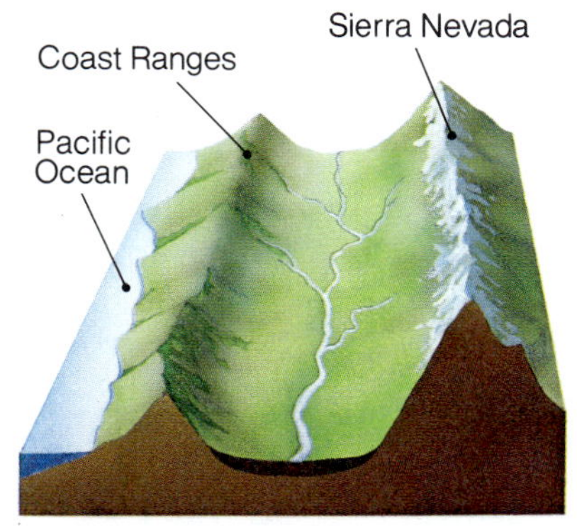

For hundreds of years before California became part of the United States, Native Americans lived in the valley. They hunted and gathered food. They found plenty of wild seeds, nuts, and roots, as well as wild game and fish. The environment made it easy to find plenty of food.

A Wild Environment

About 150 years ago, settlers tried to farm the valley. But they found only a few crops that grew well. The environment did not suit farming as well as it did hunting and gathering. It was either too wet or too dry. Rich soil was not enough.

Each spring when the snow melts in the Sierra Nevada, the mountain streams fill with water and rush down to the rivers in the valley. In the early days the low places were soon flooded with water. Unwanted and unused water flowed through the valley. The rich valley soil was swept into San Francisco Bay and the Pacific Ocean. In a few weeks the flooding was over. But large areas of muddy marshland were left behind in the low places.

Months of hot, dry weather followed the spring floods. The Central Valley has almost no rain during the summer. By early summer much of the water from the snow had already flowed to sea, and the rivers were almost dry. Small streams often dried up altogether. The wet marshes dried into areas of caked mud. Crops that were not harvested early dried up. Sometimes great grass fires burned across the land.

These great changes from season to season made much of the land impossible to farm. Large areas of land with good, rich soil had to remain unused. In many of those places where the land was farmed in spite of the problems, crops were often lost. Clearly, the water in the rivers needed to be controlled before the rich soil in the Central Valley could be used.

Farmers hoped to tame the Central Valley's wild waters. They needed dams on mountain streams to hold spring flood water and save it for summer. They needed ditches and canals to bring the flood water to their fields. They needed **levees** (LEV•eez), or raised banks of earth, to hold flooding river waters within their banks.

Using What They Had

In the early 1800s there were few settlements in the valley. In spring the high peaks of the Sierra Nevada were covered with snow. Pine forests grew on the lower slopes of the mountains. In the valley itself there were few trees. The blue water of the rivers stood out in the brown valley. Still, the rushing water was no help to the dry land.

The settlers who built their farms in the Central Valley knew the soil was good. They did not give up. Slowly, during many hard years of spring floods and dry summers, they worked to improve the land. All it needed was enough water to irrigate their crops at the right time.

They began to build dams on the rivers. They dug ditches and canals from the dams to the nearby farms. Some of the water that rushed down from the mountains in the spring now was stored behind the dams until it was needed. During the dry summer months, this supply of water was released to fill the ditches and canals. It was carried from the dams through the canals to nearby fields.

Now some of the farmers had water when their crops needed it most. With rich soil and a good water supply, more crops could be grown in the Central Valley.

Early farmers had the right idea. It took many more years and many thousands of dollars to complete a water system for the great Central Valley. The greatest changes began to take place about seventy-five years ago. Because the job was so big, help and money were needed from the government of California and from the government of the United States.

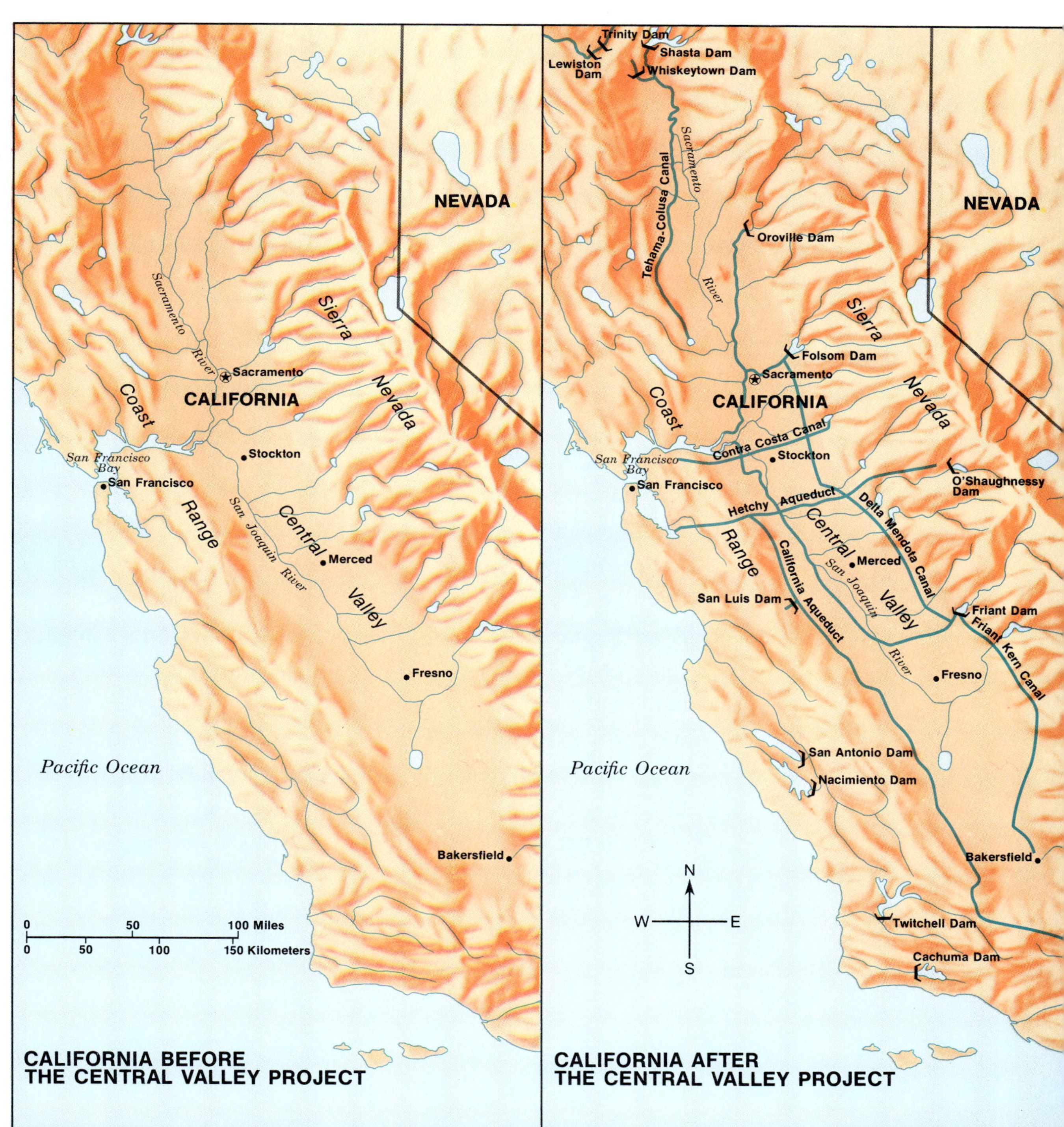

Building and Digging

New dams were built in the Central Valley. Shasta Dam is shown in the picture above. On the map at the right on page 275, you can find some of the dams that hold back the spring flood waters in California. Behind these dams, reservoirs store water until it is needed. This system of dams and reservoirs is like a set of giant faucets. Each dam can be opened when water is needed.

The northern part of the Central Valley has more water than the southern part. So water from the Sacramento River is pumped into a canal. The canal flows into a larger canal called the California Aqueduct. Study the canal system on the right-hand map on page 275. The aqueduct and the canal system carry water a long way to the south.

If you ever drive through the Central Valley, you will see the many changes brought by this huge water system. No matter what time of year it is, you will see crops growing. In the springtime the cherry and peach orchards will be in bloom. In the summer you might see fields of green ava-

cados. You might pass a truck loaded with shiny red tomatoes. The fruits and vegetables grown in the Central Valley are shipped to stores across the nation. Today people all over the United States can share in California's many food resources.

Farmers in the Central Valley of California, like farmers on the hillsides of Italy, changed their environment. But the changes made in each place differed because the resources differed. In Italy the rich soil had to be kept on the hillsides. The farmers terraced their land. In California the water had to be controlled. Dams and canals were built to store the water and carry it where it was needed.

Change for Another Reason

Other Californians changed the environment at the same time as the early settlers. In 1848 gold was found in California in the American River. This gold had been buried in the earth. But erosion of the stream beds by running water had brought it to the surface. At first miners panned in the stream beds and near the banks of streams to find gold. It did not take them long to pan most of the gold from the mountain streams and rivers.

Much gold still lay hidden deep in the earth. The miners found many ways to uncover the gold. Tunnels were carved into rocky hillsides. A great amount of earth was dug up. Powerful streams of water were used to wash away whole hillsides.

The water was carried from mountain streams through a large pipe. On the end of the pipe was a nozzle that was much bigger than the nozzle on a firefighter's hose. The nozzle forced a strong jet of water against the mountainside. The water washed away bushes, trees, earth, stones, and even big rocks.

This method was called hydraulic (hy·DRAW·lik) mining. It was one of the fastest, easiest ways to find gold. For

nearly thirty years many Californians made their fortunes from hydraulic mining. They did not know where the rocks and soil were going. They only wanted them removed. They wanted to get the gold.

The erosion caused by hydraulic mining changed the environment in ways the miners had not planned. The earth that was washed from the hillsides went into the nearest river or stream. From there it was carried down to the Central Valley. In the flat valley the rivers travel more slowly. Mud and rocks carried down from the hills settled to the bottom of the rivers.

The largest rocks were left behind as the rivers flowed on to the ocean. These rocks are still heaped on the ground over many kilometers of the Central Valley. So many smaller rocks and so much mud stayed on the river bottoms that the rivers were no longer as deep as they had been. In some places they became so shallow that boats could not carry people and supplies to and from the valley.

The **delta** is the low area of the Central Valley where the two largest rivers—the Sacramento and the San Joaquin (SAHN wah • KEEN)—come together. You can find this area on the right-hand map on page 275. Today riverbeds in the delta are higher than the land around them. Levees keep the rivers from flooding farms and towns in the delta.

Hydraulic mining caused other changes in the environment, too. Not all of the mud that was washed away from the hills settled on the river bottoms. Some of it was carried as far as San Francisco Bay. You can see this bay on the maps on page 275. The bay, too, became less deep.

Large oyster beds that had once been underwater dried up in the sun. These oyster beds had been in the bay for many hundreds of years. They had been important to the Native Americans who were living around the bay. They used the bay oysters for food and for shell beads.

Planning Ahead

Hydraulic mining was so bad for the environment that laws were passed to stop it in 1880. The miners probably never thought about the damage the mining would cause. When people use resources in new ways, they need to be careful not to damage the environment.

Sometimes, too, changes in the environment may be good for one group of people but not for another. Many peoples' lives are made safer and easier when dams are built. But a new dam may make other people unhappy. The reservoir that stores water behind a dam may cover several square kilometers of land with water. It might cover farmlands with water. The government might pay the farmers enough for their land so that they could start farming somewhere else. But it is not easy to move a family and start over. Some farmers might not want to go. They might claim that their farms are more important than a dam.

Today, with so many people living in the United States and with so many different needs to think about, it is hard to make changes that are good for everyone. Because of this problem, we all need to plan ahead in order to know the best ways to use what we have.

1. What made the topsoil in the Central Valley so rich?
2. What made it hard to farm in the Central Valley?
3. What changes were made in the Central Valley to make use of the resources there?
4. What is hydraulic mining? What are some of the harmful changes it caused in California?

When people find a new way to use a resource, they must take care not to destroy it at the same time. Central Valley water, for example, must be protected from pollution.

1. What natural resources are important in your state?
2. What is being done to protect them?

1. Use the figures below to make a graph showing the increase in world population over the past two hundred years.
   In 1900 world population was one and one-half billion.
   In 1950 population was two and one-half billion.
   In 1975 world population was four billion.
   In 2000 there will probably be six billion people.
2. What can the graph tell you about using the world's resources?

To solve the Central Valley's water problem, people had to see the problem and decide what to do about it. Then they had to raise money and plan and build the dams and canals.

1. Which of these tasks could not be done until many people agreed it should be done?
2. Which of these tasks could be done by a small group of people?

3 Sharing Resources

If you ride to school by car, bus, or bicycle, you are using steel. Trains run on steel rails, and bridges are made of steel. Tall buildings are held up by steel beams. Steel is a tough metal made from iron, other metals, and carbon. It is important to the way we live in the United States.

Riches in the Ground

Most steel made in the United States began as iron ore in Minnesota. The story of this ore begins in the hills of the Mesabi (muh•SAH•bee) Range in 1892. There Pete Helmquist began to dig a well. After digging through nearly two meters of clay, he came to some red earth. It was almost too heavy to lift with his shovel. It seemed as heavy as iron. Later Pete Helmquist's well was studied by a mining engineer who knew about rocks and minerals. The mining engineer took samples of the heavy red material Pete had found. Not only was it as heavy as iron, it *was* iron ore. Pete Helmquist's well was to become the world's largest iron mine.

The Mesabi iron mine that began as a well for Pete Helmquist is now a huge pit. It is nearly 2 kilometers wide and 5 kilometers long. Machines have dug deeper and deeper, removing the rich red ore. Mesabi iron helped the

United States become the world's leader in industry. Iron and steel are important to industry.

Little rich iron ore is left in the Mesabi Range today. Almost all the rich ore in the United States has already been mined. There is still a large amount of ore, but it must be separated from the rock that covers it. About 900 kilograms of iron ore are found in every 2700 kilograms of rock.

Most rich iron ore now comes from other nations. But in these nations, too, iron ore will not last forever. It must be used wisely and not wasted.

If you have ever helped collect empty cans, you may know that "tin" cans are mostly iron. Collecting such cans is one way to help save iron resources. The cans can be sold or traded to steel companies. The cans may then be melted, and the iron can be used over and over.

Making Steel

Iron ore is very valuable, but it cannot be used just as it comes from the earth. It is used after it is made into steel. Many things must be done to it before it becomes steel.

First the ore is mixed with limestone and **coke.** Coke is coal that has been heated to remove the gases. This mixture is then fed into a hot blast furnace. When the mixture gets very hot, unwanted materials mix with the limestone and coke and are thrown out. Pure, red-hot, melted iron is left. This melted iron is poured into molds, where it is cooled in the shape of bars.

The iron is not steel yet. It must be melted again in other furnaces. These furnaces remove more unwanted materials. At the same time other materials are added. One of these makes stainless steel, which does not rust. Another

makes steel that is tough and strong. Yet another makes steel that bends and springs back into shape.

Finished steel is made into a thousand different products. Steel cuts meat, shaves beards, supports tall buildings, and sews clothing. Without iron ore, coke, limestone, and the special materials that are added to make just the right kind of steel, you would have no steel tools.

To find out more about how these resources are supplied and shared, try the investigation on page 286.

Using the Environment

The Hopi, the Eskimo, and the people of Tepetongo depended on nearby resources to make everything they used. Their needs for food, clothing, and shelter were met by the **limited resources** of their environments. Limited means that there is only so much and no more. These people had very few choices as to how they would meet their needs.

To help increase their resources, the Hopi, the Eskimo, and the Mexicans of Tepetongo traded with other people. The Hopi, for instance, traded with other Native Americans from as far away as California.

AN INVESTIGATION
into sharing resources

Study the map of the forty-eight states on the next page. The key tells you which resource each mark stands for. Use the maps, along with what you have read in this section, to answer these questions.

1. What resources does the map show? (Use the key to help you.)
2. What industry does it show?
3. Which states have iron ore?
4. Which states have coal?
5. Which states have limestone?
6. In which states are there steel-making centers?
7. Which states have every resource they need to make steel?
8. Which steel-making states lack iron ore? coal? limestone? materials used in small amounts?
9. How do these states get these necessary materials?
10. How do you suppose steel gets to so many states?
11. In which state is the Mesabi Range? Is it near many steel-making centers?
12. What steel-making resources are in that state?
13. What steel-making resources are *not* found in that state?

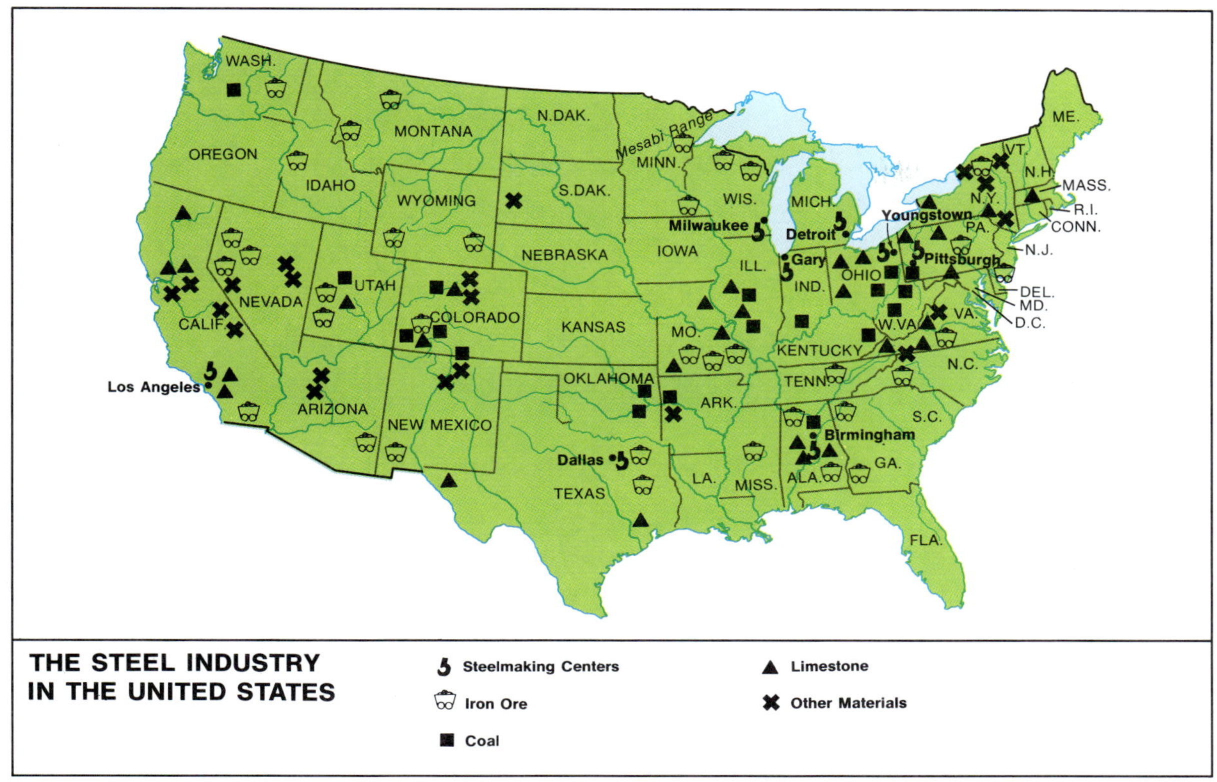

Today most people can share resources through trade with other areas. If the crops in one part of the country fail, people can usually buy food from somewhere else.

In most parts of the world there is a large supply of some resources and a small supply of others. If people are to have many choices from which to fill their needs, they must share resources. Cities, states, and nations share their natural resources by trading. In your everyday life you use resources from all parts of the United States and from many other nations, too. Some modern products, such as steel, could not be made at all if the needed materials were not brought together from many places.

People still adapt to their own environment and depend on it to supply their needs. But most people today depend on the resources of a large part of the world.

1. From what main resource is steel made?
2. Where in the United States was this resource found?
3. Where does most of this resource come from now?
4. Describe how steel is made.
5. In what states is steel made?
6. Name some ways in which steel is used.
7. What is one way you can help save iron resources?
8. Why are resources like iron ore limited?
9. How can people increase their resources?

1. Why do some parts of the United States produce no lumber?
2. Why do some places have no fish to be caught?
3. The parts of the United States where steel is made do not have all the resources needed to make steel. How can they make steel?
4. Coke, limestone, and iron ore are not of great value by themselves. How do different regions of our country share these resources? Why do they share them?

1. Use the encyclopedia or other reference books to find out which nations in the world produce oil. Make a list of the ten most important oil-producing nations.
2. Then find out which nations produce steel. Make a list of the ten most important steel-producing nations in the world.
3. Then make a map of the world to show where these nations are. You can draw the map, or you can use an outline map. Make special marks to show oil and steel. Put them on the map in the places where oil and steel are produced. Make a key to explain the special marks.

Write the names of the oil-producing and steel-producing nations, the seven large continents, and the four largest oceans on your map. Label the equator, the Tropic of Cancer, and the Tropic of Capricorn. Be sure to include a compass.

Read the following statements and decide which ones are true and which are false. Write **T** by those that you think are true and **F** by those you think are false. Then tell why you think so in each case.

1. Discovering new resources can change people's lives.
2. Each state has all the resources it needs.
3. The process of making steel proves that it is not necessary to share resources.
4. The Hopi could choose among many ways of life. They were farmers because they preferred that way of life.
5. Trading gives people more choices.

4 Making New Resources

You may remember that Pete Helmquist discovered the Mesabi Range by accident. While digging a well, some heavy red dirt got in his way. A scientist tested it and found that it was iron ore.

Suppose there had been no scientist or no way to make steel. Then the red dirt would not have been a resource. It might have been nothing more than a big problem for Pete.

Before something can be a resource, there must be a way to use it. What people think is a resource depends on what they know and what they need.

Rubber: Need and Knowledge

Natural rubber is made from a milky juice called **latex.** Latex comes from rubber trees that grow in hot, wet lands. Long ago, people learned to make rubber from latex. That rubber was soft and sticky when hot and broke easily when cold. At that time, nobody thought rubber was a very useful resource.

Then scientists began looking for a way to make rubber more useful. They added sulfur and other chemicals to it and then heated it. Then the rubber stayed firm. They called this sulfur and heat treatment the vulcanization of rubber. When automobiles came into use, there was a great need for this rubber for tires.

New Materials from Chemicals

During World War II it was dangerous for ships to bring rubber across the sea to the United States. Tires were badly needed during the war. Scientists had to find something to take the place of latex rubber.

They already knew how to make a kind of rubber from chemicals, but this rubber was not very good. They worked hard to improve it. The synthetic (sin•THET•ik) rubber they invented lasts longer than natural rubber. The rubber used today is synthetic. In boots, tires, or in the kitchen, most rubber used now is made from chemicals.

Scientists have also used the same chemicals that make rubber to invent new materials. Many of these new materials are called **plastics.** Plastics can be formed into many shapes. They can be used to make bottles, dishes, windows, and rainwear.

Plastics are not found naturally in the environment. But the chemicals they are made from do come from natural resources. One very important resource is oil. Oil is not very useful just as it comes from the earth, but it can be made into many useful goods. It is so useful to people that sometimes it is called "black gold."

Crude oil is treated in a factory called a **refinery** (rih•FY•nuh•ree). In the oil refinery it is heated and changed into such products as gasoline, grease, wax, and machine oil. After these materials are made in the refinery, many chemicals are left over. Once these were thrown away as waste materials. But now they are used to make synthetic rubber, plastic, dyes, drugs, and cloth. They have now become valuable resources, too.

A World-Wide Crisis

Oil is also an important source of energy in the United States and around the world. By the end of 1973, the United States was faced with an energy crisis. The supply of oil—so necessary to the modern world—was running low. Drivers had to slow down to 90 kilometers per hour to save gasoline. Airlines had to reduce the number of flights. All over the United States, people tried to get used to "gasless Sundays."

Families also had to get used to lower temperatures in their homes. There were no outdoor lighting displays that Christmas. Many businesses turned off their outside signs to save electricity.

The United States was not the only nation to suffer oil shortages. Japan is an island nation which has no natural iron ore or crude oil. It imports almost all of the raw materials it uses. Japanese workers turn these materials into products for other nations. With the oil shortage, Japan was fearful that its factories could not run at all. One refinery in the Netherlands, which refined much of the oil used in Europe, was cut off from its oil supplies. All over the world, it seemed, people had used their resources as if they would never run out.

About half of the energy used in the United States comes from oil. Other nations depend on oil, too. Oil is also the source of many other products—plastics, synthetic rubber and cloth, and chemicals used in products such as drugs and cosmetics. Oil is such a useful resource that there is a danger of a world-wide oil shortage.

There are still places in the United States where oil can be found. Alaska is one place. In 1974 oil companies began to build a pipeline to bring Alaska's oil to the other states. This pipeline runs 1300 kilometers from Prudhoe Bay in the north to Valdez, a seaport on Alaska's southern shore. From Valdez, oil is shipped in tankers to the Pacific Coast. Some is shipped to Japan and other countries.

Someday there may be no more oil. Nations will have to find other sources of energy and other ways to make products like plastic and drugs.

Resources in the Sea

A resource even more important than oil is fresh water. Ocean water cannot be used for drinking or watering crops unless the salt is taken out of it. Scientists have now developed a way to make water from the ocean into fresh water. Factories like the one in North Carolina pictured above are able to remove the salt from sea water.

It is very expensive to take salt from sea water. Few people are willing to pay so much for water. In Los Angeles it is cheaper to bring fresh lake and river water hundreds of kilometers than to take salt from the sea water on the city's Pacific Ocean shore. It costs so much to take salt out of water that only people in very dry places will pay the high price. They have no other way to get fresh water. The investigation on the facing page tells you how to make fresh water from salt water by yourself.

AN INVESTIGATION into making a resource useful

You can prepare fresh water from salt water. You will need a kettle with a long spout, two drinking glasses, water, and some salt.

Put the water in the kettle. Add salt until you can taste it in the water. One glass should be placed over the spout of the kettle. Place the second glass beneath the first one. Then put the kettle to boil on the stove.

What happens in the first glass as the water boils? Where is this water coming from?

When enough water collects in the second glass, cool it and taste it. Is it salty? Does it have any taste? Where is the salt now?

A Tiny Resource

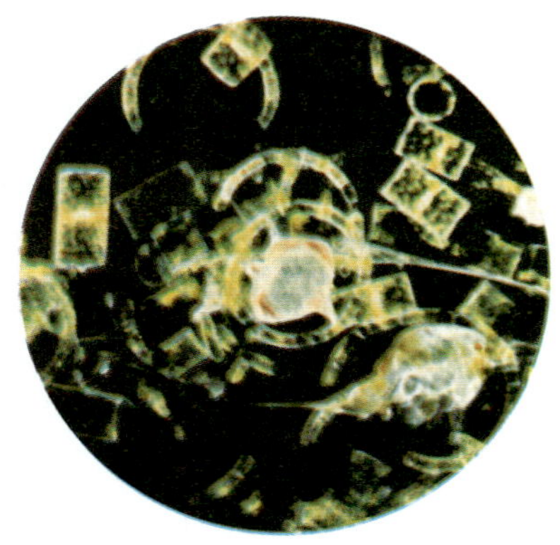

Ocean water itself cannot yet be widely used. But there are other resources in ocean water. If you look through a magnifying glass at clear ocean water, you may see tiny living plants and animals called **plankton.** Plankton grow quickly. They can be taken from the ocean, dried, and made into a kind of flour. Plankton flour is rich in protein and minerals that people need to live. In many parts of the world, people don't get enough milk, meat, fish, cheese, and eggs to keep healthy. Plankton flour could help these people. Scientists are trying to find a way to make this flour at low cost and make it taste good.

Scientists are also trying to make good flour from fish. When people catch more fish than they can sell, the extra fish can be frozen and ground into flour. Some fish that are not sold to be eaten can also be ground into fish flour. Three spoonfuls of fish flour each day will keep a person healthy even if he or she eats no milk, meat, or eggs.

In the future your supper may include foods made from plankton and fish flour. These new foods may answer the question of how to feed the growing world population.

Saving Ocean Resources

The satellite picture above shows a river emptying into the sea. Notice how the river water discolors the ocean water.

If the river water is polluted, it will carry pollution into the ocean. Parts of the ocean are now so polluted by oil and chemicals that fish and plankton can no longer live there. Scientists may learn to produce plankton or fish flour at a low cost. But there may be no fish or plankton left.

People do not eat plankton flour yet, but without plankton they would not eat other kinds of sea food. Fish and other sea life eat plankton. There are not as many shellfish in the Gulf of Mexico as there used to be. Scientists think pollution from the Mississippi River may be the reason.

Scientists have the knowledge and skills to protect the seas from pollution. What happens will depend on what people decide to do about protecting resources.

Working with Key Facts

1. Where does natural rubber come from?
2. What does vulcanization do to rubber?
3. Where does synthetic rubber come from?
4. What resource has sometimes been called "black gold"? Why?
5. Name two products that are made from oil.
6. How can plankton be made into a valuable resource?
7. Why is the use of plankton limited now?

Using What You Know

1. Name five resources that can be used the same way they are found in nature.
2. How can transportation be a resource?
3. How can the knowledge and skills of people be resources?
4. The early Eskimos did not light their homes with electricity. Today people have more ways from which to choose to get what they need. What kinds of food, shelter, clothing, water, and transportation can people choose from?

Practicing Key Skills

Many towns have pollution problems. Choose a pollution problem you know of in your own town or neighborhood. Suppose you were part of a team of social scientists who was going to study this problem. You would need to answer many questions about the problem before you could offer a solution. Begin by answering the following questions. You can work with several others in your class.

1. What is the problem?
2. Why is it a problem?
3. How did people notice the problem?
4. What harm does it do?
5. Who is hurt by it?

6. Who is in charge of the resource?
7. What people use the resource?
8. What groups want the pollution stopped?
9. Who will decide what to do about stopping the pollution?
10. What has already been done to stop the pollution?
11. Why has the pollution not been stopped yet?
12. What are possible solutions to the problem?
13. What new problems might be caused by trying to stop the pollution?
14. What will stopping the pollution cost?
15. Who will have to pay for it?
16. What will the pollution itself cost if it is allowed to go on?
17. Who will pay for the pollution if it goes on?

Write a short report telling what you think is the best solution and why. Be sure to tell how much it will cost, who will pay for it, and how the groups who use the resource will be affected by the solution.

Suppose the Food and Agricultural Organization of the United Nations were to make this report.

> The world's food supply is running out. The United States has only enough food for ten years. Europe can feed itself for only four more years. Africa, Asia, and Latin America may run out of food in two years. A good supply of fish flour and plankton flour can be made cheaply, but many people do not like the taste of these foods.

1. Is the problem one of people? things? something else?
2. How might different people see the problem?
3. How might it be solved?

Reviewing Key Ideas

Fifteen thousand years ago, early people lived where modern people live today—on North America and on other continents. The land around these early people could have been farmed. The oil far beneath the ground could have been used for cooking or lighting or running motors. The falling waters of the rivers could have been used to produce electricity. But at that time the land was not farmed. The oil was not used, and the water power did not become electricity. People did not know of these ways to use their environment. To these early people, soil, water, and oil were not resources that they could use as people do today.

Early people did not know how to make many changes in their environment. They had to adapt to their environment by using the things they found around them. They had to learn how to use their environment as they found it. Natural resources from the environment supplied their needs just as they supply people's needs today, but in different ways.

Some early people found seeds to gather. Wild plants were their main natural resources. In other places, people hunted wild game and caught shellfish. Usually people had to use what they found. Their choice of ways to supply

their needs was limited by the environment. Early farmers, for example, were able to irrigate their fields only if they had a supply of water nearby.

Using Resources Today

Today most people can add to their resources through industry and trade with other regions. But the environment still limits people. Thus you have learned this understanding about resources: People's choices depend upon the natural resources available to them.

People have always been busy learning new things about their environment. As their knowledge has grown, they have found ways to use more of the natural resources in the world

around them. Industry and science turn natural resources into useful things.

People have made many new resources. They have learned to dig minerals from the earth, to process them, and to make them into tools. By terracing hillsides, they have made new farm land. By controlling the flow of water in rivers with dams, they have made large areas of land useful for crops. They have also invented new ways to transport things and new sources of power, such as electricity and nuclear energy. People have learned to combine some materials that are not useful by themselves to make new materials. Thus you have also learned this about resources: As people develop industry, they learn new ways to use their environment and create resources.

When people change the environment, they may create problems. As they use the soil, they may also lose it to erosion. As they use water, they may also pollute it. As they use chemicals to make useful products, they may destroy life in the rivers and sea.

Today people are beginning to understand that people and their environment affect each other. People affect the natural environment, and it affects them. People have to change the land in order to mine minerals or to have lumber, more level farm land, or a steady water supply. People make changes, great or small, whenever they use their natural resources. Conservation means understanding that people depend on the environment and, as a result, must use its resources wisely.

Using Key Words

Use these key words to complete the sentences that follow.

climate	human resources
climate zones	latex
coke	levees
delta	refinery
erosion	terrace

1. The labor, skills, and knowledge that people use in their work are called ____.
2. The milky liquid in rubber trees that is used to make rubber is called ____.
3. Coal that has been heated so that all the gases are removed is called ____.
4. A factory in which crude oil is made into gasoline, plastics, wax, and other products is a ____.
5. The wearing away of soil by wind or water is called ____.
6. The part of a hillside that has been made level so that it will not wash away is called a ____.
7. The kind of weather a place has over a long period of time is its ____.
8. Mountains get colder the higher up you go. The climates at different heights on a mountain are known as ____.
9. The farmers in California's Central Valley were able to control the flooding river waters by building raised areas of earth called ____.
10. The low area of the Central Valley where the Sacramento and San Joaquin rivers join and flow into the bay is the ____.

Focus on the Social Scientist

Imagine spending two days and nights 132 meters deep in the sea, with about 11,340 kilograms of water pressing on your body, and living to tell about it! Jon Lindbergh did this in 1964.

This brave explorer is the son of another brave explorer. Captain Charles A. Lindbergh landed his tiny airplane at the Paris airport on May 21, 1927. He was the first man to fly across the Atlantic Ocean, alone and nonstop, from New York to France. Charles was an explorer of the air. His son Jon is an explorer of the environment under the ocean's waters.

Jon and another scientist were lowered in a metal diving chamber to the bottom of the sea. There they lived in a little rubber tent without a floor. Air for breathing was pumped to them through hoses. They studied ocean life and ways people could learn to work deep in the sea. They had to spend several hours in a metal chamber on their way back to the surface, so their bodies would not be hurt by the change from water to air.

Since Jon's dive, scientists have learned to make better tools to help divers adapt to the special environment under the ocean's surface. To learn about the ocean's resources, people depend on the knowledge and skills of explorers like Jon Lindbergh.

Because of them, workers now mine tin, iron ore, diamonds, and other valuable resources from the ocean floor. Under water, on land, and in the air, human knowledge and skills are important resources to help find better ways to meet people's needs.

UNIT SIX

The Consumer in the United States

At one restaurant in town hamburgers cost $2.50. At a coffee shop they cost $1.25. The fast-food chain charges sixty-five cents for hamburgers. Why is the price of hamburgers different at each place?

Two weeks before Christmas the shoes you want cost $10.95. A week after Christmas the same shoes cost $7.95. Why did the store lower the price?

Your family buys a new color television set for $400. They pay $100 now and agree to pay $15 a month for two years. You take a pencil and figure out that the television is really costing your family $460. Why does it cost the extra $60?

Prices depend on how much it costs a company to make a product. They also depend on the amount of the product that is available and how many people want to buy it. Advertising and credit can change prices, too. In this unit you will find out how businesses decide on the prices they charge for their goods and services.

The Costs of Making Things

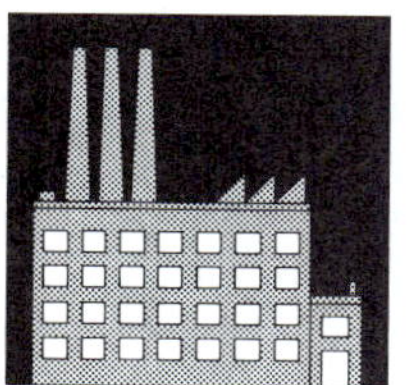

Roy's mother has sent him to the Super Giant Market with $2.00 to buy chocolate ice cream for his sister's birthday party. Several brands of ice cream are for sale at the Super Giant Market. The brands sell for many different prices. Roy has to decide which brand of ice cream to buy.

Brandex, the market's own brand, costs $1.00 for two liters. Alessi's ice cream costs twice as much, but Roy's sister likes it better. She says it has a creamier taste than Brandex ice cream.

When you decide how to use your resources to get something you need or want, you make a **choice.** Roy's resource in this case is money. If Roy's choice is Alessi's, he will get two liters of ice cream that will please his sister. If his choice is Brandex, he will get four liters of ice cream. The party guests will have bigger helpings. It is not an easy choice for Roy, but he cannot have both.

People are always making choices. The kinds of choices people make depend on what they care about. If Roy chooses to buy Alessi's ice cream, it shows that he cares about creamier ice cream. If he chooses Brandex, it shows that he cares about getting more ice cream for his money. Roy must decide which he cares about more.

Ice Cream Comes to the Market

The Super Giant Market chain has stores in three states. This chain also owns Brandex Products, where 250 people work the year around. They **produce,** or make, and package such dairy products as cream, butter, cottage cheese, yogurt, ice cream, and milk. Then they deliver them in trucks to the markets.

Mr. Alessi produces nothing but ice cream. It is his only **product.** He sells it to people at his own store. He also sells it to five stores in the same city. The stores sell it to people for him. Twenty people work for him the year around.

Roy has enough money for two liters of Alessi's ice cream or four liters of Brandex ice cream. Because Roy *wants* ice cream and *can pay* for it, he has a **demand** for it.

People have a demand for ice cream all year. Stores always keep a **supply** of it so people can buy it when they want it and can pay for it.

The demand for ice cream is not the same all the time, however. You can probably guess when during the year people demand the most ice cream. If there is a very long hot spell, some stores may actually run out of their whole supply of ice cream.

When there is little demand for ice cream, the stores order less ice cream from Mr. Alessi and Brandex. Still, on the dairy farms cows go on producing about the same amount of milk all year.

Because they make other products, Brandex keeps on buying milk and cream from the dairy farms all year. But Mr. Alessi makes only ice cream. When the demand for ice cream goes down, Mr. Alessi must buy less milk and cream. The dairy farms can count on how much milk and cream Brandex will use all year. Mr. Alessi buys less milk and cream. The dairy farms charge Brandex less than they charge Mr. Alessi.

Costs of Production

Brandex ice cream costs less to buy than Alessi's. This is partly because Brandex pays less for milk and cream than Mr. Alessi does. To make ice cream, both Brandex and Mr. Alessi must pay the costs of producing, or making, their products. They must pay their **costs of production.** These costs include the following things.

Raw materials are those things used in producing a product. Whether ice cream is made at home or in a factory, cream, milk, and sugar are needed.

Labor is work or the people who do the work. Paying people to do the labor is one of the major costs of production in a factory.

Equipment includes machines and tools. Mixers, freezers, and bowls are some equipment used to produce ice cream.

Public services include water, electricity, gas, and telephones needed to run the factory.

Property is land and buildings. Both may be either rented or bought.

To learn more about costs of production, do the investigation on the facing page.

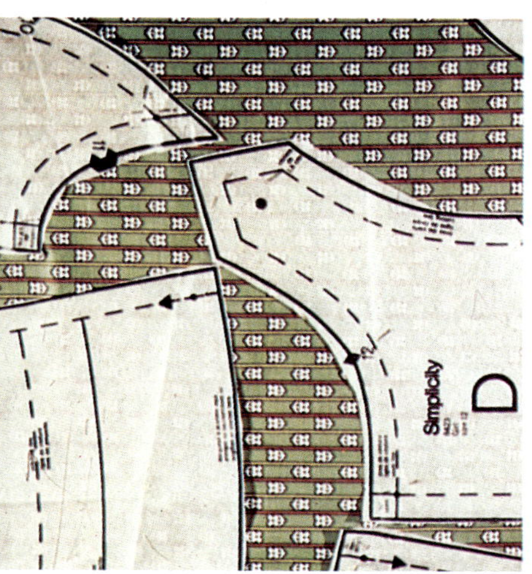

AN INVESTIGATION
into costs and price

Suppose Ann's mother is making a dress.

1. Make a list of raw materials you think she might need.
2. Find out how much each material on your list will cost her. Then find the total cost of all the raw materials.
3. Make a list of equipment you think she might need.
4. Find out the cost of each tool or machine on your list. Find the sum of the costs of equipment.
5. If Ann's mother had to buy a sewing machine, should the cost of the sewing machine be added to the other costs of the dress? Why?
6. Can you think of any other costs that should be added?
7. While she worked on the dress, did Ann's mother's time cost anything? If so, how much should be added to the cost of the dress?
8. To the costs of raw materials, add the costs of equipment, and any other costs you think are part of the total cost of the dress. What is the cost of the dress made by Ann's mother?
9. What do you think the price of such a dress would be in a store? How much profit would the store be making on the dress?

To start his own business, Mr. Alessi had to use almost all his own money and all he could borrow to pay for raw materials, labor, equipment, public services, and property. After paying these costs, he hoped to be able to earn a **profit;** that is, he hoped to have money left over after paying costs. He knew he was taking a chance. His business might fail and he would lose all he had put into it.

Costs of Distribution

The business of a dairy or any factory is producing goods. Ice cream or other goods, however, must be moved from the factory and sold to people.

The costs of moving, storing, and selling goods are the **costs of distribution.** Distribution is getting goods from the maker to the user.

The Super Giant Market pays Mr. Alessi seventy-five cents for a liter of ice cream. The store sells the same liter of ice cream for $1.00. With the twenty-five-cent difference, the market must pay its cost of distribution. When those costs have been paid, the rest is the store's profit from selling the ice cream.

When you pay for ice cream at the market, you are really paying for many things. You pay the store owners for their share of the costs of distribution. You pay the ice cream makers for their costs of production and their share of the costs of distribution. In addition, you are paying both the store owners and the ice cream makers a profit for making and selling the ice cream.

Costs of Producing a Service

Mrs. Jackson leaves her washing at a laundry. She will pay the laundry owner $2.00 to make it clean for her. The clothes, sheets, and towels are her own, but she chooses to pay to have them washed.

She is not buying goods at the laundry. She is only paying the laundry to wash for her. The laundry is selling her a **service.** She is buying the service for $2.00 so she will not have to do the washing at home herself. She may not have a washing machine. She may want to use her time to do other work. She pays the laundry to do the work of washing the clothes for her.

Like any business, a laundry has costs. It uses water and gas or oil to heat the water. It uses soap to clean the clothes. These costs add up to five or six cents a wash.

The owners have other costs, too. They must pay for machines and tools. They must pay for the land and the building and for electricity to light it. They must also pay taxes to the state government and to the government of the United States. As you can see, there are many costs in running a laundry. Still, as long as the laundry owners can make a profit, they will probably stay in business.

Most American families spend much of their money buying services. They may, for example, get the car fixed, go to the doctor, take music lessons, or go to the movies. You can probably think of many services your family buys.

Today, more people work at doing services than producing goods. Some repair shoes. Others deliver parcels. Still others keep people healthy.

1. What affects a person's buying choices?
2. Name the two things that make up a person's demand for a product.
3. Why might a store's supply of a product change at certain times of the year?
4. What are three costs of production?
5. How does a producer hope to earn a profit?
6. What are the costs of distribution?
7. What is the difference between a business that produces goods and one that sells services?

Find out the price of something your family bought this week.

1. What costs went into that price?
2. Which are costs of production? Which are costs of distribution?

Cost of raw materials

A builder made a cabinet. He sold it for $95.00. The cost of the raw materials is shown in the pie graph.

1. Which raw material cost the most?
2. Which material cost the least?
3. What was the total cost of the raw materials?
4. What was the builder's profit? (Hint: The profit is the amount of money left after all the costs have been paid.)

1. Suppose that Mr. Alessi found that his ice cream was not making a profit. What could he do?
2. It costs hundreds of dollars to send a truckload of frozen orange juice to your community. Yet the price of a small can of orange juice goes up only one cent because of shipping costs. Why does the price of one can change so little?

Supply and Demand

Last May Marty wanted a new swimsuit. Stone's Sport Shop had a bright plaid one that was just what she wanted. The price was $15.00. Marty's mother thought $15.00 was too much to pay. She didn't see why Marty couldn't wear the swimsuit her older sister had used last year. So Marty wore it for three months. Then in the middle of August, Marty and her mother went back to the store. There were still many swimsuits. But now they were selling at one-third off the regular price. The suit Marty wanted cost only $10.00.

Marty was happy that the price of her suit was less, but she did not understand why. She wondered why Mrs. Stone, the owner of the store, had decided on different prices in May and August.

Last winter Mrs. Stone had ordered a large supply of swimsuits in all sizes, styles, and colors. She knew there would be a big demand for new swimsuits in May and June when the swimming season began. She wanted a large supply of swimsuits then. She hoped that people could find just the kind of swimsuits they liked best. She hoped they would come to her shop and spend the money to buy them. So Mrs. Stone filled her racks with swimsuits in May.

In May a summer of outdoor swimming lay ahead. Mrs. Stone expected that many people would pay $15.00 so they could use their new swimsuits all summer. She guessed that the demand for swimsuits would be large then.

Many people did buy new swimsuits at that price. Still, when August came, a number of suits were left unsold. There would be only a few more weeks of weather warm enough for swimming outdoors. The suits that most people wanted were already sold. Mrs. Stone could no longer expect to sell the rest of her supply of swimsuits for $15.00. By August the demand was much smaller.

With a supply of swimsuits still on hand in August, Mrs. Stone knew she had to do something. She wanted to sell the suits and get back at least part of the money she had spent on them. So she decided to make less profit. She lowered the price of the swimsuits. Then she put an advertisement in the town newspaper. Mrs. Stone was trying to increase the demand for swimsuits in late summer by lowering the price.

Finding that swimsuits were on sale for $10.00, Marty and her mother did just what Mrs. Stone had hoped. They came in and looked through the suits that were left. They found a bright plaid suit that was one size too large for Marty. It was just what Marty and her mother wanted. They knew Marty could wear it all next year. They paid Mrs. Stone $10.00 for the suit.

Mrs. Stone, Marty, and her mother were each interested in $10.00 swimsuits for different reasons. Mrs. Stone got part of her money back. She could buy clothes to sell in the winter. Marty's mother saved $5.00. Marty got a swimming suit she liked.

Setting a Price

You can see that at $15.00 a swimsuit, Mrs. Stone's supply was greater than the demand. Not all the swimsuits sold. If she had lowered her price to $12.00 in July, she might have sold all her swimsuits then. But she might not have made much profit. What she was looking for was the price at which *supply equals demand.* In May it was $15.00. In August it was $10.00.

To learn more about setting prices, try the investigation on the facing page.

AN INVESTIGATION
into setting prices

You have read why Stone's Sport Shop changed its prices for swimsuits. Most other sellers have to change their prices, too, from time to time. What might happen to prices in each of these examples?

Crown Ranch has ten horses for sale. They are the only sellers of horses for 100 kilometers. A movie company needs twenty horses to use in a movie.

Amy's Ranch has twenty horses for sale. Her ranch is 100 kilometers off the main road. People do not often go that far away to buy horses.

Ed Kirov has fifty boxes of apples for sale. A buyer wants ten boxes.

Fran Wilson has ten boxes of apples for sale. Four buyers are each looking for ten boxes.

Act TV Company has fifteen color sets for sale. New models will come out next week.

Bob's TV Mart has two color sets left two weeks before Christmas.

1. In each example, which is greater—the supply or the demand?
2. In each pair of examples, which price might be set higher? Why?

The Only Supply in Town

Adamstown is a village 80 kilometers from the nearest city, Boston. There are few stores in Adamstown. Bailey's Nursery is the only place where people can buy plants, grass seed, garden tools, and other goods they need for their gardens. Some of the Bailey's customers know the prices of almost everything the store sells. They have shopped at Bailey's nursery for many years. They know, for example, that plant food costs $6.00 a bag.

Sometimes Adamstown people travel to shop in Boston. At the edge of Boston are several nurseries that sell goods for the garden. While they all sell mostly the same kinds of goods, each does business differently. Donati's Nursery has the best supply of garden trees and bushes. At Flowerland, Mrs. Levy knows a lot about keeping beetles and insects from eating garden plants. Mr. Arbol has a large supply of garden tools at his Garden Mart, and he fixes his customers' tools when they are broken.

All these sellers are careful to keep their prices high enough to earn a profit but low enough that people will not look for lower prices elsewhere. They offer special services. They all know that other sellers are trying to sell to the same people.

Mr. and Mrs. Bailey do not have to be this careful about setting their prices in Adamstown. Their buyers have no other place to shop. The Baileys do not have to work as hard to keep people's business.

When Business Is Slow

When a Boston garden store is not selling enough, it will have a sale. It will set prices so low that people will want to come and find a really "good buy." The other Boston nurseries might cut their prices to match the prices at the first nursery. Some might even make their prices lower.

When stores keep lowering prices to get customers away from other stores, they are in what is called a **price war.** Most price wars do not last long. Small businesses lose too much money when they sell at prices at or below their costs. Price wars usually end when each store decides to sell at about the same price as the others.

Government and Prices

Suppose you lived in Adamstown and did not want to pay the Baileys' prices. You would either have to do without rose bushes or travel to Boston to buy them.

Bailey's Nursery is the only place in Adamstown that sells rose bushes. In Adamstown the Baileys have a **monopoly** on rose bushes. Monopoly means a company is the only seller of a certain good or service in one place.

A seller with a monopoly can sell a product for a higher price than he or she might if there were other sellers nearby. If buyers will not pay what that seller asks, they have no choice but to do without the product. Such a monopoly can give a seller bigger profits.

Still, if the Baileys set their prices too high, people will not buy from them. They can do without, buy by mail order, or go to Boston. They can grow plants from seeds. As long as the Baileys' prices are not too high, people will pay a little more than they would pay in Boston. This saves them time, trouble, and the cost of going to Boston.

At one time there were many monopolies in the United States. For example, one company sold nearly all the gasoline, kerosene, and oil in America. It could set almost any price it wished. The United States government has often stepped in to break up such large, powerful monopolies.

Some monopolies are not so easily broken up. Electric, telephone, gas, and water service businesses, for example, are usually monopolies. Such public utilities are called **natural monopolies.** It is usually better and less costly to have one company's gas lines and telephone poles in a community than several.

People cannot easily do without public utilities. People need water and other utilities. If the prices are too high, people cannot simply decide not to buy these services.

Public utilities cannot set any price they wish for their services, however. The government sets the prices these companies can charge. It checks on the kind of service they give. In these ways, the government tries to keep these monopolies from charging prices that are too high.

Building a Demand

Pat O'Brien wants his mother to buy Krunchy Kool breakfast cereal. He found out there are free Secret Scanners packed in every box.

Rita and Fred want to go to the movies to see *Monsters on the Prowl.* They want their mother to take them to the 12:15 P.M. show.

Ida wants to buy the record of "Lolly Pop Corn." It's been on the Top Ten for three weeks in a row, and she does not have it yet.

Maria and Benny are sad when their family buys a new station wagon. They wanted a Flashing Fireball with a five-speed stickshift.

All of these people seem to know a lot about the goods and services they want to buy. They all seem to have made their choices even before they went to any stores.

The choices of all these people are probably shaped by **advertising.** To advertise a good or a service is to let people know about it so they will buy it. Makers of books, cereals, movies, records, and hundreds of other products need to sell what they make. They have a supply of their products. They must find or make a demand for them.

People do not demand what they do not know about. Advertising tells people about products they have not heard of before. It tells people how great these products are. Advertising tries to build a demand for a product.

A business must pay to advertise its product. Full-page ads in a magazine may cost as much as $10,000. A one-minute television ad may cost as much as $100,000. Advertising can help sell products, but it can also add to the cost of a product. But sometimes advertising can lower prices. Color television sets are an example.

When the first color television sets were produced, they were priced around $10,000. Only a few people could buy them. But advertising made more people want to buy. Soon, so many people wanted color televisions that the makers could lower prices and still make a profit. At a price of $300, the makers' profits were smaller on each set, but they sold far more sets. Advertising increased demand. And the increased demand helped lower the price. The price you pay for a product depends on you and other possible buyers and sellers as well.

1. What might happen to the price of a product if people stopped buying it?
2. What do store owners hope will happen when they lower prices?
3. What happens during a price war? What happens when a price war ends?
4. Which is likely to have lower prices: a town with a single market or one with four giant supermarkets? Why?
5. What is a monopoly?
6. What does the government do to help control monopolies?
7. What effect does advertising usually have on the demand for a product?
8. How did advertising help lower the cost of color television sets?

Gasoline is made from crude oil. There is a limited amount of crude oil in the world. At the same time, more people in more countries need more gasoline for energy every year.

1. The supply of crude oil is decreasing. What do you think this will do to the price of gasoline?
2. The number of people demanding gasoline is growing. What do you think this will do to the price of gasoline?

You can make a report on advertising. To make your report, you will need to gather information from television and magazine advertising. Your work may be easier if you take notes while you watch television commercials and look through magazines. Your notes should answer the questions on the facing page about each advertisement you use.

1. What product is being advertised?
2. What does the advertisement tell you about the product? Does it show how the product is better than other products? how the product will save money for you? how it will make people like you or admire you?
3. What evidence does the advertisement give to support what it says about the product?
4. Do you believe everything the advertisement says about the product? Why or why not?
5. Would you buy the product? Why or why not?

When you have answered these questions for several advertisements, decide on a main point you wish to make about advertising. Perhaps you want to make the point that advertising is believable or that it is not believable. Use the information in your notes to help you prepare your report. You could write a paper, make a bulletin board display, or give a talk before the class.

Suppose you work for a company that makes NoSmog smog-stoppers for cars.

1. What can your company do to get people to buy NoSmog smog-stoppers rather than another kind? List as many ways as you can.
2. What difference do you think your ideas will make to stores that sell smog-stoppers?
3. How might your ideas affect people who buy smog-stoppers?
4. How might your ideas affect newspapers, magazines, and television stations?
5. How might your ideas affect the makers of other smog-stoppers?

3 Paying the Price

In most American homes there are several machines that do the work that people once had to do themselves. Other machines provide entertainment, such as music and movies. Some of them do not cost very much at all. Others are very expensive. The expensive ones wash dishes, cook food or keep it from spoiling, and carry people places. They cost so much that most people don't have enough money at one time to pay for even one of them. Still, most people manage to buy some of these expensive machines. How do you suppose people pay for these machines?

A New Refrigerator

This is the story of the Arnesens and their new refrigerator. The old one began making loud noises. Sometimes the motor would stop altogether. Mr. Arnesen fixed it from time to time so that it still kept the food cold. But he could not stop the noise. It bothered the family night and day. They wanted a new refrigerator.

The Arnesen family had $200 in the savings bank. They looked in refrigerator stores, but all the $200 refrigerators were too small. The kind they needed cost $450. The one they liked best at that price was at Olson's Appliance Store. They decided to try to buy the $450 refrigerator.

Buying on Credit

Mrs. Arnesen talked with Mr. Olson. She told him the family needed a new refrigerator and that they had decided to buy the $450 one. Mrs. Arnesen said she could pay $200, and she wanted to turn in the old refrigerator in trade for part of the remaining cost. Mr. Olson offered $50 for the family's old refrigerator in trade for the new one. Mrs. Arnesen thought that was a fair price.

Even so, Mrs. Arnesen still did not have enough money to pay for the new refrigerator. She needed $200 more to meet the store's price.

Mr. Olson offered Mrs. Arnesen **credit** for the rest of the cost. In return, Mrs. Arnesen had to promise to pay the money by a certain date. Credit would mean that Mr. Olson was sure Mrs. Arnesen *could* keep her promise and trusted that she *would.* Credit would mean that Mrs. Arnesen could take the refrigerator home now and pay for it later.

To arrange for the credit, Mrs. Arnesen went to the store's credit clerk. She told her about her job and her husband's job and how much they each earned. She gave the credit clerk the names of other business people who had given the family credit before. The clerk called them and found that the Arnesens always paid their bills on time. The Arnesens had a good **credit record,** so Mr. Olson told Mrs. Arnesen that he trusted her to pay the $200. Mrs. Arnesen now was able to buy the refrigerator from Mr. Olson on credit.

To use the credit, Mrs. Arnesen signed a note promising to pay the store $20 a month for a year. She gave Mr. Olson $200 and said the store could take away the old refrigerator when it delivered the new one to the Arnesen home. In this way, the Arnesens could use the new refrigerator while they were paying for it. If they stopped paying for any reason, the store could take the new refrigerator back. It would not really belong to the Arnesens until they had made the last payment.

Paying for the Use of Money

That evening after supper, Mrs. Arnesen told the family how they were buying the new refrigerator. In the kitchen they could hear the noise of the old one rattling away. Mrs. Arnesen explained how the men would bring the new refrigerator tomorrow. They would take the old one away because Mr. Olson had allowed them $50 in trade for it. She also told the family about the credit. She read them the note she had signed. The Arnesen children, Joelle and Mark, got pencils and paper and began to figure out how much the new refrigerator would really cost the family.

To meet the store's price, Mrs. Arnesen had to borrow $200. To pay it back, she agreed to pay the store $20 each month for a year. This means Mrs. Arnesen would pay back $240. That is $40 more than she borrowed.

"That credit makes the refrigerator cost a lot more," said Joelle in surprise.

"You shouldn't have signed the note," said Mark. "The store cheated you!"

"Hold on!" said Mrs. Arnesen. "Do you really think it is cheating? Should the store lend us $200 for nothing? It will take us a year to pay the $200 back. In a bank, $200 can earn $10 in a year." The children thought about that.

"That may be so," said Joelle. "Just the same, the store charged you *more* than $10. It charged you $40 to lend you $200 for a year."

"Yes," said her father, "but Mr. Olson could put that $200 in the bank, too. Unless his money will earn him more than $10, why should he lend it to us? If your mother or I lose our jobs, we can't pay. Our house might burn down with the refrigerator inside. Mr. Olson's money would be safer in the bank than loaned to us. Lending money is worth the risk only if the lender makes a profit on the money."

The children were quiet for a moment. Mark had a new idea. "He says he'll give you credit. Why not use a credit card instead?"

Mrs. Arnesen took three credit cards from her wallet. The first was good only at gasoline stations. The second was for a chain of big clothing stores. The third could be used at many stores. "Olson's might accept this one," Mrs. Arnesen said. Then she did some fast arithmetic. "Over a year, credit on this card might cost us a dollar or two less than credit at Olson's," she said.

"We could also borrow the $200 from the bank," said Mr. Arnesen. "The bank charges less than Olson's for the use of its money."

"Yes, and less than the credit card, too," agreed Mrs. Arnesen. "Next time we have to buy something on credit, we will try to shop for the cheapest credit we can find. Shopping for a good credit price is as important as shopping for a good product price."

Using Money to Earn Money

Money can be used to earn money. It can do this in two ways. First, it can earn profit. After store owners have paid for all their costs, the money they have left is their profit.

Olson's store spent money to buy refrigerators from factories and to run the store. It sold refrigerators to the public for more than they cost the store. This is one way the store earned money for Mr. Olson.

Money earned money for Mr. Olson in another way, too. The store offered people credit to buy refrigerators. The people paid back a little more money than they had borrowed. This little bit more money is called **interest.**

Interest is money paid for the use of someone else's money. By offering Mrs. Arnesen credit, Mr. Olson allowed her to use some of the store's money for a time. That way, Mrs. Arnesen did not have to wait until the family had all the money to buy that new refrigerator. In return for the credit, Mrs. Arnesen was to pay the money back to Mr. Olson with interest. She paid Mr. Olson $40 interest to borrow $200. Interest on credit can be an important way for many stores to earn money and add to their profit. To find out more about credit, try the investigation on page 334.

Some businesses, like banks, earn most of their profit from interest. When you deposit money in a savings bank, you are really lending your money to the bank. The bank can use your money until you want the money back again. The bank pays interest to you for letting it use your money. The bank then uses your money to lend to other people. It lends this money to other people at higher interest than it pays you. This way the bank can make a profit. Thus, the money you put in the bank earns money for you and also for the bank.

SAVINGS ACCOUNT BOOK CERTIFICATE NO. 33-48573-57

BR	DATE	WITHDRAWAL	INTEREST	DEPOSITS	BALANCE	SYM.
33	15SEP78			$1,000.00	$1,000.00	CDP
33	31SEP78		$**2.13		$1,002.13	INT
33	11OCT78	$200.00			$**802.13	CWD
33	29NOV78			$**500.00	$1,302.13	KDP
33	17DEC78			$***75.00	$1,377.13	CDP
33	31DEC78		$*13.74		$1,390.87	INT
33	04JAN79			$**575.00	$1,965.87	KDP
33	22JAN79			$2,000.00	$3,965.87	KDP

AN INVESTIGATION
into the cost of credit

When you buy on credit, you know the price you will pay is more than the amount the price tag shows. See if you can figure what credit would cost if you were buying each of the following goods.

	Automobile	Boat	House
Advertised Price (AP)	$6,678	$1,650	$40,000
Monthly Payment (MP)	$211.54	$54.00	$322.10
Time to Pay (TP)	36 months	36 months	25 years
Total Cost (TC) = MP x TP	$	$	$
Credit Cost = TC - AP	$	$	$

When buyers are deciding how much they are willing to pay for credit, they often wonder how much the goods they are buying will be worth later.

1. Does a house become more valuable as it gets older? a boat? an automobile?
2. What difference would such a change in the value of something you were buying make in deciding whether or not to buy on credit? Explain your answer.

A Credit Economy

In our culture today, many people depend on credit. They get the things they want or need by buying them "on time." Like the Arnesen's, they pay for goods little by little over a period of time. Altogether, of course, people who buy on credit pay more for the product than they would if they paid cash for it.

Some people think they should never buy on credit because it means they must pay more. Many others feel it is worth it to pay more so they do not have to wait to have the things they need or want. Still others feel that buying on credit is all right at times, for emergencies or very costly products. In the end, whether people should buy on credit or not depends on what they value. It is something that each person must decide alone.

Personal Choices

Food to eat, water to drink, and air to breathe are very important to all people. Money is also important to people because they need it to get many of the things they want. But not everyone agrees about what is most important. A person might choose to live where the air is cleaner, even though he or she could make more money someplace else. It all depends on what the person values.

Values that differ from one person to another are **personal values.** Each person has his or her own personal values. No one can say that one set of personal values is better than another. That is a matter that each person or family must decide.

An old stamp might be worth $100 to one person, while another person might simply throw it away. Some people will pay a great deal of money for a color television set, while others do not want a television set at all. One child might buy a violin while another would buy a bicycle.

People who sell products use many ways to try to influence people's personal values. Advertising is one. Sellers hope that advertising will make many people value a product. If large numbers of people can be made to value a product and buy it, the seller will make a profit.

Other Choices

Just as values differ among people, they also differ among cultures. For example, Conchita had a baseball that mattered very much to her. Famous players had signed it. Conchita wouldn't sell it for any amount of money. This is a personal value. But many American children would feel the same way about such a ball. They all belong to a culture in which baseball is important.

Now suppose a boy from Tepetongo found Conchita's baseball. He might feel very differently about it. He might never have heard of the ballplayers whose names are on it. To him, it would be worth no more than any other ball. Since baseball players are not important in his culture, his cultural values would be different from Conchita's.

There are other values that many Americans share. For example, it is important to most American families to own a car. Most Americans like to take vacations to see other parts of the country. They like to visit friends and relatives. In a country as large as the United States, owning a car makes moving about much easier.

The kind of car a family owns depends on personal values, however. Some families like big cars. Some like station wagons or vans. Other families want smaller cars. But owning a car, no matter what kind, is a **cultural value** of most Americans.

This is not always true in other cultures. In countries where streets are narrow and towns are close together, cars are not as important. Many people have other ways to travel, like trains or bicycles. Many of these ways cost less than owning a car. Some do not dirty the air as much as cars or use as much gasoline.

Earlier in this book you read about air pollution. Most scientists believe that cars cause over half the air pollution in the United States. Owning a car is an American cultural value. But more and more people also value clean air. Which one will prove more important to Americans is a question of values.

Values, then, differ from culture to culture. Values also differ from person to person. The buying choices that people make depend on both their cultural values and their personal values.

1. How did Mrs. Arnesen get credit from Mr. Olson?
2. What is interest?
3. Give two reasons why people use credit to buy goods or services.
4. Name two ways that money can be used to earn more money.
5. What are personal values? Give an example.
6. What are cultural values? Give an example.

When you buy on credit, you get to use a product before you have paid for all of it.

1. Why might a person prefer *not* to buy on credit?
2. If you use credit, what should you do before you sign a credit note?

Listen to television and radio ads and read signs and newspapers and magazines ads to help you answer these questions.

1. Who advertises credit?
2. How is credit advertised?
3. Does the advertising say how much the credit will cost?

Mrs. Smith and Mrs. Jones both needed new tires for their cars. Mrs. Smith ordered hers from a mail-order catalog. She waited six weeks for delivery. Each tire cost $26.95.

Mrs. Jones bought new tires at a service station. She got them the day she ordered them. The station attendant put the tires on her car. Each tire cost $33.95.

1. Which person paid for extra services? What else did she get?
2. What did the other person seem to value more?

Reviewing Key Ideas

How much will you have to pay for a liter of gas, a hot dog, or a house? Can you tell? Probably not, because you have learned that there is *no one price* for any of these things. There are many prices.

Perhaps you can't tell what the price of a product will be. But you do know some of the reasons for that price. One is the cost of making a product and getting it to the final buyer. The ice-cream maker, for example, had to buy raw materials and pay workers. The owner also had to pay for the machines the workers used and the building they worked in. If the owner wanted to stay in business, she had to make a profit, too.

After goods are produced, they must get to the consumer. Other costs are added to the product while it is transported and stored. Perhaps you can now understand this about price: The price of a product depends partly upon the costs of production and the costs of distribution.

But the price you pay depends upon more than costs. It also depends upon the size of the supply from those who wish to sell. And it depends on the size of the demand, or the number of buyers and their eagerness to buy. If the supply is smaller than the demand, the price may stay the same or go up. If the supply is bigger than the demand, the price may drop.

Sometimes price is affected by competition. When a business is the only one with a certain product, it has a monopoly. Then it can control both the supply and the price of the product it sells. Thus you have also learned this about price: The price of a product depends partly on supply and demand.

In a "credit economy," customers sometimes pay more for a product than the price tag shows. Most people buy cars, for example, before they have all the money they need to pay for them. They must borrow some of the money. Then they must pay for the use of the money as well as the cost of the car. They are paying for extra services. Thus you can also make this statement about price: The price of a product depends partly on the way the buyer chooses to pay.

The Choices People Make

You have also learned that people spend their money in different ways. How people spend their money depends in part on their personal values. Some people pay a good deal for other people's labor. Other people save money by doing the jobs themselves. Some people use only their own money when they buy goods. Other people buy on credit. These are examples of economic values that are personal.

Some of our economic values are cultural. For example most Americans do not value eating truffles. Only a few Americans would pay for truffles at any price. Yet in France, many people want truffles. You can make this statement about price: The prices people are willing to pay for goods and services depend partly on their personal and cultural values.

You can express all the ideas you have learned in this unit in one general statement: Patterns of buying and selling depend upon the economic choices people make.

Using Key Words

Use these key words to complete the sentences that follow.

advertising	interest
cost of distribution	natural monopoly
cost of production	profit
credit	raw materials
demand	supply

1. When people want a product or service and can afford to pay for it, they have a ____ for it.
2. The amount of a product available to be sold to people is the ____.
3. The resources used to make goods or services are called ____.
4. The amount of money that must be spent to make a product is called the ____.
5. Money must also be spent to move, store, and sell goods. This money is the ____.
6. The money left after all the costs of producing and distributing goods have been paid is the maker's ____.
7. Telling people about a product so that they will want to buy it is called ____.
8. Sometimes people pay part of the price of something they buy and agree to pay the rest by a certain date. This buying plan is called ____.
9. The extra money that people pay when they buy on credit is called ____.
10. Sometimes it is better to have only one company supplying a service, such as electricity. An electrical company is an example of a ____.

Focus on the Social Scientist

Going shopping means making lots of choices. Choosing a loaf of bread means looking at many kinds and picking the one you want. The wrappers can tell you part of what you need to know to choose the bread you will like best.

The United States government has made laws that tell food producers they must print certain information on wrappers. In making these laws, the government uses the advice of people like Dr. Ruby Morris, an **economist.** An economist is a social scientist who studies such business matters as how goods and services are made, packaged, and sold.

Dr. Morris had learned how buyers are sometimes tricked by wrappers into getting poor buys for their money. An extra-big box may make buyers think it has more cereal in it than a smaller box. But sometimes buyers get only a bigger box for their extra money—not more cereal. Labels did not tell whether a cereal was really good for the buyer to eat, either.

Dr. Morris and other economists advise the government about what buyers need to know. They need to know more than the size of the box and the name on the wrapper. They need to know what is inside the wrapper and how much it weighs. Now the government has made laws that say the makers of foods like cereals must tell buyers what the cereal is made of, how much food value it has per serving, and how many servings are in one package.

By investigating what buyers need to know, economists like Dr. Morris give advice that helps people get the most value for their money.

A New View of Resources

Space is a valuable resource. It gets more valuable as the earth becomes more crowded. Crowded communities in the United States need to learn new ways of using their space resources. They can also learn old ways of using space carefully, ways which other peoples have used for hundreds of years.

For many years, Japan has been one of the earth's most crowded nations. The United States is almost twenty times bigger than Japan. Yet our larger nation has only twice as many people. Japanese people have had to live close together for hundreds of years, and they have learned special ways of using space.

In Japan every piece of land is used carefully. Good farm land is made to produce all the crops it can. Crops even grow on small strips of land along roads and railways. Hillsides are

carefully terraced. Young trees are planted wherever big trees have been cut for lumber so that forests are not used up. Roads and railways are carefully planned so the many people can go to and from where they live, work, and play.

Land use is important not only to the Japanese nation, but also to each Japanese family. The Tanaka family, for example, uses its space in special ways.

The Tanaka home has only three rooms, but it seems much larger inside. Instead of walls, Japanese people use sliding paper *shoji* (SHO•jee) screens to divide their homes. These screens can be opened wide to make bigger rooms or closed to make smaller rooms where family members can be alone if they like. In daytime a low table is in the middle of the largest room. The family has its meals there, sitting on straw *tatami* (tah•TAH•mee) mats on the floor. At night the table is pushed against the wall. Blankets are spread on the *tatami* mats, and the big dining room becomes a bedroom. During the day the blankets are rolled up and stored in a closet.

Behind the Tanaka home is a small garden. It is a peaceful place the family enjoys very much. In this garden are old trees, a stream, a pond, a bridge, and two benches. The garden seems very large. Yet it is only as big as most bedrooms you have seen. The garden *seems* big because everything in it is small. Old trees are kept as small as flower bushes by cutting them in special ways. The pond and stream are also small. The stream, in fact, is really only some rocks carefully placed to look like a stream.

In crowded Japan the Tanaka family has found many ways to use its space resources wisely. Space is a valuable resource in your environment, too.

How do people in your neighborhood make their space seem to grow? Choose one of the following projects and study it to help you find some ways.

1. From the sidewalk, look at yards in your neighborhood. Some yards will seem to make better use of space than others. Make drawings of two yards—one that you think uses space well and one that you think uses space poorly. Say why you think so.

2. Study the room where you sleep. Make a drawing to show how you now use the space. Show where you sleep, study, play with friends, and keep your clothes and play things. Then make another drawing to show another way you might use the space. Think about ways to make your room neater and more roomy. If you prefer, you can do the same thing for another room in your house.

3. In some communities people have made space useful by turning an empty lot into a small park. Look around your own community. Try to find an empty place where children and adults might play and relax. Make a picture or a model to show how this area could be used. Tell how this small park would improve the community. List what resources would be needed to make such a park and how they might be gotten. Do not forget that people are resources, too.

Using What You Learned

Imagine that as you walk down the street you pass several people who look exactly like you. What problems might this cause for you? Has anything ever happened that made you glad that you do things in a special way?

You have learned many reasons why people are different throughout the world. Often people in one area have special customs. Many of these ways of living are followed for years and years as traditions.

1. Can you think of examples of traditions in your community? What traditions does your school have? What traditions do you follow?

2. Do you know how any of these traditions started?

3. Why do you think they are still followed?

Most of the traditions and customs in the United States were brought here by people who came from nations all over the world. These people also learned traditions from the Native Americans, whose customs were suited to the environment of North America.

Carl Sandburg was the son of Swedish immigrants. He wrote many poems about the people who came from other nations to live and work in the United States. In one poem Sandburg described the people coming to the United States:

From six continents, seven seas, and several
  archipelagoes,
From points of land moved by wind and water
Out of where they used to be to where they are,
The people of the earth marched and travelled
To gather on a great plain.

PARADE
10:30 A.M.

Look at the map on the opposite page.

1. How was the area where each group settled like the area from which it had come? You might choose one group and find information in an encyclopedia or an atlas about the climate and resources of its homeland and the area where it settled.

2. In what ways might such likenesses make it easier for the settlers to adapt to a new land?

3. Now look around your own community. Who were the people who began your community? What evidence can you find in your community of people who brought ideas, customs, and names from different nations?

4. What is the history of the name of your community? For whom are some of the streets named?

Where Did the People Live?

As the United States grew in size and population, many people went west across the Appalachians. After the discovery of gold in California in 1848, thousands of Chinese people crossed the Pacific Ocean to California to mine gold. They also helped build the railroads. Many other people crossed the plains and mountains or came by ship to find gold.

In 1869 the transcontinental railroad joined the east and west coasts. Soon after this event, people began to settle the Great Plains. Swedes and Norwegians began to farm the fertile lands of Illinois, Wisconsin, Minnesota, Nebraska, and the Dakotas during the 1870s and 1880s. Many Mexican settlers moved into the Southwest to farm and raise cattle.

WHERE SOME IMMIGRANTS SETTLED

The story of the United States is the story of people moving, working, and building. In 1790 when the nation was newly founded, there were about four million people living in the United States. Today over two hundred million people live here.

Who Were The People?

Native American people have been living for thousands of years on the land which is now the United States. Some scientists think that the Native Americans have always lived in North and South America. Others think they began coming to North America from Asia about twenty thousand years ago. They kept coming until almost a thousand years ago. Then, about five hundred years ago, people from Europe began coming to this land. Among them were

Spanish, French, Dutch, and English explorers. These explorers learned about the people and the land of North America, but most of them did not stay.

After the explorers came the colonists. The English came to Jamestown and Plymouth. The Dutch came to New York and the Swedes to Delaware. German farmers settled on the good soil of Pennsylvania. The French came to South Carolina and later to Louisiana. Black people from Africa were brought as slaves to work on the southern rice and cotton plantations. The Scottish came to the Appalachian frontier. The Spanish came to Florida, and later the Spanish and mestizos came to California.

The people who moved into the different regions of the United States had to adapt to different climates, soils, and sources of water. Look at the relief map of the United States on pages 356–357. Choose a colored area on the map and try to answer the following questions about it.

1. How might land, climate, and waterways affect the people who live in the area you have chosen?

2. In which areas would you probably find the most people? In which would you probably find the fewest?

What Do the People Do?

In the United States today, two out of every ten people move each year. Some people move for adventure, but most people move to find the work they want.

Think about the kind of work you would like to do someday to earn a living.

Will you move from your community to do this work? Why or why not? Where might you move if you needed to move?

More scientific methods and new machinery have affected what people do and where they must live. For example, fewer farmers are needed in the United States today. With farm machinery and fertilizers, a farmer can grow more food. With new machinery, more goods can be produced, too. Thousands of people move to work in factories where these goods are made. Study the graph on this page.

1. What changes can you notice about the number of people living in the United States?

2. What can you notice about where people in the United States live?

3. What do you think has caused many of these changes?

4. What changes would you expect in the next hundred years? Why?

In the early years of this nation, most people had very little news about events in other parts of the United States. This is less true today, but people are still most interested in problems that affect them directly. Use the maps in an atlas or at the back of this book and what you know to help you answer these questions.

5. Which states would be most likely to support laws giving government aid to cities?

6. Which states would be most likely to support laws giving money for more national parks and forests?

7. Which states would be most likely to support laws giving government aid to farmers?

PHYSICAL MAP OF THE UNITED STATES
Pacific Ocean
WASHINGTON
OREGON
CALIFORNIA
NEVADA
IDAHO
MONTANA
WYOMING
UTAH
COLORADO
ARIZONA
NEW MEXICO
NORTH DAKOTA
SOUTH DAKOTA
NEBRASKA
KANSAS
OKLAHOMA
TEXAS
UNITED
MEXICO
Cascade Mountains
Coast Mountains
Columbia Plateau
Columbia River
Rocky Mountains
Missouri River
Yellowstone River
Snake River
Continental Divide
Black Hills
Great Plains
Platte River
Great Salt Lake
Great Basin
Sierra Nevada
Sacramento River
Central Valley
Colorado Plateau
Colorado River
Imperial Valley
Gila River
Salt River
Rio Grande
40°
30°
120°
Arctic Ocean
Brooks Range
Arctic Circle
Yukon River
ALASKA
Alaska Range
CANADA
70°
60°
170°
160°
150°
140°
0 250 500 Miles
0 250 500 750 Kilometers
Tropic of Cancer
Pacific Ocean
HAWAII
160°
155°
22°
20°
0 100 200 Miles
0 100 200 300 Kilometers

CANADA
Lake Superior
St. Lawrence River
MAINE
MINNESOTA
MICHIGAN
Lake Huron
VT.
Adirondack Mountains
N.H.
Central Lowlands
Mississippi River
WISCONSIN
Lake Michigan
Lake Ontario
NEW YORK
Hudson River
MASS.
CONN.
R.I.
STATES
Lake Erie
IOWA
PENNSYLVANIA
Mountains
N.J.
ILLINOIS
INDIANA
OHIO
Allegheny Mountains
MD.
DEL.
Missouri River
Ohio River
WEST VIRGINIA
Appalachian
VIRGINIA
KENTUCKY
MISSOURI
Blue Ridge Mountains
Atlantic Ocean
NORTH CAROLINA
Ozark Mountains
TENNESSEE
Tennessee River
Atlantic Coastal Plain
Arkansas River
ARKANSAS
SOUTH CAROLINA
N
W
E
S
MISSISSIPPI
ALABAMA
GEORGIA
Red River
LOUISIANA
Gulf Coastal Plain
FLORIDA
Gulf of Mexico
40°
70°
30°
80°
90°
0 100 200 300 Miles
0 100 200 300 400 Kilometers
CUBA

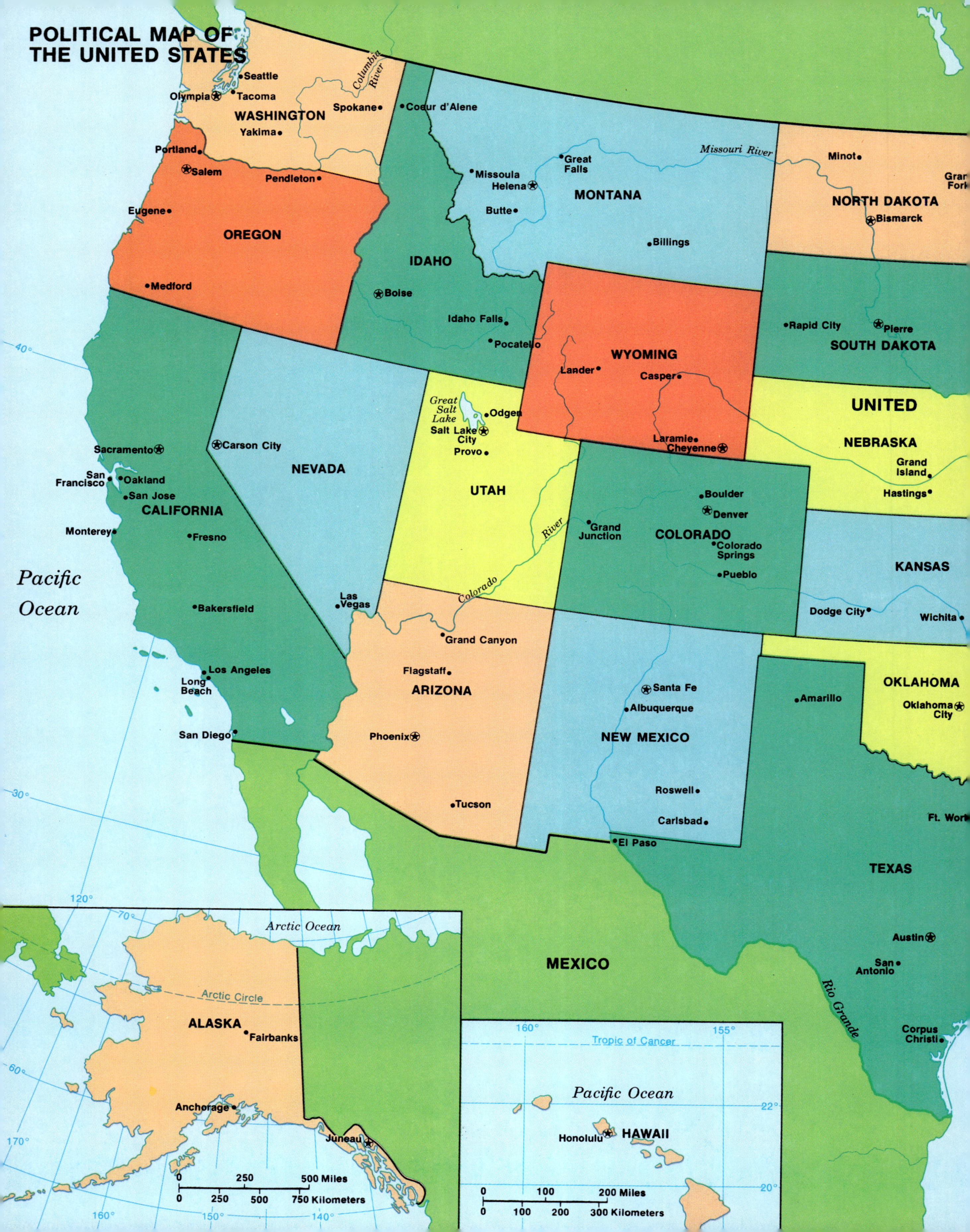
POLITICAL MAP OF THE UNITED STATES
WASHINGTON
Seattle
Olympia
Tacoma
Spokane
Yakima
Columbia River
Coeur d'Alene
OREGON
Portland
Salem
Pendleton
Eugene
Medford
IDAHO
Boise
Idaho Falls
Pocatello
MONTANA
Missoula
Helena
Great Falls
Butte
Billings
Missouri River
NORTH DAKOTA
Minot
Bismarck
SOUTH DAKOTA
Rapid City
Pierre
WYOMING
Lander
Casper
Laramie
Cheyenne
UNITED
NEBRASKA
Grand Island
Hastings
NEVADA
Carson City
Las Vegas
UTAH
Great Salt Lake
Odgen
Salt Lake City
Provo
CALIFORNIA
Sacramento
San Francisco
Oakland
San Jose
Monterey
Fresno
Bakersfield
Los Angeles
Long Beach
San Diego
Pacific Ocean
COLORADO
Boulder
Denver
Grand Junction
Colorado Springs
Pueblo
Colorado River
KANSAS
Dodge City
Wichita
ARIZONA
Grand Canyon
Flagstaff
Phoenix
Tucson
NEW MEXICO
Santa Fe
Albuquerque
Roswell
Carlsbad
El Paso
OKLAHOMA
Oklahoma City
TEXAS
Amarillo
Ft. Worth
Austin
San Antonio
Corpus Christi
Rio Grande
MEXICO
40°
30°
120°
Arctic Ocean
Arctic Circle
ALASKA
Fairbanks
Anchorage
Juneau
70°
60°
170°
160°
150°
140°
0 250 500 Miles
0 250 500 750 Kilometers
Tropic of Cancer
160°
155°
Pacific Ocean
22°
20°
Honolulu
HAWAII
0 100 200 Miles
0 100 200 300 Kilometers

CANADA
STATES
Lake Superior
Lake Michigan
Lake Huron
Lake Ontario
Lake Erie
St. Lawrence River
Missouri River
Ohio River
Mississippi River
Atlantic Ocean
Gulf of Mexico
CUBA
MINNESOTA
WISCONSIN
MICHIGAN
IOWA
ILLINOIS
INDIANA
OHIO
PENNSYLVANIA
NEW YORK
MAINE
V.T.
N.H.
MASS.
CONN.
R.I.
N.J.
DEL.
M D.
WEST VIRGINIA
VIRGINIA
KENTUCKY
MISSOURI
TENNESSEE
NORTH CAROLINA
SOUTH CAROLINA
ARKANSAS
MISSISSIPPI
ALABAMA
GEORGIA
LOUISIANA
FLORIDA
International Falls
Duluth
Minneapolis
St. Paul
Chippewa Falls
Green Bay
Sault Sainte Marie
Saginaw
Flint
Grand Rapids
Lansing
Detroit
Madison
Milwaukee
Racine
Rockford
Chicago
Sioux City
Cedar Rapids
Des Moines
Omaha
Lincoln
South Bend
Gary
Fort Wayne
Toledo
Cleveland
Akron
Peoria
Springfield
Indianapolis
Terre Haute
Columbus
Cincinnati
Huntington
Charleston
Wheeling
Pittsburgh
Harrisburg
Philadelphia
Trenton
Newark
New York
Dover
Baltimore
Annapolis
Washington D.C.
Richmond
Norfolk
Topeka
Kansas City
Jefferson City
St. Louis
Louisville
Frankfort
Lexington
Nashville
Knoxville
Memphis
Chattanooga
Winston-Salem
Durham
Raleigh
Charlotte
Greenville
Columbia
Charleston
Augusta
Atlanta
Macon
Columbus
Savannah
Birmingham
Montgomery
Mobile
Tallahassee
Jacksonville
Tampa
St. Petersburg
Miami
Tulsa
Fort Smith
Little Rock
Pine Bluff
Dallas
Shreveport
Monroe
Jackson
Biloxi
Baton Rouge
Lake Charles
New Orleans
Houston
Rochester
Buffalo
Syracuse
Albany
Burlington
Montpelier
Concord
Manchester
Bangor
Augusta
Portland
Boston
Providence
Hartford
N
S
E
W
40°
30°
70°
80°
90°
0 100 200 300 Miles
0 100 200 300 400 Kilometers

A Dictionary of Key Words

This dictionary lists the key words used in this book. Some of these words have more than one meaning. Only the meanings used in this book are given here.

Words that may be difficult to pronounce are respelled after the word. Each syllable is pronounced the way it is spelled. The accented syllable is in capital letters.

The number after each definition tells you a page where you can read more about the word. The index also lists other pages where you can find the word.

abolitionist (ab•uh•LISH•uhn•ist) An *abolitionist* is a person who wants to do away with something. In the United States, *abolitionists* wanted to do away with slavery. (p. 152)

adapt To *adapt* is to change to fit the environment. The Hopi have *adapted* to a land with little rain. (p. 8)

advertise To *advertise* a good or a service is to let people know about it so that they will want it. Stores often *advertise* their goods in newspapers, on radio, and on television. (p. 324)

amendment An *amendment* is a change or addition. As new problems and issues have arisen, *amendments* have been made to the United States Constitution. The first ten amendments are called the Bill of Rights. (p. 137)

assembly line An *assembly line* is a way of producing goods quickly. An *assembly line* in an automobile factory may have a moving conveyor belt to bring the car to each person to do his or her job. (p. 193)

boycott To *boycott* is to refuse to use or buy certain goods or services. People sometimes *boycott* goods or services as a protest. The colonists *boycotted* European goods to protest taxation without representation. (p. 92)

charter To *charter* is to give land to someone for a purpose. The King of England *chartered* companies to start colonies in America. (p. 75)

choice You make a *choice* when you choose one thing over other things that are available. People have to make *choices* about using their resources to get things they want and need. (p. 307)

clan A *clan* is a group of people belonging to the same family. A Hopi *clan* includes grandparents, aunts, uncles, and cousins. (p. 13)

climate *Climate* is the pattern of weather in a place over a year. The *climate* of places far from the equator is usually colder than the *climate* of places near the equator. (p. 263)

climate zone *Climate zones* are the climates at different heights on a mountain. The *climate zone* at the foot of a mountain has warmer weather than the *climate zone* at the top of the mountain. (p. 263)

coke *Coke* is coal that has been heated to remove the gases. *Coke* and limestone are used in the production of steel. (p. 284)

compromise (kom•pruh•myz) To *compromise* is to settle a disagreement by giving up some of the things you want in return for getting others. An agreement that is reached in this way is called a *compromise.* People in government must often *compromise* to settle their disagreements on issues. (p. 131)

Continental Congress The First *Continental Congress* was a meeting in 1774 of representatives from twelve of the thirteen colonies. The representatives at this meeting demanded their rights as English citizens. (p. 101)

corporation A *corporation* is a company in which many people invest their money and share the *corporation's* profits. A *corporation* is owned by all the people who buy shares in it. (See **stock.**) (p. 193)

costs of distribution The *costs of distribution* are the money that is spent to move, store, and sell a product after it has been manufactured. *Costs of distribution* are shared by the producer of a product and the stores that sell the product. (p. 312)

costs of production The *costs of production* are the money spent to produce, or make, goods and services. *Costs of production* include raw materials, labor, equipment, public services, and property. (p. 310)

credit *Credit* is a way of buying in which a buyer pays for a product at a later time or over a period of time. (p. 329) If a buyer has a good *credit record,* it means that he or she has used *credit* well in the past. (p. 330)

cultural trait A *cultural trait* is a special feature of a person that is learned from his or her culture. People from the same culture share many of the same *cultural traits.* The language that you speak is one of your *cultural traits.* (p. 9)

culture A *culture* is all the ways of believing and acting that belong to a certain group of people, including customs, language, and tools. You learn the *culture* of the group in which you live. (p. 8)

demand People have a *demand* for a good or service when they want it and can afford to pay for it. If you buy a record for five dollars, you have a *demand* for the record at that price. When *demand* exceeds supply, prices will usually be higher. (p. 308)

delta A *delta* is a piece of low land at the mouth of a river. A *delta* is formed by sand and soil carried by water down river. The name *delta* comes from its shape, which is like the Greek letter *delta* Δ. (p. 279)

depression A *depression* is a period when production and employment go down. During the Great *Depression* in the United States in 1929, many people lost their jobs. (p. 226)

dictator A *dictator* is a leader of a nation who takes away the people's freedoms. Mussolini and Hitler were *dictators.* (p. 228)

equipment *Equipment* is machines, tools, or other things needed to do a job. Mixers, bowls, and ovens are some of the *equipment* used to make bread. (p. 310)

erosion (i•ROH•zhun) *Erosion* is the wearing away of soil by water and wind. One way farmers try to prevent soil *erosion* is by building terraces on hills. (p. 261)

executive branch The *executive branch* is the part of the United States government which directs the government and puts the laws into effect. The *executive branch* is led by the President. (p. 134)

federal government A *federal government* is a form of government in which the national and state governments each have some powers. The United States government is a *federal government.* (p. 137)

gross national product *Gross National Product,* or *GNP,* is the value in dollars of all the goods and services produced by a nation in a year. The *GNP* of the United States in 1978 was over one trillion dollars. (p. 196)

human resources *Human resources* are the labor, skills, and knowledge that people use in their work. *Human resources,* natural resources, and resources made by people are all needed to produce goods and services. (p. 269)

inaugurate (in•AW•gyuh•rayt) To *inaugurate* is to swear into office. Presidents of the United States and governors of the fifty states are *inaugurated* after they are elected. (p. 160)

indentured servant An *indentured servant* is a person who agrees to work for someone for a certain period of time. Many people paid for their passage to America by becoming *indentured servants.* (p. 75)

integrate (IN•tuh•grayt) To *integrate* is to make the use of something, such as a school, neighborhood, or bus system, available to persons of all races. Civil rights groups in the United States work for racial equality and *integration.* (p. 240)

interact To *interact* is to act on each other. Two or more people *interact* when they do things that affect each other. You *interact* with a friend when you talk or play together. (p. 16)

interest *Interest* is money paid for the use of someone else's money. When a person buys goods or services on credit, he or she must pay additional money, or *interest,* for the credit. (See **credit.**) (p. 332)

judicial branch The *judicial branch* is the part of the United States government which decides how laws work. The *judicial branch* is a series of courts of law. The Supreme Court is the highest court. (p. 134)

labor *Labor* is work or the people who do work. A producer pays for *labor* by paying wages. (p. 310)

latex *Latex* is a milky liquid that comes from rubber trees. Rubber can be made from *latex.* (p. 290)

legislative branch The *legislative branch* is the part of the United States government which makes laws. The *legislative branch* is made up of the Senate and the House of Representatives. Together they are called Congress. (p. 134)

levee (LEV•ee) A *levee* is a raised bank of soil. Farmers build *levees* to hold river waters within their banks so the waters will not flood nearby fields. (p. 273)

loyalist A *Loyalist* was a colonist who did not agree with Parliament's laws but wanted to remain loyal to England and the king. (p. 100)

mesa (MAY•suh) A *mesa* is a flat-topped hill. *Mesa* is a Spanish word for table. Some Hopi villages are on *mesas.* (p. 3)

militia (muh•LISH•uh) A *militia* is a citizens' army. Towns had local *militia* called "Minute Men" who fought against the British in the American Revolution. (p. 100)

monopoly A business has a *monopoly* when it is the only seller of a certain good or service in one place. Most *monopolies* result in high prices. (p. 195) A *natural monopoly* is a *monopoly* such as a public utility. *Natural monopolies* are allowed by law because some services are better and less costly if supplied by one company. Telephone and utility companies are examples of *natural monopolies.* (p. 323)

override To *override* is to overcome something. Congress can sometimes pass a bill by *overriding* the President's veto. (p. 137)

Parliament *Parliament* is the legislature, or law-making branch, of the English government. Colonists in America wanted to govern themselves because they had no representatives in *Parliament.* (p. 75)

patriot A *Patriot* was a colonist who thought the colonies should govern themselves. *Patriots* fought the English in the American Revolution. (p. 100)

persecute To *persecute* is to punish. Some religious groups came to America because they had been *persecuted* in England for their beliefs. (p. 81)

physical trait A *physical trait* is a feature of a person's body. The shape of your nose and the color of your eyes are two of your *physical traits.* (p. 9)

plantation A *plantation* is a large farm. Tobacco *plantations* in Virginia produced the colonists' first cash crops to sell to England. (p. 76)

popular sovereignty (SOV•rin•tee) *Popular sovereignty* is the idea that people have the right to make decisions that are important to them. (p. 153)

produce To *produce* is to make. A dairy company might *produce* ice cream, cheese, and butter. (p. 308)

profit *Profit* is the money left over after a producer has sold his or her goods or services and has paid for the costs of production and distribution. Businesses try to sell at a price high enough to leave a *profit.* (p. 312)

property *Property* is land and buildings. *Property* can either be bought or rented. (p. 310)

protectorate (pruh•TEK•tuhr•it) A *protectorate* is a nation or territory to which a stronger nation gives military protection in return for some economic and political control over it. Half of the Virgin Islands is a *protectorate* of the United States. (p. 215)

public services *Public services* are services that everyone needs. Water, gas, and electricity are *public services.* (p. 310)

raw materials *Raw materials* are resources that can be used as they are or treated to make other goods or services. Milk, wood, and oil are *raw materials.* (p. 310)

refinery (rih•FY•nuh•ree) A *refinery* is a factory in which crude oil is treated and changed into products such as gasoline, plastic, and machine oil. (p. 292)

role A *role* is all the ways of acting that make up one of the parts a person plays in life. People play a number of different *roles* during their lives. In your family, you may have the roles of daughter and sister or son and brother. (p. 42)

secede (si•SEED) To *secede* is to withdraw from a group. In 1850 southern leaders warned that southern states might *secede* from the Union. In 1861, southern states did secede. (p. 147) *Secession* is the withdrawing, or *seceding,* of a state from the union. The *secession* of southern states led to the Civil War. (p. 162)

segregate To *segregate* is to keep some racial, religious, or ethnic groups apart from the rest of society. In 1896 the Supreme Court ruled that segregation laws were constitutional. In 1954 the Supreme Court changed its ruling and decided that segregation in schools, restaurants, or other public places was unconstitutional. (p. 240)

service A *service* is any work someone is paid to do that does not produce goods you can see or touch. A laundry does a *service* when it washes people's clothes. You do a *service* when someone pays you to babysit or rake leaves. (p. 313)

stock *Stock* is shares of a corporation that are sold to people. *Stockholders* are part-owners of a corporation. (See **corporation.**) (p. 193)

supply *Supply* is the amount of goods or services for sale at a certain price. When *supply* exceeds demand, prices will usually be lower. (p. 308)

tariff (TAR•if) A *tariff* is a tax on goods. A *tariff* could make foreign goods more costly than goods made within a country. (p. 146)

terrace (TER•uhs) A *terrace* is a level place on a hillside. *Terraces* are cut into hills to stop erosion. (p. 262)

truce A *truce* is an agreement between both sides in a conflict to stop fighting. A *truce* was declared in Korea in 1950. (p. 241)

trust A *trust* is formed by the joining of two or more companies in the same industry in order to share resources. There were once many *trusts,* such as sugar, oil, and steel *trusts,* in the United States. Because a *trust* can drive smaller companies out of business, *trusts* are now limited by the Sherman Antitrust Act. (p. 195)

tundra *Tundra* is grassy, treeless land. *Tundra* in the Arctic is frozen most of the year. (p. 24)

unconstitutional A law is *unconstitutional* when it violates the meaning of the Constitution. The Supreme Court has the power to decide when a law is *unconstitutional.* (p. 155)

values *Values* are the ideas, beliefs, and ways of acting that are important to people. You learn some *values* from your culture. People living in one culture usually share many *values.* (p. 41) *Personal values* differ from one person to another. (p. 336) *Cultural values* differ from one culture to another. (p. 337)

zone A *zone* is an area set aside for a special purpose. A city may divide its land into factory *zones* and residential, or housing, *zones.* (p. 91)

Index

Pronunciation Key[1]

In this book, pronunciations are given for some of the more difficult words. Each word is respelled as it is usually pronounced. The accented syllable of a word is in capital letters.

The list below shows how a dictionary helps you to pronounce words. Each dictionary symbol stands for a sound in the English language. Beside each dictionary symbol is a word or words with a respelling. The respelling shows how the sounds in the word are shown in this book.

a	add or Aztec (AZ•tek)
ā	ace or claim (KLAYM)
ä	father or kiva (KEE•vah)
b	bat or budget (BUJ•it)
ch	catch or check (CHEK)
d	dog or debt (DET)
e	end or ebb (EB)
ē	tree or chief (CHEEF)
f	fit or family (FAM•uh•lee)
g	log or goal (GOHL)
h	hope or habit (HAB•it)
i	it or igloo (IG•loo)
ī	ice or climate (CLY•mit)
j	joy or jail (JAYL)
k	cool or culture (KUL•chur)
l	look or rule (ROOL)
m	move or compass (KUM•pus)
n	nice or nation (NAY•shun)
ng	ring or trading (TRAYD•ing)
o	odd or column (KOL•um)
ō	open or ocean (OH•shun)
ô	order or off (AWF)
oi	oil, boy, or Iroquois (EAR•uh•kwoi)
oo	pool or feud (FYOOD)
o͝o	took or Blackfoot (BLAK•fuht)
p	pit or people (PEE•puhl)
r	run or right (RIYT)
s	see or service (sur • vis)
sh	sure, rush, or shame (SHAYM)
t	talk or trait (TRAYT)
th	thin or authority (uh•THOR•uh•tee)
u	up or son (SUN)
û(r)	term or conserve (kuhn•SURV)
yoo	few or useful (YOOS•fuhl)
v	eve or vote (VOHT)
w	away or work (WURK)
y	yet or yield (YEELD)
z	zest or charisma (kuh•RIZ•muh)
zh	vision or measure (MEZH•uhr)
ə	the schwa, an unstressed vowel representing the sounds a in above (uh•BUV) e in sicken (SIK•uhn) i in possible (POS•uh•buhl) o in melon (MEL•uhn) u in circus (SUR•kuhs)

A 9
B 0
C 1
D 2
E 3
F 4
G 5
H 6
I 7
J 8

1 Adapted from *The HBJ School Dictionary*, published by Harcourt Brace Jovanovich, Inc., 1977